T0313929

# GENDERED
# TRAJECTORIES

# GENDERED TRAJECTORIES

*Women, Work, and Social Change
in Japan and Taiwan*

*Wei-hsin Yu*

STANFORD UNIVERSITY PRESS
STANFORD, CALIFORNIA

Stanford University Press
Stanford, California

Library of Congress Cataloging-in-Publication Data

Yu, Wei-hsin.
   Gendered trajectories : women, work, and social change in Japan
and Taiwan / Wei-hsin Yu.
      p. cm.
   Includes bibliographical references and index.
   ISBN 978-0-8047-6009-6 (cloth : alk. paper)
   1. Women—Employment—Japan.   2. Women—Employment—Taiwan.
3. Sex discrimination in employment—Japan.   4. Sex discrimination in
employment—Taiwan.   5. Sex discrimination against women—Japan.
6. Sex discrimination against women—Taiwan.   I. Title.
   HD6197.Y8 2009
   331.4095124'9—dc22                                    2008036648

Typeset by Publishers' Design and Production Services, Inc.
in 10/13 Sabon

*To my family, past and present*

# CONTENTS

*Figures*

*Tables*

ACKNOWLEDGMENTS

Having lived in four different countries during the past decade and a half, I find myself constantly observing national differences in institutions, norms, and practices, and I often think about how these differences shape our actions, views, and actual life chances. Many of my daily observations turn into conversation starters or, less frequently, sources for mildly intellectual debates. This book, however, is a product of a more serious attempt to satisfy my curiosity regarding why people from different societies face different choices and constraints. The comparison between Japan and Taiwan began to make sense to me when I first visited Tokyo in 1995. I remember how everything seemed so familiar yet different from that in Taiwan, where I grew up. Immediately I wanted to tell a story about the differences I observed. As years went by, I learned more about both societies and came to the realization that providing explanations for the observed differences between them was not as easy as I originally thought. A turning point occurred in late 2002, when I returned to Japan to observe changes it had experienced due to the economic turmoil of the late 1990s. As I recognized the influences of previously set conditions on recent development, it became clear to me that a complete understanding of women's employment in Japan and Taiwan requires a careful look into history. Rather than asking why these countries are so different today, I decided to uncover the processes of change that led to the different levels of gender inequality in the two economies.

My intention of exploring changes in women's economic opportunities over time eventually became this book—one about gender and social change in Japan and Taiwan. The task of examining two countries across several decades of time was not a simple one; it would not be possible without support from numerous people. To begin, Mary Brinton played an important role in realizing my wish to study and experience Japanese society at an early point of my career, and has provided invaluable help and suggestions throughout various stages of this project. Her constant encouragement convinced me that the rather long journey I took to complete this book was worthwhile. The constructive criticism Bill Parish provided early on helped develop the book by making me rethink about the research questions and arguments. From him I also learned to organize and present the results in a more accessible fashion. Linda Waite and Kazuo Yamaguchi also provided useful feedback on methodological and conceptual issues during early stages of the project.

Various people from Japan and Taiwan, academics or otherwise, have greatly contributed to my understanding of these countries. Friends I made while living in Tokyo not only have been important sources of information for a foreigner like me, but have also given me many precious memories of Japan. Among them, I especially thank Yoshie Arita, Sanae Isozumi, Chiaki Sekiguchi, and Takashi Kusaka for helping me locate informants for my fieldwork in Tokyo during 1996–1997. Shih-min Wang, Lung-yu Tsai, Ling-yi Lee, Bo-rong Pan, Hui-jun Liu, Mei-yaw Yeh, Chong-ying Niou, and Hui-ju Wu did the same for my fieldwork in Taipei, for which I am thankful. In addition, Shuichi Hirata and Reiko Yamato were incredibly helpful when I returned to Japan to conduct more field research in 2002. Shuichi was instrumental for my obtaining institutional affiliation, important contacts, and even a place to stay. Despite having hardly known me at the time, Reiko went through enormous trouble to arrange my visits to various government offices and related institutions in the Kansai area. I am deeply indebted to their kindness. Furthermore, I am grateful to Ming-Ching Luoh for offering critical data for my analysis regarding entry into Taiwan's elite universities (Chapter 7). This book has also benefited from indispensable inputs from Kuo-hsien Su, Nan Lin, Yoshimichi Sato, Fumiaki Ojima, and Hiroshi Ishida. Of course, I owe a tremendous thank you to all the women and men I interviewed in Japan and Taiwan, who squeezed time out of their busy schedules to share their life stories and insights with me.

During the process of carrying out this project, I was fortunate to receive extensive institutional support. My early fieldwork in Japan and Taiwan was funded by Hosei University in Japan, Academia Sinica in Taiwan, and the Chiang Ching-kuo Foundation. Generous grants from the National Science Council in Taiwan, the Center for Asian and Pacific Studies and Institution of Sociology at Academia Sinica, and the Matsushida Foundation allowed me to obtain research assistance and take another extended field trip to Japan in 2002–2003. The Japan Institute of Labour hosted me during my stay in Tokyo in 2002, and enabled my access to several government institutions and a vast amount of research materials. A research grant from the Vice President's Office at the University of Texas at Austin came in at a later stage and provided the help I needed to bring the book into shape.

I started this book while working at Academia Sinica and finished it at the University of Texas at Austin. Both institutions provided friendly yet intellectually challenging working environments, which eased my pursuit of this work considerably. I am grateful to all my colleagues at these institutions for their support, encouragement, and feedback at various stages of the project. I extend special thanks to Ari Adut, Art Sakamoto, Kelly Raley, Christine Williams, and Yun Fan for their helpful suggestions as well as for their friendship.

Several people provided crucial research and editorial assistance that prompted completion of the book. In particular, I thank Chih-yao Chang, Daisuke Wakamatsu, Pei-lin Lee, and Shannon Shen, who helped collect much of the aggregate statistics and policy details presented herein. I also appreciate Donna Maurer for copyediting early drafts of the book. She patiently went through several rounds of editing with me and made the book better as a result.

My thanks also go to Kate Wahl and Joa Suorez at Stanford University Press. Along with Denise Botelho, they provided superb assistance that was critical in turning this project into a published work. In addition, I am grateful to James Raymo and the other reader for Stanford University Press, who gave not only positive reviews but also very thoughtful comments on an earlier version of the book. I believe that the revisions I made based on their suggestions have improved the book substantially.

Finally, like many people who have spent years pursuing a project, I strongly believe that the love and encouragement from my family were what kept me going throughout my long journey. Thus, my ultimate gratitude goes to my family, past and present. In addition to his or her unconditional support, each member contributed to this work in many different ways. For instance, my mother's stories from work, which I heard often while growing up, were what inspired me to study gender stratification in the first place. My father and brothers enthusiastically mobilized their social networks to find people with whom I could speak about the project, among other things. Although I feel equally indebted to each member of my family, I should note that my wonderful spouse, Andrés Villarreal, made significant contributions to the book also as an insightful sociologist. Our discussions from theoretical and methodological issues to ways of presentation helped me make many decisions that critically improved content. Moreover, his infinite confidence in me made it easy for me to stay on track even when things seemed rather disappointing. I simply cannot thank him enough for everything he has done.

*Wei-hsin Yu*
*Austin, October 2008*

# GENDERED
# TRAJECTORIES

## CHAPTER ONE

# Gender Inequality and Social Change in Japan and Taiwan

The past century has witnessed dramatic changes in women's work outside the home across a wide range of societies. Despite its initial negative effect on female labor force participation, industrialization has nearly universally increased women's involvement in nonagricultural work over the long run (Goldin 1995; Pampel and Tanaka 1986). This overall impact of industrialization, however, has not led to an equivalent degree of improvement in women's socioeconomic status in all countries. There remain significant differences in the gender wage gap, women's employment rates and trajectories, as well as gender distributions across occupations and employment status among countries with similar levels of economic development (Charles and Grusky 2004; Rosenfeld and Birkelund 1995; Stier, Lewin-Epstein, and Braun 2001; Wright, Baxter, and Birkelund 1995). The discrepancy between economic development and gender inequality is well illustrated in the global ranking of gender gaps published by the World Economic Forum (Zahidi 2007). In 2006, less industrialized countries such as Tanzania, the Philippines, and Ghana outranked a few advanced economies (including Sweden, Norway, and Canada) in terms of women's economic opportunities relative to men's. The same report indicates that despite being one of the wealthiest countries in the world, Japan ranked 79 among the 115 countries included with respect to the overall gender gap—far behind many low- and middle-income countries.

Why does women's economic status improve rapidly with industrialization in some countries but slowly in others? Answering this question requires a careful comparison of the evolution of women's employment opportunities as broader economic shifts take place in different countries. Previous research on the long-term development of the opportunity structure for women's gainful employment, however, has disproportionately focused on the U.S. context (e.g., Goldin 1990; Rosenfeld 1996; Thistle 2006). Knowledge of how macroeconomic changes shape the transformation of women's employment opportunities is particularly scarce outside of Western Europe and the United States (Van der Lippe and Van Dijk 2002). Also rare are comparative–historical analyses of gender inequality in the labor market. The shortage of systematic comparisons of the development of women's labor market opportunities makes it difficult to identify the social and institutional forces that account for changes in women's economic roles and opportunities across the industrialized world.

This book addresses how social institutions affect women's employment during economic development by comparing changes in women's job opportunities in Japan and Taiwan during the second half of the twentieth century. Although these two East Asian countries differ in their levels of development, they share several important features that make such a comparison particularly relevant. Many of the similarities between Japan and Taiwan can be traced back to the historical, political, and cultural intermixing in the region. Japan's fifty-year colonial rule in Taiwan (1895–1945) shaped Taiwan's modern bureaucratic institutions and educational system, and contributed to a convergence in the two countries' paths of economic development (Gold 1988; Hamilton and Biggart 1988; Mizoguchi and Yamamoto 1984). Among their shared features of economic development is a history of patriarchal policies, particularly the exploitation of female labor (Brinton 1993; Cheng and Hsiung 1994; Cumings 1987; Hsiung 1996). Culturally, aspects of the Confucian and Buddhist traditions have influenced both societies, leading to similar gender ideologies (Brinton 2001; Greenhalgh 1985). Also notable is that both educational systems are highly stratified and standardized (see Chapter 7), resulting in a strong emphasis on educational credentials in both labor markets (Brinton 1993; Huang 2001; Ishida 1993; Rohlen 1983; Yu and Su 2008).

What makes these two cases interesting is that, despite their many similarities, by the end of the twentieth century they differed substantially in their levels of gender inequality in the labor market. Although closely following Japan's steps in economic development, Taiwan has seen more drastic changes in women's employment opportunities than Japan during the past several decades. This different pace of change has led Taiwan to have a smaller gender gap in economic status than Japan. As the following section shows, the discrepancy in gender inequality between these two countries today is not easily attributable to their differences in macroeconomic conditions, demographic characteristics, social norms, or even policies and legislation. Using a comparative–historical approach, this book specifically addresses how Japanese and Taiwanese women came to their current places. The story I tell links macrolevel institutions to individual experiences and elucidates how individuals' decisions and actions at key moments in their lives contribute to broader changes in women's status in society. In telling such a story, this book aims not only to explain the puzzling difference in gender inequality between Japan and Taiwan, but also to provide a general understanding of gender and social change in industrial societies.

Japan and Taiwan are both known for their phenomenal rates of economic growth during the second half of the twentieth century. Moreover, both countries achieved their postwar economic success through exports under single-party dominance (Johnson 1987). Nevertheless, Japan began its industrialization long before World War II and experienced the transition to a postindustrial economy beginning in the mid 1970s, whereas Taiwan's trajectory of industrialization started later and was more condensed (Brinton 2001; Cumings 1987). Considering their different stages of economic development, one may question whether Japan and Taiwan are indeed comparable. This book, however, does not focus on the different levels of gender inequality between Japan and Taiwan at the *present*. Rather, the puzzle I intend to explain concerns the fact that Taiwan has veered away from Japan's path in terms of gender inequality in the labor market, despite following Japan closely in the trajectory of industrialization. As later chapters in this book show, Taiwanese women did not start from a much different place, as far as their employment opportunities are concerned, from that of Japanese women. Yet, while still catching up with Japan economically, Taiwan has experienced greater changes in women's economic roles and status than Japan. In this sense, the two countries' different economic stages actually make the comparison of gender inequality in the workplace more interesting.

To illustrate the similar trajectories of economic development in Japan and Taiwan, Figure 1.1 shows the annual economic growth rates of the two countries throughout time. There is a clear convergence in the two countries' experiences. Taiwan's rapid industrial expansion from the mid 1960s to the mid 1980s roughly resembles Japan's period of high economic growth from the mid 1950s to the early 1970s, whereas Taiwan's slower economic growth since the late 1980s appears to have followed Japan's experience from the mid 1970s to the 1980s. Taiwan's "catching up" has resulted in a national income level approaching Japan's today. As Table 1.1 shows, Taiwan's gross domestic product (GDP) per capita at purchasing power parity in 2005 was estimated to be $27,721 (in international dollars), about 90 percent of Japan's and higher than those of several other members of the Organisation for Economic Co-operation and Development (OECD), including Spain, New Zealand, and South Korea. Other socioeconomic indicators presented in Table 1.1 also suggest that Taiwan has come to be comparable with Japan. The Gini indexes indicate that the two countries have similar levels of household income inequality. In addition, both countries have moderate

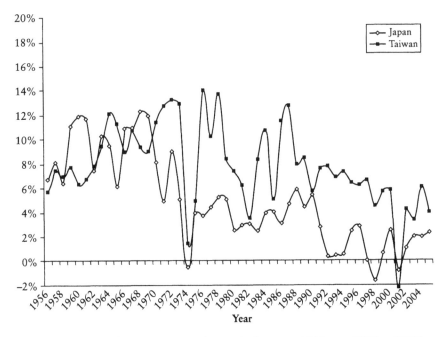

*Figure 1.1.*    Annual economic growth rates in Japan and Taiwan, 1956 to 2005.

SOURCE: Cabinet Office, Government of Japan, *Annual report on national accounts*, various years; Directorate-General of Budget, Accounting and Statistics (DGBAS), Executive Yuan, Republic of China, *National income of Taiwan area, the Republic of China*, various years; Statistics Bureau, Management and Coordination Agency, Japan, *Historical statistics of Japan*, 1987.

rates of unemployment, a relatively high average age of first marriage and childbirth, very low fertility rates, and medium divorce rates compared with other industrialized countries (based on country statistics reported by the OECD [2006] and the United Nations [2007b]).

Despite their various similarities, Japan and Taiwan differ in women's educational attainment and economic status, as shown in the bottom half of Table 1.1. The educational opportunities for Japanese women appear to exceed those for their Taiwanese counterparts. The percentage of Japanese women whose highest educational level completed was the upper secondary level was nearly 20 percent more than that of Taiwanese women as of 2005. There was also a slightly greater proportion of the female population with tertiary education in Japan than in Taiwan.[1] The percentage of women with four years of university education, however, was nearly identical in the two countries.

Given Japanese women's somewhat higher educational attainment, it is rather surprising that they occupy a smaller share of managerial and administrative positions than their Taiwanese counterparts. Furthermore, the dif-

TABLE I.I
*Comparison of Japan and Taiwan.*

|  | Japan | Taiwan |
|---|---|---|
| Selected socioeconomic indicators, 2005 |  |  |
| GDP per capita at purchasing power parity, in international dollars | $30,615 | $27,572 |
| Gini index* | 31.4 | 34.0 |
| Unemployment rate, per 100 people | 4.3 | 4.1 |
| Mean age at first marriage, y |  |  |
| Men | 29.8 | 29.7 |
| Women | 28.0 | 27.1 |
| Mean age of mothers first giving birth, y | 29.1 | 27.7 |
| Crude marriage rate, per 1,000 people | 5.7 | 6.3 |
| Crude divorce rate, per 1,000 people | 2.1 | 2.8 |
| Total fertility rate | 1.3 | 1.1 |
| Women's education and economic status, 1995–2005, % |  |  |
| Highest educational level[†‡] |  |  |
| Upper secondary | 46.6 | 28.4 |
| Tertiary | 24.3 | 21.9 |
| University and above | 7.5 | 7.4 |
| Female managers/senior officers, % |  |  |
| 1995 | 8.9 | 13.1 |
| 2005 | 10.1 | 16.5 |
| Female-to-male wage ratio, % |  |  |
| 1995 | 62.5 | 70.0 |
| 2005 | 65.9 | 78.2 |
| Percent of women with part-time jobs[‡] | 36.1 | 6.3 |
| Female share of part-time workers, %[‡] | 73.8 | 46.7 |

SOURCE: Department of Household Registration Affairs, Ministry of Interior, Republic of China, Household registration statistics (http://sowf.moi.gov.tw/stat/year/y02-02.xls). DGBAS, Executive Yuan, Republic of China, *Yearbook of manpower survey statistics, Taiwan area, Republic of China,* various years; Social indicators, 2005 (www.dgbas.gov.tw/public/Data/411711484071.xls). International Monetary Fund, World economic outlook database (www.imf.org/external/ns/cs.aspx?id=28). OECD, *OECD factbook 2006: Economic, environmental and social statistics,* 2006. Statistics and Information Department, Minister's Secretariat, Ministry of Health, Labour and Welfare, Japan, Vital statistics database (www.mhlw.go.jp/english/database/db-hw/index.html). Statistics Bureau, Ministry of Internal Affairs and Communications, Japan, The 2005 population census, 2007 (www.e-stat.go.jp/SG1/estat/NewList.do?tid=000001007251), and Labour Force Survey, various years (www.stat.go.jp/data/roudou/2.htm).

*Data for Japan from 2000.
†Among the population older than 15 years, excluding those in school.
‡Data from 2000.

ferences between 1995 and 2005 indicate that the pace of growth of women in managerial positions has been faster in Taiwan. The same can be said for the average wages of women relative to those of men. Not only were Taiwan's gender wage gaps smaller than Japan's in both 1995 and 2005, but Taiwan's wage gap shrank at a greater rate over time. By 2005, Taiwanese women received almost 80 percent of men's pay on average, whereas Japanese women were paid less than two thirds of men's wages.

Because the gender pay ratios shown in Table 1.1 are based on wages paid to regular full-time employees, the difference in such ratios between Japan and Taiwan represents only part of the difference in the gender wage gap. To be specific, although 36.1 percent of working Japanese women held part-time jobs in 2000, only 6.3 percent of Taiwanese working women did so. This difference is consistent with the fact that part-time workers are predominantly female in Japan (73.8% were women in 2000), but not in Taiwan (46.7%). Because part-time jobs generally pay lower wages even after taking women's skills and working hours into account (Houseman and Osawa 1995; Yu 2002), the difference in women's relative economic status between the two countries should be greater if part-time workers are included in estimating the gender pay gap. In other words, the fact that Japanese women are more likely to hold part-time jobs implies that their relative economic status lags behind Taiwanese women's even more than suggested by the levels of gender wage parity presented in Table 1.1.

In addition to differences in the economic gender gaps, women's employment trajectories in Japan and Taiwan also differ over their lifetimes. Figure 1.2 shows the female employment rate by age group in Japan and Taiwan, as well as in the respective major urban centers (the Tokyo metropolitan area and Taipei city).[2] The employment rates are lower among Japanese women in their thirties and early forties compared with those ages 25 to 29 years and 45 to 49 years, suggesting that women have a tendency to withdraw from the labor force during the early years of child rearing. The levels of employment are noticeably higher among Taiwanese women in their thirties than their Japanese counterparts. Interestingly, this difference cannot be explained by the possibility that Taiwanese women time their childbearing differently than Japanese women. Figure 1.3 presents the age distributions of brides and mothers who had live births in a recent year. The distributions are amazingly similar for Japan and Taiwan, especially when we contrast them with the age distribution of mothers in the United States (data on the U.S. age distribution of brides are unavailable). The mothers who gave birth recently in Japan and Taiwan were concentrated between 25 and 34 years of age, whereas their U.S. counterparts' age profile was clearly more diverse. Japanese and Taiwanese women appear to exhibit what Mary Brinton (1988, 1993) calls "condensed (rigid)" life cycle patterns, characterized by relatively little variation in the age at which individuals undergo major life course events, such as marriage and childbirth.

Given that the vast majority of women experience childbearing from their late twenties to early thirties in Japan and Taiwan, it is reasonable to argue that the difference in the employment rates among women in their thirties between these countries reflects women's different tendencies to remain in their jobs upon marriage and childbirth. That is to say, Taiwanese women seem more likely to continue their employment careers than Japanese women during their childbearing and early child-rearing years. It is noteworthy that U.S.-based research on female employment has suggested a

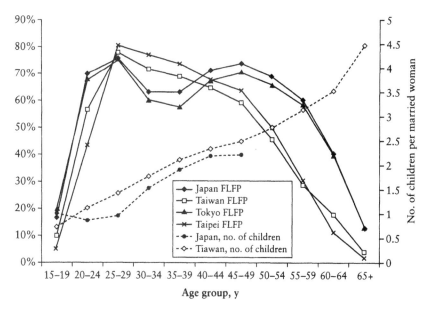

*Figure 1.2.* Women's labor force participation and number of children by age group.

SOURCE: DGBAS, Executive Yuan, Republic of China, Manpower Survey, 2005 (www.dgbas.gov.tw/ct.asp?xItem=17286&ctNode=3246), and Women's Marriage, Fertility, and Employment Survey, 2003 (www.dgbas.gov.tw/public/data/dgbas04/bc4/wtable3.xls); National Institute of Population and Social Security Research, Japan, *The processes of marriage and fertility among married couples in our country, 2002,* 2004; Statistics Bureau, Ministry of Internal Affairs and Communications, Japan, Labour Force Survey for 2005 (www.stat.go.jp/data/roudou/2.htm).

*Note:* The female labor force participation (FLFP) rates are calculated for all women, whereas the average number of children is calculated for married women only. The Tokyo metropolitan area includes Tokyo city and the surrounding urban areas—specifically, the Yokohama, Saitama, and Chiba prefectures. The FLFP rates in both Japan and Taiwan are based on 2005 data. The number of children among married women is based on 2002 data for Japan and 2003 data for Taiwan.

decline in women's postmarital retreat from the labor force during economic development, particularly with a shift to a service economy (Goldin 1990; Oppenheimer 1970). Yet, despite its more advanced economic stage and larger service sector (see Chapter 3), Japan demonstrates a greater tendency for women's postmarital retreat from the labor force than Taiwan.

The patterns of female employment by age group are generally similar in the major urban area and in the country as a whole for both Japan and Taiwan (Figure 1.2). The tendency of continuous employment, however, appears to be particularly strong among urban Taiwanese women, as the employment rate among women in their thirties is particularly high in Taipei. Conversely, women in the Tokyo metropolitan area have lower employment

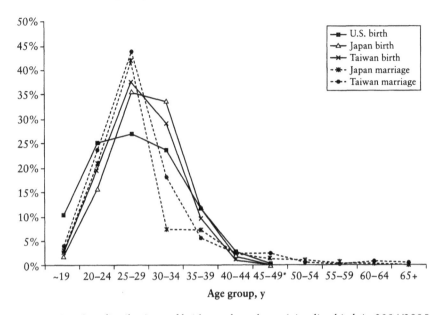

*Figure 1.3.*    Age distributions of brides and mothers giving live birth in 2004/2005.

S O U R C E : Department of Household Registration Affairs, Ministry of the Interior, Republic of China, Household registration statistics (www.ris.gov.tw/ch4/static/st10-10.xls; www.ris.gov.tw/ch4/static/st10-17.xls). United Nations, *Demographic yearbook 2004*, 2007.

*Note:* The data for the United States and Japan are from 2004, whereas the data for Taiwan are from 2005.

*The category includes all women 45 years of age and older for the statistics regarding age at giving live birth.

rates during their child-rearing years than the national average. Such opposite urban–rural gaps in female employment rates add further to the list of the two countries' striking differences regarding women's employment.

Figure 1.2 seemingly indicates that Taiwanese women's labor force participation only continues until their mid forties, given the female employment rate declines among older women. An analysis in Chapter 6 that uses life history data nevertheless shows that this is not the case. Therefore, for now, I focus on Taiwanese women's greater tendency than Japanese women to participate in the labor force after marriage. This Japan–Taiwan gap cannot be easily explained by differences in women's family responsibilities. First, the two countries are similar in terms of the availability of domestic labor for hire. Unlike in countries with extremely high levels of urban–rural inequality (e.g., China) or relatively open immigration policies (e.g., Singapore), there has been limited reliance on cheap domestic labor supplied by women from rural areas or lower income countries in Japanese and Taiwanese households (Loveband 2006; Mori 1997).[3] In the vast majority of these households, the wife shoulders nearly all responsibility for domestic chores (Gender Equality Bureau 2003; Lee, Yang, and Yi 2000; Tang and Parish 2000; Tsuya and Bumpass 1998). Second, as Figure 1.2 shows, married women in all age groups have fewer children in Japan than in Taiwan. Although having fewer children should enable Japanese women to participate in more labor force activities than Taiwanese women, the employment rate is higher among women in their thirties and early forties in Taiwan. Thus, despite the relatively low fertility rate, Japanese women appear to have difficulty continuing their careers upon marriage and childbirth.

Another possible explanation for the differences in women's economic status and employment trajectories between Japan and Taiwan has to do with the prevalent gender roles and attitudes in the two societies. While the historical and cultural intermixing in East Asia is conducive to the development of shared norms and values in Japan and Taiwan, their cultures are certainly not identical. Therefore, it might be that Taiwanese women are less likely to believe in the "separate sphere" ideology, which prescribes men's primary role to be market workers, with women acting as caretakers for their family members. Such a difference would explain why Taiwanese women participate more continuously and achieve higher status in the labor market than Japanese women.

To demonstrate gender beliefs in the two countries, Figure 1.4 shows the distributions of responses toward a series of questions regarding gender roles among Japanese and Taiwanese adults in the International Social Survey Programme (ISSP) conducted during 2002. The responses suggest that the predominant gender attitudes in Taiwan are actually more consistent with the separate sphere ideology than those in Japan. A greater proportion of Taiwanese people reported agreeing with the statement that a man's job is to earn money whereas a woman's job is to look after the home and family. Similarly, a greater percentage of Taiwanese respondents expressed that a preschool child will suffer if his or her mother works, even though mothers of preschool children appear to work more frequently in Taiwan than in Japan. The notion that what women really want is a home and children was also more popular in Taiwan. Nevertheless, Taiwanese respondents were more likely than Japanese respondents to consider employment as the best way for women to gain independence. This difference might result from the fact that there is more gender inequality in the workplace in Japan. Hence, women's employment is considered less beneficial in that country. Although the responses shown in Figure 1.4 are from both men and women, examining women's responses alone does not alter the differences between Japan and Taiwan.[4] Overall, contrary to the speculation that Taiwanese women might hold less traditional gender beliefs, they show greater support for the separate sphere ideology than their Japanese counterparts.

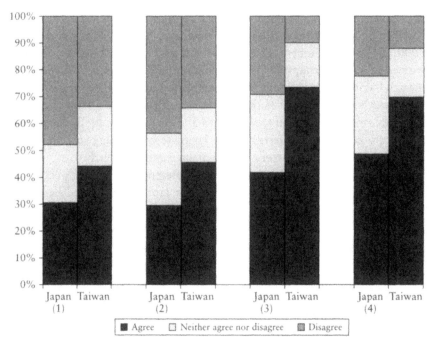

*Figure 1.4.*   Attitudes regarding gender roles in Japan and Taiwan.

SOURCE: ISSP, 2002.

*Note:* The bars indicate the percentage of respondents who agree/disagree with (1) "a man's job is to earn money; a woman's job is to look after the home and family"; (2) "a preschool child is likely to suffer if his or her mother works"; (3) "a job is all right, but what most women really want is a home and children"; and (4) "having a job is the best way for a woman to be an independent person."

In addition to gender beliefs, national policies and legislation are also potentially important to explaining cross-national differences in gender inequality in the labor market (Chang 2004; Gustafsson 1995; Van der Lippe and Van Dijk 2002). For example, countries that provide childcare subsidies make new mothers' employment less costly than in other countries, resulting in a greater likelihood for women to continue their jobs after childbirth (Gustafsson 1995). At the same time, job retention for married women is likely to be lower in countries that require husbands and wives to pay income tax jointly (Eissa 1996; Feldstein and Feenberg 1996; Gustafsson 1992; Pyle 1990). Moreover, employment policies ensuring equal access to jobs for men and women and permitting relatively lengthy leave for childbirth are thought to enhance the labor supply of married women, particularly those with young children (Glass and Estes 1997; Glass and Riley 1998).

There is, however, little evidence showing that government policies and regulations have made it easier for women to continue their jobs after marriage and childbearing in Taiwan than in Japan. First, while the critics often charge the Japanese government with providing insufficient childcare facilities, public childcare centers are even scarcer in Taiwan. Childcare provided by public facilities has been the primary alternative to maternal care in Japan, whereas it has played a relatively small role in relieving the childcare burden of Taiwanese mothers (Chen 2000; Yi 1994; Yu 2001a). As discussed in Chapter 5, the lack of public childcare centers does not necessarily mean that Taiwanese mothers are short of childcare options. As far as state childcare subsidies are concerned, however, the Japanese government has been providing more for working mothers of young children than the Taiwanese government.

Second, the two countries currently share similar tax systems, according to which husbands and wives can file wages apart, but must file property income together.[5] A "marriage penalty" nevertheless existed in Taiwan before the revision of the tax law in 1990. Until the revision, Taiwanese wives were not allowed to separate their wage income from their husbands' for tax purposes, resulting in higher tax rates among dual-income families. Although such a marriage penalty is thought to discourage married women's employment, it appears not to have been the case in Taiwan. As Chapter 2 shows, Taiwanese women began to increase their postmarital participation in the labor force around the mid 1970s, long before the government lifted the marriage penalty in the tax system. More important, because Taiwan's tax law actually provided a disincentive for married women to work, differences in tax regulations cannot account for the divergence in women's economic opportunities between Japan and Taiwan.

Third, with regard to regulations for workplace gender equality, Japan passed the Equal Employment Opportunity Act (EEOA) in 1986, whereas there was no similar legislation in Taiwan until 2002. Although Japan's EEOA has been criticized for being ineffective, it does prohibit blatant forms of gender discrimination, such as reserving certain jobs for men only (Lam 1993; Upham 1987). By contrast, Taiwan had no law against any form of gender discrimination through the twentieth century (Chen 2000). Last, Japanese women are entitled to fourteen weeks of maternity leave (six weeks before delivery and eight weeks after), but Taiwanese women are given only eight weeks of maternity leave in total. In fact, until 1985, Taiwan had no legal provision for maternity leave; hence, most women were unable to take such leave for more than four weeks. Even after Taiwan's Labor Standard Law mandated eight weeks of maternity leave in 1985, not all industries had to comply with this law. For example, until 1998, the Labor Standard Law did not apply to tertiary industries, such as finance and services industries (which are highly feminized). In addition, while the EEOA has enabled Japanese employees to take unpaid childcare leave for at least one year since

1986, it was not until sixteen years later that this leave became possible for Taiwanese employees.[6] Thus, whatever small effect Japan's policies may have on gender equality, Taiwan's provisions to advance working women's welfare are worse. The policy differences between the two countries only make it more surprising that Taiwanese women seem to have higher economic status and more continuous employment careers.

In summary, the comparison of Japan and Taiwan poses an interesting puzzle that needs to be explained. Despite their similar patterns of economic development, demographic trends, and social norms, women's employment opportunities have clearly diverged between these two countries. Compared with their Japanese counterparts, Taiwanese women have more equal economic status in relation to men, and they also appear to participate in the labor force in a more continuous fashion. Such differences are particularly puzzling given that Japanese women, on average, have higher educational levels, fewer children, and less traditional views toward women's involvement in the labor market than Taiwanese women. Moreover, although the Japanese state is thought to put little effort into enhancing gender equality (Chang 2000; Edwards 1988; Schoppa 2006), its welfare provision for working mothers is still more extensive than that in Taiwan. Because of all the commonalities and discrepancies between Japan and Taiwan, comparing the development of women's market opportunities in these countries is not only relevant, but also important for understanding differences in gender inequality across industrial societies.

## GENDER INEQUALITY AS A DYNAMIC SOCIAL PROCESS

A central focus of this book is social change. Although Japan and Taiwan both have experienced rapid economic and demographic changes since World War II, women's employment opportunities in these two countries have evolved at remarkably different rates. As later chapters in this book demonstrate, Taiwanese women's employment trajectories have become increasingly similar to men's over time, leading to greater gender equality in the labor market in that country. Conversely, changes in Japanese women's employment careers have been less dramatic and hence less consequential for workplace inequality between men and women. Although each generation of Japanese women generally spends more years of their lives in the labor force than the previous one, women's employment trajectories in Japan remain distinctly different from men's. This lack of convergence between men's and women's employment careers largely contributes to Japan's relatively wide gender gap in economic status.

Why do the two countries differ in the rates at which they reduce gender inequality in the workplace? What happened? I seek answers to these questions by conducting a comparative analysis of women's employment throughout the past half century. I argue that gender inequality in the labor market is a result of a long-term social process that involves both market forces and institutional responses to the market. Previous attempts to explain cross-national differences in gender inequality have predominantly relied on comparisons made at a single time point, and have considered the institutional arrangements and social conditions affecting women's economic opportunities as fixed (e.g., Chang 2004; Stier et al. 2001). My study will broaden our understanding of worldwide differences in gender inequality by considering such differences as results of dynamic social processes. As social values and institutions change over time, the gender gap in economic opportunities may also narrow or widen. The analysis results presented in this volume show that the pace and direction in which a society transforms often depends on preexisting institutional arrangements. Moreover, the outcomes of social change can then become part of the social forces that either accelerate or hamper further transformations of women's labor market opportunities. Thus, only by comparing the long-term development of women's employment opportunities across countries can we accurately identify the factors contributing to worldwide differences in gender inequality in the labor market.

While there is no shortage of studies documenting the evolution of women's economic lives (e.g., Goldin 1990; Oppenheimer 1970; Rosenfeld 1996; Thistle 2006), few of these studies are based on non-Western societies, and even fewer adopt a comparative perspective. Contrasting the pace and direction of changes in women's employment in Japan and Taiwan during the past half century enables me to reveal an untold story regarding gender and social change. Specifically, this story tells how change is possible even in societies in which cultural values and social policies tend to deter gender equality. Thus, this is a story that cannot be told by previous studies that compare Western and East Asian countries (usually Japan) (e.g., Brinton 1993; Chang 2000; Esping-Anderson 1990). Moreover, the similar trajectories of socioeconomic development in Japan and Taiwan make it possible to isolate what precisely motivates or impedes changes in gender inequality in a way that an East–West comparison cannot. Finally, although there has been increasing attention paid to differences within East Asia, rather than East–West discrepancies (e.g., Brinton 2001), this book is the first to offer a systematic analysis of the historical change in women's employment behavior in two East Asian countries. By taking into account changes in women's economic opportunities over time, this analysis extends beyond research focusing on cross-sectional differences and uncovers the broader dynamics that shape gender inequality and social change in Japan and Taiwan.

## LINKING MACROLEVEL FACTORS TO WOMEN'S EMPLOYMENT OVER THEIR LIFE COURSE

Historical time is not the only temporal dimension emphasized in this study. The individual's lifetime constitutes another temporal dimension on which this book focuses. Women's decisions about employment at key moments of their lives make up the patterns of female employment at the aggregate level. Explaining the divergence in women's employment patterns between Japan and Taiwan therefore requires a comparative analysis of the constraints and opportunities women face at different points of their life course. Furthermore, because women's employment opportunities vary substantially throughout their lifetimes, examining these opportunities at a single point in their lives provides only partial evidence of the differences in the gender gap in economic status between Japan and Taiwan. As Chapter 2 shows, the gap between men's and women's economic conditions varies throughout their life course in both countries, but the extent to which it changes differs by country. Specifically, Japan's gender gap in wages widens at a faster pace than Taiwan's as individuals move further along their life course. A thorough understanding of the differences in women's economic opportunities between Japan and Taiwan thus requires an explanation for why they differ in the rates at which gender inequality increases or decreases with various life course stages.

I therefore use a life course approach to examine women's employment decisions and their economic consequences, instead of assessing women's occupational status at a single point in their lives. In particular, I compare Japanese women's employment trajectories with those of women in Taiwan and highlight the cross-national differences in the factors affecting women's decisions to participate in the labor force at crucial points in their lives. At the same time, I emphasize the mechanisms linking macrolevel influences to the microlevel decision-making processes that women face. I argue that country-specific organizational arrangements, industrial policies, social norms, and labor market conditions affect women's employment decisions by shaping their work and home environments, and hence their assessments of the feasibility of combining work and family life. Prior studies comparing women's employment in East Asia and elsewhere have paid insufficient attention to these microlevel social dynamics that directly influence women's lives (e.g., Brinton 1993; Esping-Anderson 1990; Schoppa 2006). As a result, not only do the mechanisms translating macrolevel barriers into microlevel behavior remain unspecified, but the implicit assumption of an automatic macro–micro link generally leads researchers to neglect the variation in women's responses to macrolevel constraints within a country. My analysis expands previous research on gender and work by showing how macrolevel conditions shape within-country differences in women's employment decisions and how such within-country patterns then account for the aggregate-level discrepancies between Japan and Taiwan regarding women's employment.

As my analysis unfolds, it should become clear that telling a complete story about gender and social change in Japan and Taiwan requires taking into account both macro- and microlevel dynamics, as well as the span of individuals' lifetimes and historical time. Although macrolevel conditions such as aggregate labor demand and industrial policies shape women's decisions about labor force participation at the microlevel, women's employment behavior throughout their life course also forms social patterns at the aggregate level. Such aggregate patterns can further shape country-level norms, discourses, and even institutional arrangements, which then become an important part of what women of the next generation must consider when making decisions about their employment careers. That is to say, not only do opportunities and constraints existing in the social context shape individuals' decisions and behaviors, but the aggregate result of individuals' actual behaviors can also influence the directions of social change.

## A NOTE ON WOMEN'S WORK AND ECONOMIC STATUS

This study is about women's employment, or women's participation in market work. For simplicity I use a rather narrow definition of work throughout this book. Unless otherwise specified as, for example, domestic work, the term *work* refers exclusively to market work. This does not mean to imply that women perform work only in the market. Women across the world devote a tremendous amount of time and labor producing goods and services at home, to the extent that unpaid domestic work constitutes the "second shift" for those who also participate in the labor market (Hochschild 1989). In fact, as this book shows, it is precisely because women work so hard at home that the conflict between their jobs and family obligations seems inevitable.

Market work in the contexts of Japan and Taiwan is not necessarily paid work or work outside the home. For example, women might perform piecework at home for pay (Hsiung 1996). This job option has nevertheless become increasingly unavailable with the shrinking of the manufacturing sector in both countries.[7] Still relatively common is for married women to work at family-owned (usually their husbands') enterprises with either irregular or no pay (Yu 2001b, 2004). Despite their lack of regular wages, such women's labor contributes directly to the production of the family enterprise. My definition of work considers all that involves a person's direct participation in economic activities, since such participation has the potential to enhance a woman's marketable skills and expand her social contacts beyond the domestic realm.[8]

Because I am primarily interested in gender inequality in the workplace, women's economic opportunities in this book generally refer to their chances of obtaining higher income and occupational status in the labor market. Similarly, my assessment of women's economic status is based on their own jobs, regardless of what their husbands do. Some of the people I spoke with in Japan and Taiwan expressed the sentiment that nonemployed women with husbands who have high earnings are truly better off than married women with jobs. Indeed, nonworking wives of relatively wealthy men may enjoy better economic conditions than many women who do work. Using family as the unit to assess women's economic well-being seems to make sense, especially in these countries, since they traditionally have low divorce rates. My ultimate concern, however, is with the opportunities the economy affords women to pursue labor market achievement as individuals. A statement from one Japanese woman I interviewed, who held a clerical job at a large firm, illustrates just how much women's own job opportunities and economic achievements mean to them:

> The reason I decided to come back to work after giving birth—it is hard to explain. How do I put it? I am always part of my social relations on other occasions. I am my husband's *wife* for my neighbors and other relatives. When I send my child to daycare, I am the *mother*. It is only at work I am *Tanaka Keiko* [name changed], myself. I continue this job because I want to maintain being myself.

### RESEARCH DESIGN AND OUTLINE OF THE BOOK

The analysis presented in this book is based on data from multiple sources, including aggregate statistics published by government offices and related agencies, individual-level surveys, and in-depth personal interviews. Generally speaking, I use aggregate statistics to show macrolevel trends, and survey and interview data to demonstrate microlevel responses to macrolevel conditions. With the individual-level survey data, I compare the work and life experiences of women born during various decades since 1935. Most chapters of this book focus on changes in women's employment from the 1950s to the mid 1990s—the period when Japan and Taiwan both underwent remarkably rapid and constant economic growth. By focusing on this period, I am able to demonstrate the conditions that mediate the effects of industrial expansion on gender inequality in the labor market. In addition, the period through the mid 1990s was one in which women's employment opportunities diverged between Japan and Taiwan. As the final chapter of the book shows, the development of workplace inequality between men and women in the decade since the mid 1990s is largely a continuation of that of the previous decades in both countries. Separating the past decade from the previous period, however, allows me to differentiate the effects of Japan's unprecedented economic recession (and its associated reforms) since the 1990s on women's employment from those of other structural factors that play key roles in explaining the divergence in gender inequality between the two countries.

Throughout this book I seek to combine statistical analysis with ethnographic observations and women's life stories that I obtained through in-depth personal interviews conducted in major metropolitan areas in Japan and Taiwan.[9] Such qualitative material not only helps substantiate my arguments, but also adds meaning to the social patterns observed with survey data. To learn about how women's family concerns shape their employment trajectories, the women I interviewed were all married with children, held a job at the time of their interview, and had premarital employment experience. Most of them were in their mid-thirties to mid-forties. The interview topics generally included their detailed job experiences and their reasons for making employment- or family-related decisions at different points of their lives. I also conducted interviews with firm managers, labor union officers, government officials, and workers at daycare centers to understand the difficulties women face in managing work and family life. All these informants were located through snowball sampling, with the help of my acquaintances (to start). Altogether, I conducted intensive interviews with more than eighty individuals. My personal observations and others' views that were revealed to me on informal occasions are also used to illustrate the conditions that working women often confront in Japan and Taiwan.

The central questions of this study are how and why Japan and Taiwan diverged with regard to women's employment opportunities during their life course. The remaining chapters of the book address these two questions with a series of comparative analyses utilizing the multiple data sources just described. I begin in Chapter 2 by documenting how women's employment trajectories have differed between Japan and Taiwan, as well as the consequences of these differences. Using survey data containing individuals' detailed work histories, I show changes in women's timing and duration of labor force participation, as well as their frequency of job shifts over time. This analysis helps establish the critical time points when women in these two countries began to diverge in their patterns of labor force participation. In the same chapter I compare men's and women's career processes in both countries. In particular, I examine the implications of the gender difference in work trajectories for women's income and occupational attainment over the long run. I find evidence that women's decisions to continue their jobs after marriage and childbirth play a crucial role in shaping their lifetime economic status.

In Chapter 3, I develop the explanations for the differences in women's employment trajectories in Japan and Taiwan. The emphasis of this chapter is to show how specific differences between the two national labor markets contribute to the different work environments women face in the two countries. The macrolevel differences I discuss center on the two countries' industrial strategies, predominant employment practices, and structures of business organizations. I pay particular attention to how preexisting structural conditions contributed to the different strategies that employers adopted in response to market shifts during the two economies' development. Such strategies had important implications for working women by shaping their job demands and workplace dynamics. I argue that women's working conditions and workplace atmosphere affect their perceptions of the feasibility of combining their job and family responsibilities. The perceived level of compatibility between work and family directly affects women's decisions about employment at key moments of their lives.

To examine systematically the theoretical framework just described, in Chapter 4 I provide an individual-level analysis of women's decisions to leave the labor force after marriage and childbirth. This analysis reveals that the factors contributing to women's exit from the labor force tend to differ between Japan and Taiwan. The differences in the dynamics of women's postmarital job exits are consistent with the discrepancies in working conditions that women with differing types of jobs in these countries experience. The evidence also supports the claim that, because of divergent labor market conditions, women generally face greater difficulties combining their family and job responsibilities in Japan than in Taiwan. I then link the individual-level results to aggregate-level changes over time. I demonstrate that the observed labor force exit dynamics, along with broader economic and demographic shifts, account for the historical change in women's employment behavior in the two countries.

I turn to the family side of the story in Chapter 5, where I discuss child-care options, maternal obligations, and women's domestic responsibilities. Using aggregate statistics and qualitative data, I show that the greater conflict between family and job responsibilities Japanese women experience also arises from their family's higher demand for their time and labor. An examination of the historical changes in family spending, gender attitudes, and child-rearing time presented in the second half of Chapter 5, however, suggests that the differing job demands and workplace atmosphere for women are primarily responsible for the different rates at which women's employment behaviors change between the two countries. Shifts in female employment behavior can nevertheless lead to other societal transformations that have reciprocal effects on women's employment.

Chapter 6 focuses on married women's decisions to return to the workforce. Not only does labor force reentry constitute a major transition in women's working and family lives, it is also closely associated with women's economic status at a later stage of their life course. I begin the chapter by analyzing the timing of women's reentry into the labor market, using work history data. This analysis reveals how the differing levels of conflict between job and family responsibilities for women shape the pace at which they return to the labor force in Japan and Taiwan. Additionally, I show that married women's timing of resuming employment also depends on how the labor market they face may penalize their work interruption. Based on whether their job opportunities decrease significantly with their time away from the labor force, women are likely to time their labor market returns differently. The second part of the chapter analyzes the types of jobs available for women returning to the labor force. I find striking differences between Japan and Taiwan in women's destinations upon employment reentry. I argue that Japan's rigid labor market practices, along with its dualist work structure that offers sharply different rewards to employees in regular full-time status versus those on a contingent or part-time basis, essentially account for married women's highly restricted job options upon labor force reentry.

I turn my attention to these countries' educational systems in Chapter 7 because they play a part in shaping workplace dynamics for women. The quality and composition of a country's labor supply largely depend on women's and men's educational opportunities. In particular, whether a country's labor supply consists of a sufficient number of qualified men is thought to affect the overall likelihood for managers to accommodate women in the workplace, since managers generally prefer hiring men over women given the same qualifications (Brinton, Lee, and Parish 1995; Reskin 2001). Chapter 7 shows that Japan and Taiwan differ in their educational opportunities for men and women, resulting in differing compositions of their overall labor queues. Specifically, the analysis demonstrates how a strong emphasis on vocational education and gender segregation in elite high schools actually enhanced women's access to higher education in Taiwan. This greater access, along with Taiwan's relatively restricted number of university students, compelled Taiwanese employers to utilize highly educated women more than in Japan. In addition, I discuss how the small differences in the design of the school entrance examinations between Japan and Taiwan had critical implications for girls' chances of entering prestigious universities. The remarkable discrepancy in women's representation in elite universities is among the key factors contributing to the gap in women's economic opportunities between the two countries.

Finally, Chapter 8 concludes this study by first summarizing the findings and overall arguments presented in the previous chapters. Following this, I describe changes in women's employment opportunities since the mid 1990s using more recent survey data. I then assess whether a further divergence or a future convergence can be expected between the two countries by evaluating recent policy changes and their implications for gender inequality in the workplace. I pay special attention to how broader economic shifts, resulting from the slowdown of both economies since the late 1990s, may transform workplaces and gender inequality in the years to come. Last, beyond the specific cases of Japan and Taiwan, this chapter ends with a discussion of this study's general implications for understanding the different paces at which the economic gender gaps close across the industrialized world.

## CHAPTER TWO

# The Development of Women's Labor Market Experiences

The remarkable speed of economic development that Japan and Taiwan experienced after World War II ensured rapid changes in women's labor market experiences. In both countries, women had virtually moved out of the agricultural sector by the late 1970s. They had become more frequently involved in office work rather than factory work by the end of the twentieth century (Brinton 2001). Despite these shared trends, there are considerable differences between Japan and Taiwan in the development of women's economic roles. The objective of this chapter is to explain how women from these two countries diverged in their employment behaviors, as well as the economic consequences of this divergence. To this end, I compare the employment trajectories of women from different birth cohorts in Japan and Taiwan. *Birth cohorts* refer to individuals who were born during the same time period within a population. Members of a birth cohort experience the same historical events at similar time points of their lives. I focus on the experiences of the birth cohorts that entered adulthood and became eligible for market work from the early 1950s to the early 1990s to delineate labor market and social changes during the second half of the twentieth century.

Although I focus on the post-World War II development of women's work opportunities and experiences in Japan and Taiwan, it is noteworthy that Japan's industrialization started long before the war (Cumings 1987; Pyle 1978). It was not unusual for Japanese women with some formal schooling to hold modern industrial jobs even before World War II (Brinton 1993). By contrast, the Taiwanese economy was primarily agrarian in the aftermath of World War II, despite the onset of its industrialization under prewar Japanese colonial rule (Cumings 1987). Because of their different paces of economic development, it is expected that Japan and Taiwan would differ in the magnitude of change in women's market activities since the 1950s. This chapter, however, shows that the divergent histories of industrialization between the two countries do not account for all the differences in the patterns of female labor force participation.

The trends and analysis presented here are based on data from two nationally representative surveys. Specifically, the data for Japan are from the Social Stratification and Social Mobility Survey (SSM) conducted in 1995, and the data for Taiwan are from the Taiwan Social Change Survey (TSC) conducted in 1996. These surveys asked respondents to report their entire employment careers and information about each job retrospectively (see Appendix A for more details). Using such job history records, I first describe changes in women's employment trajectories over time in the two countries. Second, I explore gender differences in career processes and compare the gender gap in economic conditions between the two countries. In particular, I examine the earnings of men and women, with an emphasis on the implications of women's employment trajectories for their income. Taken together, the analysis presented in this chapter addresses the following questions: How did women's career processes evolve during the second half of the twentieth century in Japan and Taiwan? To what extent did men and women differ in their employment trajectories? Have women and men converged or diverged in their labor market experiences over time? Finally, how different have Japan and Taiwan been with regard to the gender gap in economic opportunities?

## TRENDS IN WOMEN'S PARTICIPATION
## IN THE LABOR FORCE

This section focuses on the labor market experiences of women from different birth cohorts. Survey respondents from Japan and Taiwan are divided into four cohorts based on whether they were born in the 1930s, 1940s, 1950s, or 1960s.[1] Differences in the experiences of these four groups, taken together, indicate how women's working lives have changed in the two countries throughout time.

### Changes in Women's Work Experience

Today, most people have been or expect to be engaged in market work at some point in their lives. This has not always been the case historically. Although few men in the samples for Japan and Taiwan reported that they had never participated in any market work, nearly one fifth of Taiwanese women born 1936 to 1941 had never held any job.[2] Conversely, less than 8 percent of Japanese women born during the same period reported not having any job experience throughout their lifetime. Taiwanese women's likelihood of ever participating in the labor force, however, increased rapidly with time. When the cohort born in the 1960s reached working age, there was virtually no difference between Japan and Taiwan, or between women and men.

Gender differences in the length of work experience nevertheless remain in the two countries. According to the survey data, the average proportion of time Japanese men spent on market work since their first entry into the labor market was close to 100 percent.[3] It was extremely rare for Japanese men to discontinue their employment careers. Taiwanese men had a greater tendency for work interruptions than Japanese men, but their career trajectories were still relatively continuous. On average, a Taiwanese man who had his first job at age twenty would have had only one year of absence from the labor force by age 40, after excluding the time he had to be away from the labor market for his mandatory military service.[4] By contrast, Japanese women who started their first job soon after leaving school were in the labor force for about 66 percent of the time, whereas Taiwanese women were employed for 69 percent of the time after their first job. Based on these percentages, a woman who began her working life at twenty years of age would have accumulated about twenty years of work experience by age 50 in both countries. This length of work experience, though lower than what a similar man would have accumulated, is comparable with that of U.S. women born in the 1970s (Rosenfeld 1996:204). Thus, although market work was once viewed as a short-term activity before marriage for women in both Japan and Taiwan (Brinton 1993; Diamond 1973; Hunter 2003; Kung 1994), most women born during the postwar decades participated in the labor force for an extensive proportion of their lives.

Women's timing of labor force participation has also changed over time, especially in Taiwan. To illustrate, Figure 2.1 shows by birth cohort the percentages of women in the labor force at seven time points in their lives: before marriage, at first marriage, at first childbirth, at last childbirth, at last child 3 years old, at last child 6 years old, and at last child 6 years old.[5] Because a considerable number of women born in the 1960s had not completed their childbearing by the survey years (1995 in Japan and 1996 in Taiwan), I present their work experience only up to the point of having their first child. Likewise, I do not present the proportion of women born in the 1950s in the labor force when their last child was 12 years of age, because only a small proportion of them would have experienced this life course stage by the time of the survey.

Reflecting its rapid industrialization during the postwar decades, Taiwan witnessed a 30 percent increase in women's labor force participation before marriage. In comparison, the increase in Japanese women's premarital labor force participation seems small. This small increase has to do with the fact that even those born in the 1930s had a participation rate as high as 91 percent. Women's premarital work experience nevertheless converged in the two countries during the late twentieth century. Taiwanese women born in the 1960s, who finished their education roughly in the 1980s, had

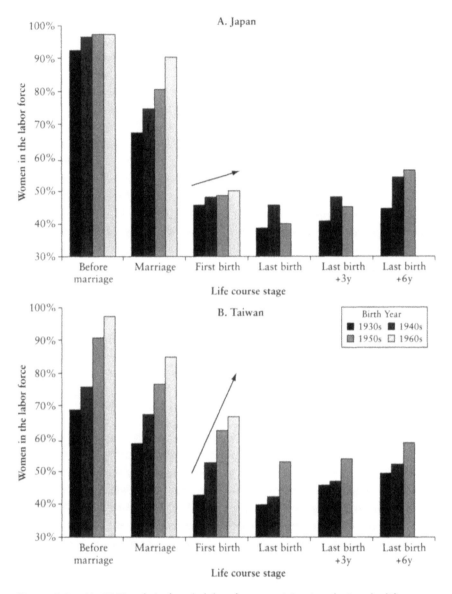

*Figure 2.1.* (A, B) Trends in female labor force participation during the life course for Japan (A) and Taiwan (B).

SOURCE: Japan, 1995 SSM, part A; Taiwan, 1996 TSC, part II.

*Note:* The life course stages included in the figure are before marriage, at first marriage (current marriage for Japanese respondents who had remarried), at first childbirth, at last childbirth, last child 3 years old, and last child 6 years old. Respondents who had not reached the given life course stage by the survey year were censored in the calculation.

a comparable premarital employment rate with that of their Japanese coun-terparts. In fact, by the 1980s, not only women's rates of premarital em-ployment were similar, but single women in both countries also worked as frequently and as continuously as their male counterparts.

While the work experience of single women in the two countries has converged with economic development, women's employment trajectories since marriage have not. In particular, the growing labor force participation among single women had a lasting effect on their employment throughout their life course in Taiwan, but not in Japan (illustrated by the arrows in Figure 2.1). The employment rates at first marriage and first childbirth for Taiwanese women increased to a similar extent as newer cohorts gained more work experience while single. By contrast, although the proportion of Japanese women who worked through marriage increased across cohorts, there was little change in the labor force participation rates in the year of first childbirth. In other words, Taiwanese women with young children have become increasingly active in the labor market, but this has not been the case in Japan.

Comparing different groups' participation in the labor force through the life course helps me identify the critical time point at which women's employment behaviors diverged between the two countries. Although Tai-wanese women born in the 1930s had a slightly lower employment rate around their first childbirth than their Japanese counterparts, those born during the next several decades generally participated in the labor market at a higher rate at that stage. Hence, as early as the 1960s, when women born in the 1940s began to enter motherhood, there emerged a difference in mar-ried women's employment behavior between Japan and Taiwan. However, Taiwanese women born in the 1950s were the ones who had higher em-ployment rates than those in Japan throughout their years of rearing young children (i.e., the period from their first childbirth to the time when their last child entered school). This trend suggests that around the mid 1970s, when women born in the 1950s were about to become mothers, the increase in the proportion of married women who continuously participated in the labor market became substantial in Taiwan.

### Labor Force Exit and Reentry

In addition to the length of work experience, the frequency of exits from the labor force also characterizes individuals' employment careers throughout their life course. In Japan and Taiwan, most of the labor force exits made by women are related to changes in their family status. Among all the labor force exits experienced by women in the samples before the age of 50, more than 70 percent of such exits occurred around the years of marriage and childbearing for Japan, and more than 60 percent for Taiwan.[6] Although women in these countries left their jobs more frequently than men, they tended not to move in and out of the labor force frequently. Among ever-married Japanese women who had left the labor force at least once by the survey time, only 12 percent exited the labor market more than once. By contrast, Taiwanese women had slightly more employment interruptions throughout their working lives. About 17 percent of ever-married Taiwanese women who had ever left the labor market had done so more than once. In short, had it been not for marriage or childbearing, women in these countries would rarely interrupt their employment careers.

A sizable proportion of Japanese and Taiwanese women who left the labor force at one point returned. Based on their experiences of labor force exits and returns, I divide women in the two countries into three groups: (1) those with continuous careers that involve no interruption, (2) those with interrupted careers that contain both labor exit and reentry, and (3) those with short-lived careers that end with a labor exit at a relatively early time point in their lives. Figure 2.2 presents the distribution of these three types of careers among women by age group. Because this characterization is based on events of labor force exit and reentry that occurred by the current age, the frequency distribution for the younger groups is less accurate. Specifically, women of younger age could potentially return to the labor force after the survey was conducted. Hence, the percentages presented in Figure 2.2 underestimate the proportion of those women who will eventually have intermittent careers. It is also likely that, within the youngest age group (25–34 years), the proportion of women with continuous careers is overestimated, because not all of them have experienced marriage and motherhood. I therefore include the distribution of the three types of careers among women age 25 to 34 who were mothers. Their patterns of careers might be closer to those of all members of this birth cohort had they all undergone marriage and childbirth.

Interestingly, the differences in the distribution of careers between the two older age groups are similar in both countries. Japanese and Taiwanese women born in the 1940s (i.e., age group 45–55) were more likely to have continuous or interrupted careers, rather than early retirements, than those born in the 1930s (i.e., age group 55–60). The distribution of continuous, interrupted, and short-lived careers among Taiwanese women born in the succeeding decade (i.e., age group 35–44) was nearly identical. The distribution for the next birth cohort of women, however, suggests a substantial increase in women's tendency to have continuous employment careers. Almost 50 percent of Taiwanese mothers between 25 and 34 years of age had been working continuously as of 1996. By contrast, in Japan, the increase in women's likelihood to work continuously reversed for those born since 1950 (i.e., age groups 25–34 and 35–44). A smaller proportion of

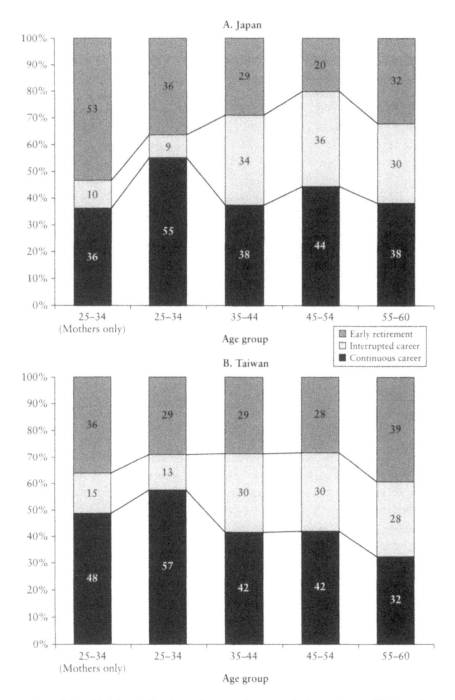

*Figure 2.2.* (A, B) Distributions of women's careers in Japan (A) and Taiwan (B).
SOURCE: Japan, 1995 SSM, part A; Taiwan, 1996 TSC, part II.

Japanese women born in the 1950s experienced continuous careers compared with those born a decade earlier. Only 36 percent of Japanese women born in the 1960s had worked continuously, if nonmothers from this group are excluded. This percentage was even smaller than those among members of previous cohorts who had been in the labor force for longer.

The reversal of Japanese women's tendency toward continuous employment, as revealed in Figure 2.2, coincided with two broader economic changes. One has to do with Japan's overall economic growth. Born in the 1940s, women in the 45- to 54-year age group faced Japan's high growth period (from the mid 1950s to the early 1970s) as they stepped into marriage and motherhood. The rapidly increasing demand for labor during this period made women born in the 1940s exceptional in terms of their likelihood of continuous employment. Second, the late 1960s was when women's participation in wage employment surpassed that in family enterprise employment and self-employment (Brinton 2001; Yu 1999). Soon afterward, when those born in the 1950s began to enter marriage, the reversal of women's continuous employment occurred. An increase in wage employment appears to be associated with Japanese women's declining tendency to work continuously.

Although the proportion of Japanese women with continuous careers hardly increased, they extended their working lives by returning to the labor force more frequently and at a faster rate. Figure 2.3 compares the percentages of women who had returned to the labor force by ages 35, 40, and 45 years. A relatively high percentage of ever-married women returned to market work in Japan. For example, more than 50 percent of Japanese women born in 1946 to 1950 had returned to the labor market by age 40. More than 60 percent of this same cohort of women had reentered the labor force by 45 years of age. Moreover, not only were Japanese women increasingly likely to return to the labor market, but their age of employment reentry had become younger. A greater percentage of women born in 1951 to 1955 had reentered the labor market by age 40 than that of women born a decade earlier who had returned by age 45. For the youngest group shown in Figure 2.3 (women born 1956–1960), more than 40 percent had returned by the time they turned thirty-five years old in Japan. Thus, nearly every cohort of women returned to the labor force at a higher and faster rate than the previous one in postwar Japan.

Figure 2.3 also indicates that, at least for those born before 1956, Taiwanese women who had once left the labor force were less likely to return than Japanese women. Although the percentage of Taiwanese women who had reentered the labor market by age 35 was similar to that of their Japanese counterparts, the proportion of women who returned to the labor force after age 35 was much smaller in Taiwan. Nevertheless, Taiwanese women did return to the labor market at higher and faster rates over time.

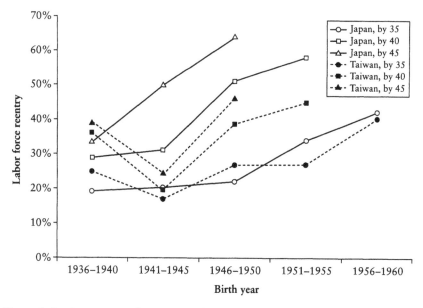

*Figure 2.3.* Proportion of ever-married women returning to the labor force by various ages.

SOURCE: Japan, 1995 SSM, part A; Taiwan, 1996 TSC, part II.

*Note:* The percentages of labor force returns are calculated only among those who had left the labor force. Women who worked continuously are not included in the figure. Also, those born after 1960 are not included in the figure because many of them were less than 35 years old when the surveys were conducted.

The increase in the proportion of women who returned to the labor force somewhat coincided with Taiwan's drastically declining fertility rates in the 1960s and 1970s. As the average number of children in Taiwanese families decreased to less than three during the late 1970s (Chang, Freedman, and Sun 1987), women born in the 1950s, who were likely to enter motherhood around this time, displayed a significant increase in the rate of labor force reentry.

To summarize, the postwar changes in female employment patterns in the two countries had shortened the gap in the length of work experience between men and women throughout their lifetimes, especially for Taiwan. The evolution of Japanese women's employment trajectories featured relatively constant rates of work interruptions, but increases in labor force returns. Despite a rise in women's employment continuity during Japan's period of rapid economic growth, women of the succeeding cohorts failed to continue increasing their participation in the labor market after marriage and childbearing.[7] In fact, they became more likely to withdraw from the labor force. This trend is consistent with aggregate statistics that show a steady decline of women ages 25 to 34 in the labor force from the 1960s to the late 1970s in Japan (International Labour Office 1990). Thus, the change in the employment behavior of Japanese women born in the 1940s was exceptional and had to do with that country's unprecedented economic growth in the 1960s. Japanese women, however, had extended their working lives during the second half of the twentieth century by increasing their rates of reentering the labor market. Not only were Japanese women more likely to return to work, but they also reentered the labor force more promptly.

Taiwanese women's work trajectories transformed roughly at the same time that their Japanese counterparts increased their rate of employment interruptions—around the late 1970s.[8] I have shown that Taiwanese women born since 1950 generally have had longer and more continuous working lives. In particular, these women were more likely to remain in their jobs upon marriage and childbearing. Taiwanese women's rates of labor force returns also increased over time, even though the amount of increase was not as high as that in Japan. It is noteworthy that a steady rise in female participation in wage employment accompanied these changes in women's work experience. Taiwan's proportion of the female labor force in wage employment surpassed that in family enterprise employment and self-employment during the early 1970s (Brinton 2001; Yu 1999). Interestingly, although the increase in women's wage employment was associated with their greater tendency to interrupt work for child rearing in Japan, it appears to have coincided with the growth of working mothers in Taiwan.

GENDER DIFFERENCES IN CAREER PROCESSES

The length of work experience is not the only aspect that distinguishes men's employment careers from women's. Men and women often differ in their occupation, employment status, job tenure, frequency of employer changes, and the timing of job turnover, among other variables (Padavic and Reskin 2003; Reskin 1993; Yamagata, Yeh, Stewman, and Dodge 1997; Yu 2004). These gender differences, taken together, shape the gap in economic well-being between men and women throughout their lifetime (Rosenfeld 1992). Thus, whereas examining work experience helps determine the gender gap in the quantity of work, comparing women's and men's career processes informs the gap in the quality of work. In the following, I examine gender differences in employment trajectories, as well as the economic consequences associated with these differences in Japan and Taiwan.

*Job Mobility and Labor Market Outcomes*

I begin the analysis of women's and men's career processes by revealing their respective job mobility, measured by the number of employers they have

TABLE 2.1
*Average number of jobs experienced throughout men's and women's employment careers.*

| | JAPAN | | | | TAIWAN | | | |
|---|---|---|---|---|---|---|---|---|
| | Men | Women | Employed men | Employed women | Men | Women | Employed men | Employed women |
| No. of job spells | 2.20 | 2.16 | 2.22 | 2.49* | 2.90 | 2.47* | 2.94 | 2.87 |
| | (1.52) | (1.35) | (1.52) | (1.34) | (1.77) | (1.67) | (1.75) | (1.65) |
| N | 891 | 1016 | 864 | 634 | 1377 | 1452 | 1313 | 837 |

SOURCE: Japan, 1995 SSM, part A; Taiwan, 1996 TSC, part II.

Numbers in parentheses are standard deviations.

*The difference between the female group and its corresponding male group is statistically significant at the 0.05 level based on a two-tailed *t*-test.

had. In labor markets in which employers generally prefer stable workers, high job mobility across organizations may send a negative signal about workers and may lead to diminished career outcomes. At the same time, frequent employer changes can be an indicator of individuals' desirability in the labor market in societies in which cross-organizational job mobility is common. In either case, job mobility may be associated with individuals' economic conditions over the long run.

Table 2.1 reports, by gender, the total number of job episodes respondents experienced in the Japanese and Taiwanese samples. Here, a job episode refers to a period of time when an individual works for the same employer, and the average number of job spells is an indicator of interfirm job mobility. I also present in Table 2.1 the job mobility of men and women currently in the labor force (i.e., "employed men" and "employed women"), because nonemployed women are likely to have particularly short work experiences and thus unusually few employer changes. Taiwanese adults, on average, experienced more job episodes than their Japanese counterparts. The average number of jobs for men and women, however, is small in both countries. About 87 percent and 76 percent of Japanese and Taiwanese respondents, respectively, had worked for three or fewer employers. Such levels of job mobility are low compared with that in the United States, where the majority of adults hold more than five jobs throughout their lifetime (Allmendinger 1989). The similarity in the level of job mobility in Japan and Taiwan is particularly interesting given Taiwan's lack of a "permanent employment" system, in which employers are expected to retain workers throughout their working lives (Cole 1971; Crawcour 1978; Taira 1970). Thus, while Taiwanese employers made no explicit promise of long-term employment, workers generally experienced nearly the same level of job stability as in Japan. Perhaps Taiwan's rapid economic growth has contributed to this high level of job stability.

Despite their similarity in the overall level of employment stability, Japan and Taiwan differ in gender differences in job mobility. On average, Japanese men had a nearly equivalent level of job mobility as women, whereas Taiwanese men experienced greater interfirm mobility than women. However, after excluding those who were not currently in the labor force, Japanese men generally had fewer employers than women. Conversely, there was no difference in job mobility between working men and women in Taiwan. One reason why Japanese working women had more job spells throughout their lives is that they were more likely than men to interrupt their employment careers during their early child-rearing years. Although Taiwanese women were also more likely than men to withdraw from the labor force, it appears that Taiwanese men moved between organizations frequently enough to offset this gender difference.

Do frequent employer changes result in better or worse jobs for individuals? Are Japan and Taiwan different in this regard? To answer these questions, I explored how the frequency of employer changes is associated with occupational status in each country. I found no clear relation between employer changes and occupational status.[9] The experience of job shifting within the same organization, however, connects closely with occupational attainment. Figure 2.4 shows the distribution of current occupations

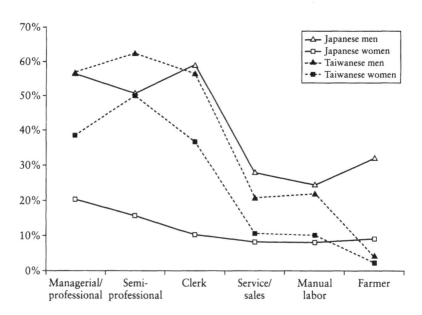

*Figure 2.4.*  Percentage of workers with experience of within-organization job shifting by current occupation.

SOURCE: Japan, 1995 SSM, part A; Taiwan, 1996 TSC, part II.

by workers who experienced within-organization job changes, regardless of whether such changes were promotions. White-collar workers, particularly those in managerial and professional occupations, were much more likely than blue-collar or service and sales workers to report having had this experience. In other words, intrafirm job mobility is positively associated with occupational attainment. Moreover, women in every occupation were less likely than men to report any experience of intrafirm job changes, suggesting that they were less likely to move up job ladders within firms. The gender gap in intrafirm job mobility is particularly wide for Japan.

Occupational status is not the only measure for labor market outcomes. Frequent employer changes may also affect one's chance of obtaining certain types of jobs. I categorize five groups of workers based on firm size and employment status: (1) self-employed and family enterprise workers, (2) part-time or temporary workers, (3) "regular" full-time employees in small firms (<30 employees), (4) regular employees in medium-size firms (30–499 employees), and (5) regular employees in large firms (≥500 employees). The labor market positions each of these groups occupies imply different levels of job stability and overall welfare for individuals. Table 2.2 reports the distribution of the five worker groups by interfirm job mobility. I consider individuals with only one job as having no job mobility, those who had two or three jobs as having medium job mobility, and those who had more than three jobs as having high job mobility.

As Table 2.2 indicates, employees' levels of job mobility reduced considerably as firm size increased in Japan. It was extremely rare for those with high job mobility to work in medium to large firms. The relation between job mobility and firm size was particularly apparent among Japanese women. Fifty-nine percent of women in medium and large Japanese firms were in their first jobs. This finding suggests that women who interrupted their employment careers would be unlikely to work as regular employees in sizable firms later in their lives. By contrast, 30 percent of men and 27 percent of women employed by large Taiwanese firms had never changed employers. About one fifth to one fourth of Taiwanese men and women with high job mobility were working at large firms as regular full-time employees. Taken together, these results indicate that job mobility was more strongly associated with individuals' chances of obtaining standard full-time jobs in medium to large firms in Japan than in Taiwan.

It is possible that regular employees in large Japanese firms have particularly low interfirm mobility because there is little incentive to leave their "good" jobs—that is, jobs with high stability and potential for upward mobility. The fact that it is much rarer to find workers with high job mobility in large firms in Japan than in Taiwan, however, suggests that large Japanese firms are more strongly against hiring workers with a history of frequent

TABLE 2.2

Distribution of current labor market position by gender and frequency of employer changes.

| | JAPAN | | | | | | TAIWAN | | | | | |
| | Men | | | Women | | | Men | | | Women | | |
| | None‡ | Medium§ | High¶ | None | Medium | High | None | Medium | High | None | Medium | High |
|---|---|---|---|---|---|---|---|---|---|---|---|---|
| Family/self-emp.* | 18.4 | 69.5 | 12.1 | 26.2 | 56.0 | 17.8 | 10.5 | 63.7 | 25.8 | 18.5 | 58.2 | 23.3 |
| Part time, temp.† | 5.7 | 68.9 | 25.4 | 18.2 | 45.5 | 36.4 | 20.0 | 50.0 | 30.0 | 37.1 | 51.4 | 11.4 |
| Regular, <30 employees | 19.2 | 64.1 | 16.7 | 22.7 | 52.6 | 24.7 | 12.7 | 47.5 | 39.8 | 12.2 | 51.2 | 36.6 |
| Regular, 30–499 employees | 33.3 | 42.3 | 24.4 | 29.3 | 53.8 | 17.0 | 17.7 | 58.4 | 23.9 | 19.9 | 48.9 | 31.3 |
| Regular, ≥500 employees | 49.4 | 47.2 | 3.4 | 59.3 | 36.3 | 4.4 | 29.9 | 49.6 | 20.5 | 27.1 | 46.4 | 26.4 |

SOURCE: Japan, 1995 SSM, part A; Taiwan, 1996 TSC, part II.

*Family employment or self-employment.

†Employed as part-time or temporary workers.

‡Never had any employer change.

§Changed employers once or twice.

¶Changed employers more than twice.

employer changes. Women with such a history appear to be particularly unlikely to be hired as regular workers by large firms in Japan.

### Shifting between Standard and Nonstandard Employment

I have shown that regular full-time employees generally had a history of fewer employer changes than workers with "nonstandard" jobs, such as temporary and part-time jobs, self-employed work, and jobs at family enterprises, especially for Japan (Table 2.2). Do workers in nonstandard types of employment relations change jobs more often? Or are they likely to hold these types of jobs because their employer change histories make it difficult for them to find regular full-time jobs in firms that prioritize low turnover rates? To answer these questions, I examined the work histories of respondents in the Japanese and Taiwanese samples, with an emphasis on individuals' shifts to nonstandard employment. The results indicate that Japanese men were much less likely than their female counterparts to move from standard to nonstandard jobs. For instance, about 45 percent of the Japanese women between 35 and 54 years old reported that they began their working lives as regular full-time employees and shifted to nonstandard jobs later on, whereas less than 20 percent of their male counterparts reported this.[10] Interestingly, moving from nonstandard to standard forms of employment is not nearly as common as transitioning in the opposite direction in Japan, particularly for women. For example, among Japanese women age 35 to 44 years, only 8 percent engaged in nonstandard types of employment first and then became full-time employees. This unidirectional movement suggests that, in Japan, the nonstandard employment sector is likely to absorb workers rejected by the standard employment sector, and women are more likely than men to be among such workers (see Chapter 6 for more details).

The unequal flow between standard and nonstandard employment occurred for Taiwanese men and women as well, but the difference in percentages between these two types of flow is not as great as it is for Japanese women. Taiwanese women age 45 and older actually were almost as likely to have moved from nonstandard to standard jobs as to have shifted in the opposite direction. In addition, unlike in Japan, a greater proportion of men than women shifted from standard to nonstandard employment in Taiwan. What makes the two countries differ in this regard may have to do with whether moving to the nonstandard employment sector is likely to involve greater gain or loss in each country. I examine this issue later in a section concerning the relation between earnings and job mobility.

Not only do women and men differ in the likelihood of shifting between standard and nonstandard jobs, they also experience job shifts at different points during their life course. My earlier work (Yu 2004) shows that, in both countries, changes in family status (such as entry into parenthood) tend to increase women's likelihood of shifting to nonstandard employment, but not men's. As men move along their life course, however, the proportion of them in full-time employment decreases gradually, whereas self-employment increases. It appears that men are likely to become entrepreneurs after they have accumulated some experience in firms owned by others.

The likelihood of becoming self-employed is generally stronger in Taiwan than in Japan. In addition, Taiwanese men are able to move on to self-employment earlier than Japanese men. To give an example, when looking at the work histories of respondents age 45 to 60 in the samples, I found that by the time of marriage, the percentage of full-time employees among Taiwanese men dropped from 61 percent to 47 percent, whereas the percentage of self-employed Taiwanese men increased from 26 percent to 34 percent. Only 13 percent of Japanese men, by contrast, were self-employed at the time of marriage. Taiwan's smaller scale of businesses is likely to account for men's stronger tendency and earlier age of moving into self-employment in that country than in Japan. Because it requires less capital and fewer skills to start a small-scale enterprise, Taiwanese men are more able to move into self-employment than Japanese men (Yu 2004; Yu and Su 2004; also see Chapter 3).

Although men who leave standard employment generally move to self-employment, women increasingly participate in various types of nonstandard employment, including self-employment, family enterprise employment, and part-time and temporary employment, as they move through the stages of marriage, childbearing, and child rearing. In particular, women in Japan are highly likely to hold part-time or temporary jobs during later stages of their lives. Among women age 45 to 60 in the Japanese sample, the percentage of them in temporary or part-time employment increased nearly twice as much when their children were out of preschool. The percentage increased to 18 percent, which is 28 percent of the women in the labor force, by the time their last child went to middle school. Among the rest of the female workers at this family stage, 38 percent of them held standard full-time jobs, whereas 34 percent of them were in family enterprise employment or self-employment. The finding that many Japanese women with school-age children held part-time jobs is distinctively different from what is usually observed in Western countries, where women shift to part-time or temporary work when their children are in preschool (Drobinič, Blossfeld, and Rohwer 1999; Mincer 1985; Moen 1985; Walsh 1999).

Compared with their Japanese counterparts, Taiwanese women's participation in nonstandard types of employment increase less as they go through the family cycle. Based on the work histories of women in the Taiwanese sample, the percentage of female workers with standard full-time jobs did become smaller after they had their first child, but it increased again at later family stages. Furthermore, more than 50 percent of the female labor force in

Taiwan had full-time jobs, and only a small proportion was in part-time and temporary employment, regardless of family stage. Women in Taiwan, however, are found to be far more likely than men to become family enterprise workers, especially after marriage (Yu 1999, 2001b). Despite some positive effects of marriage and child rearing on Taiwanese women's likelihood of holding nonstandard jobs, my earlier work (Yu 2004) shows that family status is a less powerful predictor of women's participation in standard and nonstandard employment, as well as nonemployment, in Taiwan than in Japan. This finding is consistent with previous research arguing that Taiwanese women's shifting to nonstandard work is associated with their social ties and economic opportunities in the nonstandard employment sector, rather than family concerns alone (Lu 2001; Yu 2001b; Yu and Su 2004).

### Earnings and Job Mobility

I have shown a few differences between women's and men's employment careers in Japan and Taiwan. To shed light on the implications of these differences, I turn my attention to earnings. I first investigate how earnings are associated with the frequency of job mobility. Figure 2.5 shows the percent

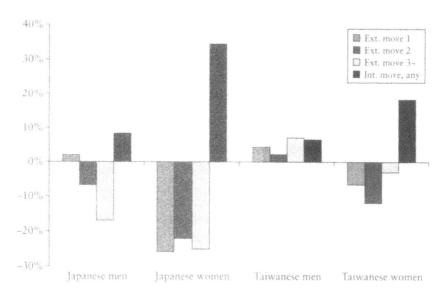

*Figure 2.5.* Job mobility and percent changes in annual earnings.

SOURCE: Japan, 1995 SSM, part A; Taiwan, 1996 TSC, part II.

Note: The baseline is the annual earnings of a hypothetical person who never experienced an employer change ("Ext. move") or within-organization job shift ("Int. move"). Each bar indicates the percent change in this same person's annual earnings with each type of job movement experienced.

changes in annual earnings for a "baseline" person who is married and has a high school education, fourteen years of work experience, no job change experience either within or between organizations, and a full-time clerical job in a medium-size firm (with 30–99 employees), if this person begins to change employers or moves to a different job within the firm. These earnings changes are calculated from the annual incomes predicted for men and women with the designated characteristics in Japan and Taiwan, using coefficients from a regression analysis of earnings for each of the gender and national groups separately (see Appendix B, Table B.2 for the regression results).

In Japan, employer changes generally lead to earnings decreases. Compared with the baseline person, a Japanese man who changes employers once would make similar earnings, all else being equal. Changing employers more than once, however, is associated with a wage penalty. The more external job shifts he undergoes, the lower his earnings would be. A Japanese woman's earnings are likely to be penalized as soon as she begins to change jobs between organizations, and the penalties are greater than those for men. In other words, the cost of a job exit is much higher for women than men in Japan. What is also interesting is that the association between the frequency of job changes and Japanese women's earnings is nonlinear. A woman who has the same characteristics as the baseline person faces a 26 percent earnings loss as soon as she leaves her first job. However, changing employers any more frequently would have only a small effect on her earnings. Thus, whereas the Japanese labor market penalizes men based on how frequently they change employers, it penalizes women based on *whether* they ever exit their first job. Apparently, as far as Japanese employers are concerned, any experience of employer change demonstrates that a woman is not a stable worker.

In contrast, moving between organizations might actually help Taiwanese men, although their percent increases in annual earnings with job mobility are small and statistically nonsignificant. Similar to Japan, employer changes are more harmful for women's economic well-being, but the percent decreases in earnings with women's increasing job mobility are smaller in Taiwan than in Japan. Interestingly, for both men and women in Taiwan, having high levels of job mobility is just as good as having no job mobility at all. For both genders, the differences in earnings between a baseline person and one with the same characteristics who changed employers three times or more are small and statistically nonsignificant at the 0.05 level. Therefore, although Taiwanese workers on average do not change employers often, those who do are unlikely to be penalized in terms of earnings. This finding suggests that an individual can possibly move up internal job ladders within organizations or seek better jobs in the open market for upward mobility in

Taiwan. Thus, compared with Japan, employer turnover is more acceptable in the Taiwanese labor market.

Also notable is that the experience of internal job movement is associated with earnings gains for both genders across countries. Although it was more common for men than women to change jobs within an organization (Figure 2.4), the benefit of internal job mobility on earnings was greater for women in both countries. A Japanese woman with the same characteristics as the baseline person would earn 34 percent more if she had ever been transferred or promoted to a different job within the organization. The same experience leads to an 18 percent earnings increase among Taiwanese women.

The reason why women with the experience of internal job mobility make particularly high earnings compared with other women may have to do with how rare it is for women to be placed in the "internal labor markets" in these two countries (Doeringer and Piore 1971; Kalleberg and Sørensen 1979). Labor market researchers have long argued that not all workers compete equally in an open labor market. Employers may select workers into internal labor markets and offer additional training and promotion opportunities for the chosen ones. As a result, those selected early on into internal labor markets tend to have higher occupational attainment in the long run. The internal labor market perspective also contends that women are less likely than men to be selected into the internal labor market because employers tend to view men as more suitable workers and consider them more worthy of investment (Brinton 1989; Kalleberg and Lincoln 1988). Opportunities for internal job changes are often provided to employees in the internal labor market within the firm, especially in Japan (Brinton 1993; Koike 1983). Because women are often excluded from internal labor markets, those who are able to enter such markets may be exceptionally outstanding and thus rewarded more substantially.

The increase in earnings associated with internal job mobility is greater in Japan than in Taiwan for both gender groups. This cross-national difference can be explained by the greater importance of entering firms' internal labor markets for an individual's long-term occupational achievement in Japan than in Taiwan. Unlike their Taiwanese counterparts, Japanese workers were unlikely to move up by changing jobs frequently across firms. Because climbing up the firm's job ladders is almost key to upward mobility, those who are assigned to the "fast track" with the firm are likely to have a particularly greater advantage over others.

In addition to the associations between the frequency of job changes and earnings, I also examine the effects on earnings of moving into different types of employment. As stated earlier, in both countries, individuals' likelihood of taking a nonstandard job increases with age. I focus now on how such career paths affect their economic well-being. Figure 2.6 shows

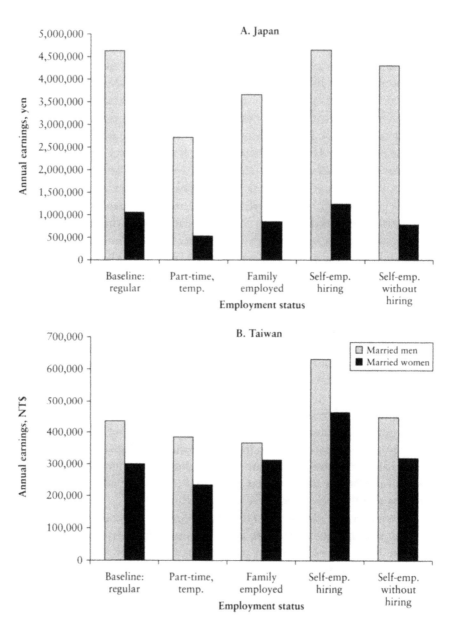

*Figure 2.6.* (A, B) Predicted annual earnings by gender and employment status for Japan (A) and Taiwan (B).

SOURCE: Japan, 1995 SSM, part A; Taiwan, 1996 TSC, part II.

*Note:* The status of self-employment is divided into two types based on whether a self-employed person hires others to work in the same establishment.

the predicted earnings for a hypothetical person in different types of employment.[11] This person is assumed to be married and to have a high school education, fourteen years of work experience, no job change experience either within or between organizations, and to hold a clerical occupation in a small firm (with 1–29 employees). In Japan, this worker is likely to fare better economically as a full-time regular employee, rather than as any type of nonstandard worker (i.e., family enterprise worker, self-employed worker, part-time temporary worker).[12] Although there is a large gap in earnings between Japanese men and women, the general pattern with regard to how employment status is associated with earnings is similar for both groups.

By contrast, standard wage employment is not always the best option for Taiwanese workers. The hypothetical person would make the most earnings as an entrepreneur who employs others. Although other nonstandard employment options do not necessarily lead to higher earnings than standard full-time employment, taking these nonstandard jobs rather than standard full-time jobs is not as detrimental to one's income in Taiwan as in Japan. This cross-national difference is particularly pronounced for women. In Taiwan, other than taking a part-time or temporary job, which usually involves fewer hours of work, a woman with the same characteristics as the hypothetical person would make as much or even more earnings holding a nonstandard job compared with holding a standard job. In Japan, however, this same woman would fare much worse if she were to take almost any nonstandard rather than standard job. In particular, a Japanese woman with a part-time or temporary job would receive no more than half the annual earnings of one who has the same individual characteristics and a full-time regular job. Although part-time workers generally spend fewer hours at work than full-time employees, aggregate statistics indicate that the average working hours of part-time and temporary employees were close to three fourths of those of full-time employees (Ministry of Labour, Japan 1996).[13] Thus, the number of working hours cannot fully account for the extremely low earnings of Japanese women with part-time and temporary jobs.

I stated earlier that women were more likely than men to move to the nonstandard employment sector over their life cycles, and that this tendency was stronger in Japan. An analysis of the effect of employment types on earnings indicates that such job movement is associated with particularly substantial income loss in Japan. Taken together, these findings suggest that the gap in economic well-being between Japanese men and women widens over their life course, as women increasingly shift to nonstandard jobs. Women's decreasing likelihood of holding full-time regular jobs throughout their life course affects their well-being to a relatively small extent in Taiwan, since a nonstandard job is not necessarily associated with lower earnings. Perhaps because shifting to nonstandard employment, particularly self-employment, may actually enable financial gain, Taiwanese men are almost as likely to do so as their female counterparts.

Another notable finding from the two-country comparison in Figure 2.6 is that the gap in the predicted earnings between a man and a woman with the same individual characteristics is much larger in Japan than in Taiwan, regardless of employment status. Part of the reason for Japan's greater gender gap in earnings is that the hypothetical person is assumed to be married, and the marriage penalty is particularly great for Japanese women.[14] Estimates from the regression analyses of earnings (Appendix B, Table B.2) indicate that Japanese men's earnings were likely to increase by 26 percent when they became married, after controlling for various individual and job characteristics. Conversely, Japanese women's earnings decreased by about 25 percent when they married. In contrast, both Taiwanese men and women had higher earnings if they were married, rather than single, but the benefit of marriage for male workers was twice that for female workers (18% vs. 8% increases). Hence, not only were Japanese women more likely than Taiwanese women to be harmed financially by shifting to the nonstandard employment sector, they were also penalized more substantially for being married. As a result, the gender gap in earnings widens over women's life cycles to a greater extent in Japan than in Taiwan.

SUMMARY

This chapter provides a detailed picture of the development of men's and women's career trajectories during the second half of the twentieth century in Japan and Taiwan. Overall, women exhibited a stronger attachment to the labor force during this period. By the end of the past century, not only was it nearly universal for women to participate in the labor market at some point in their lives, there was virtually no difference in the rate of employment between men and women before marriage. Married women's participation in the labor market has also increased over time. Consequently, the total length of women's employment careers has extended in both countries. In this regard, women's labor market experiences have become more similar to men's during these decades.

Despite the similarity in women's increasing labor force attachment, married women's career trajectories differed considerably in Taiwan and Japan. In Taiwan, the increase in single women's labor force participation has led to fundamental changes in female employment behavior. Taiwanese women began to increase employment rates upon marriage and childbearing in the 1970s and, since then, their frequency of having continuous employment careers has increased constantly. By contrast, there has been little change in Japanese women's tendency to continue their jobs after marriage and childbearing. The proportion of married women who participate in the labor market during their childbearing and early child-rearing years rose somewhat during Japan's period of rapid economic growth in the 1960s, but this trend did not last. Japanese women's rates of continuous employment decreased after the high growth period and have become stagnant since the beginning of the recessionary period in the early 1970s. Nevertheless, this decrease did not reduce Japanese women's postmarital work experience dramatically, because those of later cohorts returned to the labor force more frequently and at a younger age.

The two countries' divergent development of women's career trajectories, starting from the 1970s, eventually led to Taiwan's higher rate of women's employment during their prime working age—in their thirties and forties—despite Japanese women's longer history of industrial employment. The gender differences in employment continuity became smaller in Taiwan than in Japan, because Taiwanese women were more likely to continue their jobs upon marriage and childbirth. Although Japanese women's labor market experience was likely to grow considerably later in their lives, after labor force reentry, they fell behind men in the length of work experience during their prime working age to a greater degree than their Taiwanese counterparts.

In addition to women's more frequent employment interruptions, there are a few key differences in career processes between men and women in the two countries. First, Japanese women have experienced more jobs than men in their lifetimes, partly because they are more likely to interrupt their employment careers. While greater job mobility is generally associated with worse career outcomes for both Japanese men and women, the penalty of leaving an organization is far greater for women. For this reason, an interruption of an employment career is particularly harmful for Japanese women's long-term occupational attainment and economic status. In comparison, Taiwan's difference in job mobility between men and women has been smaller. Moreover, the association between job mobility and labor market outcomes is relatively weak. Taiwanese men who change employers frequently are even likely to have a small economic gain. Thus, although Taiwanese women generally have more continuous careers than Japanese women, they paradoxically would have been penalized less had they decided to exit their jobs and enter different firms at a later time.

Second, Japanese women are more likely to move to nonstandard jobs than men. This gender gap is particularly wide among older adults, because Japanese women frequently enter the nonstandard employment sector after their childbearing and early child-rearing years. In fact, among female Japanese workers with school-age children, those holding regular full-time jobs are the minority. This is not the case for Taiwan. Although the proportion of nonstandard workers among married women is greater than that among single women, the majority of Taiwan's married female labor force holds regular full-time jobs. Moreover, the gender difference in the rate of shifting to the nonstandard employment sector is relatively small in Taiwan. Nevertheless, men and women tend to move to different types of nonstandard jobs. Taiwanese men are much more likely than women to hold nonstandard jobs that can potentially lead to higher earnings than standard paid jobs, such as self-employed work. Conversely, Taiwanese women are more likely than men to be family enterprise workers if they leave regular full-time jobs. Despite this gender difference, the overall consequences for women who move to the nonstandard employment sector are less negative in Taiwan than in Japan.

In conclusion, the results of this chapter point to the importance of using a life course approach to assess gender inequality in labor markets cross-nationally. More commonly in Japan than in Taiwan, women encounter a growing number of obstacles in the labor market as they age. Not only are Japanese women more prone to leave their premarital jobs than Taiwanese women, but they also tend to move to nonstandard jobs at later life course stages. Because both frequent employer changes and nonstandard employment status are associated with severe financial penalties for Japanese women, their economic status is likely to diminish as they progress through their life course. In contrast, Taiwanese women's career trajectories have been more similar to men's in terms of their tendencies of having continuous careers, changing jobs across organizations, and staying with standard full-time jobs. Interestingly, when Taiwanese women did change organizations or employment sectors, perhaps because such behaviors are not as strongly labeled as "women's behaviors" as in Japan, the penalties associated with these types of movements were smaller in that country.

The findings regarding female employment behaviors and their consequences naturally lead to the following questions: Why do Japanese women interrupt their employment careers more frequently than Taiwanese women, despite the greater penalty in Japan? Similarly, why do Japanese women shift to nonstandard employment more frequently than Taiwanese women? The answers to these questions are essential for elucidating the divergence in women's employment opportunities between Japan and Taiwan. The remainder of this book is devoted to addressing these questions by examining the differences between the two countries in women's employment behaviors over their life course.

## CHAPTER THREE

# Comparing Labor Market Structures and Workplace Dynamics

The cases of Japan and Taiwan demonstrate two different ways in which women gain work experience in a society. In Japan, women's more frequent and faster returns to the labor force after marriage and childbearing have increased their average years of employment during the past several decades. Despite this change, Japanese women's tendency to interrupt their employment careers during childbearing and the early child-rearing years has remained high. By contrast, the increasing job attachment among younger cohorts of women has largely contributed to the rise in Taiwanese women's work experience. Not only has single women's labor force participation become a norm in postwar Taiwan, but more recent cohorts of women also are more likely to extend their labor market experience by remaining in their jobs after marriage and childbearing.

These two patterns of female labor force participation have different implications for women's economic well-being. In explaining gender discrimination in the United States, Claudia Goldin (1990) argues that an increase in training costs in modern work organizations leads employers to prefer those who are likely to stay at one organization for a long period of time. The history of women's lower labor force attachment in comparison with men's provides the foundation for managers to use gender as a predictor for a worker's probability of job turnover. Women, therefore, are less preferred than men for relatively promising jobs. Such "statistical discrimination" can be expected to decline as women's work experience increases. Nevertheless, managers' prejudice against female workers is often based on not only their total years of participation in the labor force, but also their likelihood of work interruptions. Married women's propensity for leaving the labor market, even for a short period of time, makes it difficult for employers to estimate and maximize their productivity, which often depends on workers' age and job tenure. Consequently, the more likely it is for women to work discontinuously in a society, the less incentive there is for employers to abandon differential treatment for men and women in the workplace. Thus, as long as Japanese women continue to exit the labor force after marriage and childbearing, their increasing labor force participation is unlikely to alter employers' prejudice against them.

Given the implications of women's employment patterns for gender inequality, it is important to ask: Why has married women's tendency of continuous employment increased in Taiwan but remained low in Japan? The career trajectories of women shown in the previous chapter seem to suggest that women in these two countries have made different *choices* concerning the timing of their employment over their life cycle. However, as sociologists have long noted, individuals often make choices under the *constraints* embedded in their social context. The objective of this chapter is to reveal how Japan and Taiwan have developed different constraints under which women make decisions about their employment. I begin with an overview of theories about the changes in married women's employment patterns. In particular, I discuss how the comparison between Japan and Taiwan challenges existing research that focuses on the effects of women's occupational opportunities, job segregation, and social norms on their postmarital job retention. To offer an alternative framework, I argue that labor market arrangements and workplace dynamics in the two countries explain the differences in women's employment trajectories over their life course. I then use historical trends drawn from aggregate statistics to demonstrate how different labor market practices that affect women's employment behaviors were developed in the two countries. This comparison of national labor market characteristics is followed by an individual-level analysis that links macrolevel forces with women's employment exits in the next chapter.

### EMPIRICAL CHALLENGES FOR EXISTING THEORIES

Research documenting married women's employment histories in the United States shows the importance of the shift to a service economy and increases in women's education. Industrial changes at the macrolevel are thought to have caused growth in U.S. clerical and sales sectors, which in turn increased the number of jobs that were more "feminine" by conventional definitions (Cotter, Defiore, Hermsen, Kowalewski, and Vanneman 1998; Oppenheimer 1970). Meanwhile, as women increased their educational attainment, they became better equipped for office jobs. This increase in women's qualifications and skills enabled them to take advantage of the new job opportunities made available by economic changes. Compared with factory jobs, not only did office jobs pay better, but they were also considered "clean and decent," hence more suitable for women. The improvement in women's occupational opportunities thus increased their income potential and alleviated the social stigma against the employment of wives and mothers (Goldin 1990, 1995; Leibowitz and Klerman 1995). Consequently, U.S. women's likelihood of leaving the labor force upon marriage or childbearing has decreased over time (Rosenfeld 1996).

Japan and Taiwan experienced similar social and economic changes that led to the improvement of women's occupational opportunities in the United States, though at different times. Figure 3.1 shows trends in the percentages

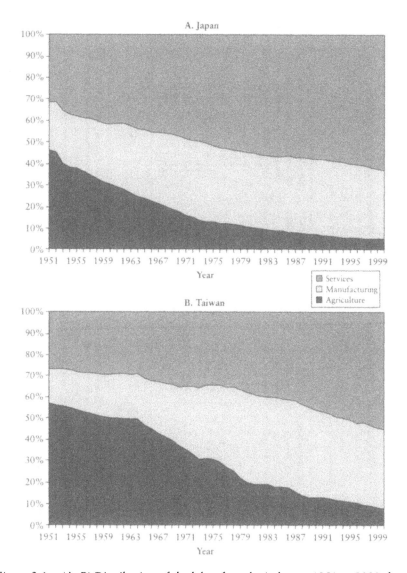

*Figure 3.1.* (A, B) Distribution of the labor force by industry, 1951 to 2000, for Japan (A) and Taiwan (B).

SOURCE: DGBAS, Executive Yuan, Republic of China *Yearbook of manpower survey statistics, Taiwan area, Republic of China,* various years; Statistics Bureau, Management and Coordination Agency, Japan, *Historical statistics of Japan,* 1987, *Annual report on the Labour Force Survey,* various years.

TABLE 3.1
Occupational distributions of the female labor force in Japan and Taiwan.

| | JAPAN | | | | TAIWAN | | | |
| | 1970 | | 2000 | | 1970 | | 2000 | |
| Occupational categories | Distribution of female workers | Female share within occupation | Distribution of female workers | Female share within occupation | Distribution of female workers | Female share within occupation | Distribution of female workers | Female share within occupation |
|---|---|---|---|---|---|---|---|---|
| Managerial | 0.5 | 4.8 | 0.8 | 10.9 | 2.9 | 17.8 | 1.4 | 13.5 |
| Professional | 2.7 | 21.1 | 9.8 | 35.7 | 6.2 | 32.1 | 8.0 | 50.0 |
| Semiprofessional | 4.7 | 47.1 | 5.3 | 25.1 | 0.3 | 4.9 | 15.8 | 39.7 |
| Clerical | 17.8 | 49.2 | 30.2 | 61.1 | 8.7 | 28.5 | 18.8 | 76.3 |
| Sales and service | 23.1 | 52.2 | 27.2 | 56.7 | 11.3 | 13.6 | 25.3 | 53.5 |
| Agriculture | 26.1 | 53.1 | 5.5 | 43.0 | 48.6 | 30.9 | 7.1 | 28.9 |
| Skilled labor | 21.7 | 26.2 | 15.1 | 23.5 | 16.5 | 19.7 | 17.5 | 21.7 |
| Unskilled labor | 3.4 | 33.7 | 6.1 | 43.4 | 5.5 | 35.6 | 6.3 | 46.4 |
| Total | 100.0 | 39.1 | 100.0 | 41.0 | 100.0 | 24.3 | 100.0 | 39.0 |
| Index of gender segregation* | | | | | | | | |
| All (36 occupations) | 35.9 | | 39.8 | | 33.0 | | 43.4 | |
| White-collar occupations | 37.8 | | 45.3 | | 23.0 | | 48.2 | |

SOURCE: Calculations based on Bureau of Statistics, Office of the Prime Minister, Japan, 1970 population census of Japan, 1971, DGBAS, Executive Yuan, Republic of China, Yearbook of manpower survey statistics, Taiwan area, Republic of China, 2000, Ministry of Interior, Republic of China, Household and residence census, 1970, and Statistics Bureau, Ministry of Public Management, Home Affairs, and Posts and Communications, Japan, 2000 population census of Japan, 2001.

All values are in percentages. The category of skilled blue-collar occupations includes both skilled and semiskilled manufacturing work.

*I used the index of dissimilarity for measuring occupational gender segregation. The index score can be interpreted as the percentage of men or women that would have to move to different occupations to be evenly represented in all occupations. This index uses 36 occupations made comparable by recoding detailed occupational categories across time and countries: four in the managerial category, seven in the professional occupational category, eight in the associate professional category, two for clerical work, three for sales and services work, four skilled blue-collar occupations, four semiskilled blue-collar occupations, three unskilled blue-collar occupations, and one occupation for agriculture jobs.

of the labor force in agricultural, manufacturing, and service industries in both countries. The share of the Japanese labor force in service industries has grown rapidly since 1950. By contrast, Taiwan first experienced an expansion of manufacturing industries from the mid 1960s and then shifted to a service economy during the mid 1980s. Overall, while the economic transformation occurred at different times in the two countries, their patterns of change were similar.

Also similar to the U.S. experience, the economic development coincided with increases in women's educational attainment in both Japan and Taiwan (Brinton and Lee 2001; Yu and Su 2006; also see Chapter 7 for details). The changing availability of office jobs, along with the improvement in female education, eventually enhanced women's occupational status in Japan and Taiwan, just like in the United States. Table 3.1 presents Japanese and Taiwanese women's occupational distributions in 1970 and 2000. The proportion of the female labor force in white-collar occupations, including managerial, professional, semiprofessional, and clerical occupations, clearly rose with time; so did the female share within these occupations. Thus, in both countries, women have experienced increases in occupational prestige and earning potential over time.

Table 3.1 also shows that, by the year 2000, Japan and Taiwan had converged in the share of the labor force constituted by women, despite Japan's more advanced development. With respect to the quality of women's occupations, trends in occupational gender segregation were also converging in the two countries. The number of women grew more sharply in those occupations that were considered relatively feminine, such as office clerk, nurse, and teacher. Overall, the index of gender segregation for white-collar occupations increased from 37.8 to 45.3 in Japan and from 23.0 to 48.2 in Taiwan from 1970 to 2000, which is closely correlated with the magnitude of the growth of female labor force participation in white-collar occupations in each society. These statistics on female employment suggest that women's occupational opportunities are not sufficiently different between Japan and Taiwan to explain the divergence in the rate at which women leave the labor market upon marriage or childbearing. Furthermore, Taiwan experienced more changes in women's employment patterns during the postwar period while otherwise following Japan's path of industrialization. Industrial changes and the subsequent growth of clerical and service jobs cannot account for the more dramatic increase in married women's continuous employment in Taiwan.

When explaining why Japan failed to replicate the historical experience of the United States concerning gender and work, Mary Brinton (1988, 1993) argues that Japan's educational system, social and family norms, and employment practices together have woven a unique system in which individuals have little control over their accumulation of "human capital" (Becker 1964), defined as marketable skills acquired through education and training. To elaborate, because the educational system tracks students from the high school level onward, and encourages built-in age barriers for all levels of schooling, individuals are unlikely to return to school after starting a job in Japan. Hence, individuals must rely heavily on their families to invest in their schooling. At the same time, the prevalence of life course norms regarding the appropriate ages for experiencing major life course events (such as schooling, employment, marriage, and childbearing) restrict the available timing for individuals to improve their education or job-related training over their life course. This inability to control their own human capital development hampers Japanese women's economic opportunities because, from family to workplace, they are thought to "need" less education and training than men. Parents tend to invest in sons' schooling preferentially because of the strong family norms for sons to support aging parents financially. Even relatively altruistic parents are likely to invest in their sons rather than in their daughters, because they sense that discrimination against women in the workplace will lower the return to their educational investment in their daughters. Similarly, employers tend to provide more on-the-job training to men because job turnover rates are likely to be higher for women. In turn, Japanese women have little chance to compete successfully with men in the labor market.

Although Brinton (1988, 1993) offers a useful framework for explaining the life chances of Japanese women, she does not fully explain why Japanese women have failed to develop more continuous employment careers during the past several decades. In her framework, Japanese women's high job turnover rates around marriage and childbearing are taken as given, as such rates constitute an explanatory factor for employers' discriminatory practices. Even if we were to link this human capital-based explanation to women's employment behaviors, there are still three potential problems. First, women may alter their employment behaviors despite the lack of change in the level of gender inequality in society. For example, from the 1950s to the 1980s, there was only a small decrease in the gender gap in earnings in the United States. The labor force participation of young married women and new mothers nevertheless grew during this period in response to increases in women's real wages (Goldin 1990; Rosenfeld 1996). Second, if women's employment decisions are explained by their relatively low human capital, Japan's increases in female education over time should still raise the employment rates among women with young children. Third, Taiwan shares with Japan a number of features that, according to Brinton (1988, 1993), constrain women's human capital development. These features include the highly standardized, strictly examination-based school systems; strong family norms for sons' support for aging parents; and intense life course norms with respect to the proper timing for schooling, employment, marriage, and childbearing (Greenhalgh 1985; Yu and Su 2006; also see Chapter 7). These broader norms and social institutions appear to affect Taiwanese women's career trajectories differently. Why have Taiwanese women's rates of employment interruptions decreased despite the social institutions that tend to obstruct women's life chances? Why was Japan's experience different? The literature reviewed so far has failed to provide satisfactory answers to these questions.

## JOB CONTEXT AND THE CONFLICT BETWEEN WORK AND FAMILY

To provide an understanding of the divergence in female employment behavior between Japan and Taiwan, I draw on research that emphasizes the job conditions that contribute to the level of compatibility between women's work and family responsibilities. Women face decisions about whether to continue their jobs upon marriage and childbearing, because these changes in family status require them to balance their roles as workers, wives, and mothers. The conflict among these roles for women leads to their decision to leave the labor force. Certainly not all women find their jobs equally incompatible with their family roles. Women are prone to leave the labor force after marriage and childbearing if the characteristics of their jobs and workplaces are likely to make it difficult to combine their work with family obligations (Desai and Waite 1991; Glass and Riley 1998; Glass and Camarigg 1992). Jobs that lack schedule flexibility and reasonable work hours—that is, no mandatory overtime or night shifts—are relatively incompatible with women's roles as wives or mothers (Glass and Estes 1997). In addition to the time demand associated with a job, a work environment that provides social support for, or at least is not hostile toward, wives and mothers generally enhances women's continuous employment. For example, Glass and Riley (1998) show that supervisors and coworkers' reactions to a woman's pregnancy affect her job retention following childbirth, even after controlling for schedule flexibility. Married women are also more likely to continue working when their workplace climates do not convey disapproval for the employment of mothers with young children (Rindfuss and Brewster 1996).

I argue that job requirements and workplace dynamics are the key to explaining the divergent patterns of women's employment between Japan and Taiwan. I stress the importance of implicit workplace norms and other workers' attitudes on women's job retention in Japan and Taiwan—societies that have relatively low tolerance for individualistic behavior. During my interviews with women in these two countries about their employment experiences, many brought up their workplace climate when explaining their past decisions. For example, one Japanese woman in her early fifties told me that she probably would have quit her first job as a clerk at a major automobile company around the time of her marriage had she not done so earlier for other personal reasons. Her reasoning was that almost all female workers left their jobs upon marriage in that company. This woman married and had her first child during her second job at a foreign-owned company. I asked why she did not consider leaving her job to take care of her child like many other women of her generation did. She paused for a moment and said, "I don't know. It didn't occur to me. Many other women in the company were married with children, so my instinct was to find a nanny to look after my daughter and continue to work."

Two other Japanese women also commented on how their employment decisions were affected by the "tradition" in their workplaces. They both were employed by large-scale enterprises that used to be owned by the government. As such, their workplaces still more or less resemble those in the public sector in terms of the overall atmosphere. According to these women, because the public sector traditionally retained more married women with young children (also see the analysis in Chapter 4), it seemed natural for them to remain in their jobs after childbirth.

Another example illustrating how workplace norms affect women's decisions about employment came from a Taiwanese bookkeeper in her mid forties, who had been employed continuously by a large jewelry chain since before her marriage. She mentioned that she might retire in a few years, by age 50 or so. I asked why she would retire, since she seemed content with her job. She explained, "You don't see many older women, women in their fifties, in office jobs in private companies. No woman in my office is that old. I would feel strange to remain in the company at that age." The same concern was also expressed by another Taiwanese woman of about the same age working at a smaller, international trade company. Similarly, a Japanese woman told me that she shifted to a less prestigious and lower paying job at a smaller firm affiliated with her previous firm after she reached her late forties because it was the norm for older employees in her previous workplace to do so. What is considered appropriate and customary in the workplace appears to play an essential role in women's decisions to continue their jobs.

In addition to the cultural tendency to comply with implicit rules in the workplace, I argue that relatively low family dissolution rates and the prevalence of traditional gender relations have further encouraged women in the two countries to make decisions about postmarital employment continuity based on their working conditions and workplace altomosphere.[1] A low divorce rate and a prevalent male-breadwinner ideology both lessen the long-term benefit of economic independence for married women. Consequently, married women's decisions regarding job retention largely depend on more immediate concerns, such as their job demands and the hostility they face in the workplace. Thus, in societies like Japan and Taiwan, the specific contexts in which women work are particularly worthy of our attention.

While previous research on working conditions and women's employment generally concerns microlevel processes, I argue for the need to bring in macro-institutional contexts. In particular, I emphasize how cross-national differences in institutional arrangements lead to differing workplace norms and dynamics. These norms and dynamics shape the level of compatibility between women's jobs and family responsibilities, thus explaining differences in female employment behaviors across countries. Based on this general framework, I develop explanations for the differences in women's employment trajectories between Japan and Taiwan. In the remainder of this chapter, I examine the macrolevel labor market conditions that have contributed to the development of the overall workplace climate and job norms in the two countries. I also discuss how the differences in working environments and job obligations between Japan and Taiwan account for their divergent levels of women's work–family conflicts. The primary focus of the discussion, however, is the macrolevel conditions that should affect workplace dynamics in the two countries. I leave to the next chapter a more detailed, microlevel analysis of the effects of women's work environments on their rates of exit from the labor force.

## NATIONAL LABOR MARKETS AND WORKPLACE DYNAMICS

Despite having converged in many other respects, Japan and Taiwan have differed substantially in their overall labor demand–supply conditions, structures of business organizations, and within-firm employment practices. These differences have led to divergent workplace dynamics for individual workers between the two national labor markets. In the following, I elucidate the connection between macrolevel labor market conditions and microlevel workplace dynamics that shape the level of role conflict that working mothers experience. The questions guiding the analysis are: Why have labor market characteristics differed between Japan and Taiwan? How have these structural differences shaped general working conditions and workplace dynamics? Specifically, how have these different working conditions between the two countries affected women?

### Industrial Strategies and Labor Demand

Research on female labor force participation has long emphasized the importance of labor demand. As reviewed earlier in this chapter, the growth of clerical and sales jobs is thought to affect the demand for female labor (Cotter et al. 1998; Oppenheimer 1970). Although this theory concerning female labor demand does not fully explain the discrepancy between Japan and Taiwan, we should not overlook the impact of labor demand on married women's employment. High labor demand should have an overall effect on workplace dynamics. A labor shortage encourages employers to make adjustments in the workplace to reduce job turnover. Employers are also more likely to give jobs to, or even to accommodate, the less preferred when facing labor shortages.

Economic incentives created by labor demand constituted a major force behind changes made to the workplace to increase women's postmarital job retention in Japan and Taiwan, as there was relatively little legal or ideological support for gender equality in the workplace through the late 1980s (see Chapters 1 and 5). I should note that employers have not considered married women as a preferable source of labor in these two countries for at least two reasons. First, married women as a group began to participate in the labor force later than men and single women. As newcomers in a labor market, they lacked a credible history as workers from employers' point of view. Second, the shared belief that women's ultimate place is at home in these Confucianism-influenced societies strengthened employers' bias against married women as potential workers. However, as postwar development led to different levels of labor demand between Japan and Taiwan, it became necessary for Taiwanese employers to make more adjustments than their Japanese counterparts.

Postwar development in Taiwan resulted in a higher labor demand than in Japan. To elaborate, the economic success of both countries relied heavily on industrial exports, but their roles in the global economy were quite different. Through the mid 1980s, Taiwan's exports concentrated in commodities that required intensive labor but low skill, such as textiles, electronic parts, and plastic products. As the value of Taiwan's exports rose from US$450,000,000 to US$30,456,000,000 from 1965 to 1984, that country experienced rapid growth in labor-intensive industries and labor demand (Hamilton and Biggart 1988).

In contrast to Taiwan, Japan's economic success during the postwar period relied mostly on exports from capital- and skill-intensive industries. Light industries had lost their dominance to heavy industries in the Japanese economy since before World War II (Brinton 1993). Commodities such as automobiles and machines contributed to Japan's remarkable economic growth through the late 1980s (Hamilton and Biggart 1988). These types of industrial exports generally required the input of skilled labor. At the same time, they were conducive to relatively small increases in labor demand in the economy.

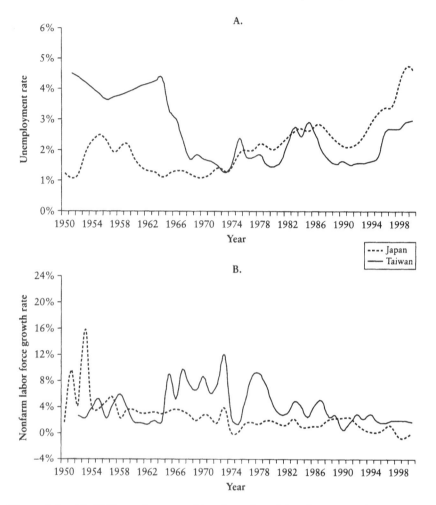

*Figure 3.2.* (A, B) Unemployment (A) and nonfarm labor force growth (B) rates, 1950 to 2000.

SOURCE: DGBAS, Executive Yuan, R.O.C., *Yearbook of manpower survey statistics, Taiwan area, Republic of China*, various years. Statistics Bureau, Management and Coordination Agency, Japan, *Historical statistics of Japan*, 1987, *Annual report on the Labour Force Survey*, various years.

Note: The nonfarm labor force growth rate is calculated as the percentage increase in the number of workers in the nonagricultural sector from the previous year.

To demonstrate the effects of these different industrial strategies on labor demand, Figure 3.2 presents trends in unemployment and nonfarm labor force growth rates from 1950 to 2000 in Japan and Taiwan. Reflecting their miraculous speeds of economic growth during the past half century, both countries had relatively low levels of unemployment through the late 1990s.

Nevertheless, the growth of the nonfarm labor force was more dramatic in Taiwan. This growth was particularly remarkable from the mid 1960s to the early 1990s, a period when Taiwan's manufacturing sector expanded rapidly (Figure 3.1). In other words, the dominance of labor-intensive industries created a large number of new jobs in Taiwan during those decades.

Taiwan's rapid increase of new jobs made it necessary to recruit new members into the labor force. While the agricultural sector shrank during Taiwan's economic development, the decrease in agricultural workers accounted for only a small proportion of the increase in the nonfarm labor force. Taiwan's nonfarm labor force grew at an average rate of 6 percent per year from 1965 to 1985, but the agricultural labor force shrank by only 1 percent per year during the same time. Moreover, despite overall population growth during this period, the supply of men of working age was not sufficient to meet the increasing labor demand. As shown in Figure 3.3, the male population age 15 to 59 years rose by merely 3 percent per year, on average, from 1965 to 1985. Thus, the natural growth of the male population and the labor released from the agricultural sector, taken together, were still not enough to fill all the positions created from the rapid expansion of labor-intensive industries during Taiwan's high-growth period.

A few ethnographic studies have documented how the demographic composition of the Taiwanese labor force has changed with the growth of

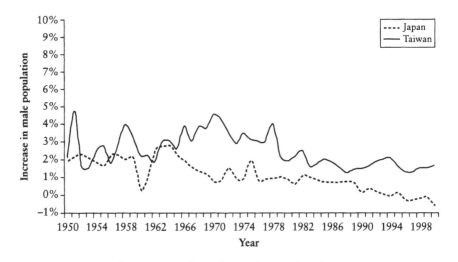

*Figure 3.3.* Annual increases in the male population of working age, 1950 to 2000.

SOURCE: DGBAS, Executive Yuan, Republic of China, *Yearbook of manpower survey statistics, Taiwan area, Republic of China*, various years; Statistics Bureau, Management and Coordination Agency, Japan, *Historical statistics of Japan, 1987, Annual report on the Labour Force Survey*, various years.

*Note:* "Male population of working age" is defined as men age 15 to 59 years.

light industries (e.g., Diamond 1979; Hsiung 1996; Kung 1994). As described in Lydia Kung's (1994) study of female factory workers in the mid 1970s, industrialization first incorporated single women from rural areas, in addition to men, into Taiwan's workforce. These "working daughters" viewed employment as an extension of their family obligations, gave a sizable proportion of their wages to their parents, and expected their working lives to end upon marriage. As the economy continued to grow and mandatory education was extended, the labor supply of single women became less than sufficient to meet the rapidly increasing labor demand. To resolve the problem of labor shortages, the government initiated the "Living Rooms as Factories" campaign to urge homemaking women to contribute their labor to the economy by performing piecework at home for neighborhood factories in the mid 1970s (Hsiung 1996). Despite this effort, employers' complaints about labor shortages and the need to hire illegal foreign labor remained common in the early to mid 1980s (Brinton et al. 1995). Desperately needing labor, Taiwanese employers began to alter their expectations of their employees in the mid 1970s, as Janet Salaff (1994) observed:

> By the mid 1970s, factories had mushroomed and competed for workers. Village girls no longer needed to leave the south to find industrial work. . . . As the pool of female workers grew smaller in the early 1970s [as a result of the increase in girls' education], married women who had finished bearing children joined the labor market. . . . In this era, management no longer drew on unskilled young women as their primary labor force. Instead, they sought reliable and steady workers. . . . Married women from nearby neighborhoods were a main source of new labor to this firm. (p. xiii)

By contrast, trends relevant to Japan's labor demand suggest that labor shortages have rarely been a problem in that economy since 1950. Figure 3.2 indicates that the growth of the nonfarm labor force was much slower in Japan than in Taiwan. Japan's lower labor demand reflected its focus on capital-intensive industries and innovative commodities during this period. Even when Japan achieved its most remarkable economic growth, from 1955 to 1973, the average growth rate for the nonfarm labor force was only 3 percent per year.[2] Accompanying this increase in nonfarm employment was a near 3 percent annual decrease in agricultural workers. Plus, the male population of working age rose by an average rate of more than 2 percent per year from 1950 to 2000, as shown in Figure 3.3. The shrinkage of the agricultural sector and the growth of the male population together provided a sufficient labor supply for the industrial sector, which grew rather moderately despite Japan's economic growth.

Because the market could generate a sufficient labor supply from existing sources, Japanese employers found little need to accommodate newcomers, such as married women, in the labor market. In fact, as previous studies indicate, labor surplus conditions have been common in the Japanese labor market since the mid 1970s, except for a brief period when there was an economic bubble in the late 1980s (Brinton 1993; Gao 2001). Given this, Japanese employees generally had restricted leverage with respect to their working conditions. Traditionally not part of the labor force, married women in particular had little with which to bargain. The experience of a nurse whom I interviewed illustrates how Japanese workplaces might be different had there been a greater demand for women's labor. Like elsewhere in the world, being a nurse is considered a women's job in Japan. Nursing is therefore one of the few occupations that frequently faces labor shortages in that country. The Japanese nurse I talked to confirmed the overall shortage of nurses in nearly all hospitals where she had worked. While Japanese workplaces rarely provide childcare assistance (see Chapter 5), she mentioned that many hospitals she knew of had on-site childcare facilities to retain married female nurses. The labor shortage apparently compels managers of these hospitals to make an extra effort to accommodate married women in the workplace.

Needless to say, throughout Japan's history there was also a time when labor-intensive industries predominated in the economy. Before the 1930s, the textile industry played a critical role in Japan's industrializing economy, and single women constituted the majority of the industry's workers during that period (Brinton 1993; Hunter 2003). Nevertheless, Japan's labor demand at that time did not increase as much as it did in postwar Taiwan—that is, not to the extent that the workplace had to accommodate married women. Why? We need to keep in mind that the global economy changed during the prewar and postwar periods. International trade grew faster during the postwar era. As the developed world relied increasingly on less industrialized countries for labor-intensive manufacturing (Wood 1994), exports from Taiwan's light industries had a greater potential for growth than Japan's during the first couple of decades of the twentieth century. As a result, the growth of overall labor demand that Taiwan experienced during the postwar period surpassed that of Japan during the same phase of industrialization. Moreover, even when the Japanese economy did encounter severe labor shortages, its particular structure made it possible for employers to adopt a solution other than utilizing married women's labor. The different solutions to the problem of labor shortages led the two countries to diverge in women's working conditions. I elaborate on Japanese management's solution and its long-term implications in a later section.

*Demand and supply of skilled labor.* If the labor shortages caused by the expansion of Taiwan's labor-intensive industries were the only reason why married women's labor supply increased, then we would expect Taiwanese employers to have reverted to their preferences for male and single workers after the economy shifted its industrial focus. According to Figures 3.1 and 3.2, both the manufacturing sector and nonfarm labor forces have grown relatively little since the late 1980s in Taiwan. These trends suggest that after the mid 1980s, there was no longer much of a shortage of low-skilled labor in that country. Indeed, Gindling and Sun (2002) found that the relative demand for workers with higher education compared with those with high school or equivalent education increased steadily from the late 1970s to the late 1980s, and it has increased sharply since the late 1980s (Gindling and Sun 2002:164, Figure 4). The considerable rise in demand for workers with higher education also coincided with when exports from technology-based industries, such as the computer industry, began to exceed those from light, labor-intensive industries, around the 1990s. That is to say, since the 1980s, Taiwan has steadily moved away from labor-intensive industries and become more like Japan during the early postwar decades. Why did Taiwan not follow Japan's path regarding women's employment opportunities despite these changes in economic activities and labor demand conditions?

To explain Taiwan's continuing divergence from Japan from 1980 onward, it is important to compare the supply of skilled labor between the two countries. Educational opportunities were more widespread in Japan than in Taiwan during the decades after World War II. This difference resulted partly from Japan's more advanced development and partly from the Taiwanese government's deliberate restriction of university access to ensure an abundant labor supply for jobs requiring low- to mid-level skills (Woo 1991). Although Japan requires education only through junior high school, the percentage advancing to senior high school has been more than 90 percent since the 1970s (Brinton and Lee 2001). By contrast, only 70 percent and 62 percent of boys and girls age 12 to 17, respectively, were in secondary education in 1975 in Taiwan (Brinton et al. 1995). Japan also has higher advancement rates to tertiary education than Taiwan throughout last half century (see Chapter 7).

One might argue that a discrepancy in educational opportunities between Japan and Taiwan is to be expected because of their different levels of economic development. To assess better the differences in educational opportunities between Japan and Taiwan, I compare access to higher education while the two countries were at similar economic stages. In 1980, when the focus of Taiwan's economy began to shift to skill- and capital-intensive industries, only about 11 percent of those age 18 to 21 were in higher education (Directorate-General of Budget, Accounting and Statistics [DGBAS] 1996). By contrast, Japan had reached a comparable percentage of higher education attainment as early as 1955, when a sizable proportion of the Japanese labor force was still in the agricultural sector.[3] Higher education also expanded rapidly in the 1960s and 1970s in Japan. Almost two fifths of Japanese students were able to attain higher education by 1975 (Yanotsuneta Kinenkai 2000:532). This advancement rate was considerably higher than the rates in Taiwan, even in the 1990s. About 20 percent of the Taiwanese population age 18 to 21 were in higher education in 1990, and the percentage rose to 28 in 1995 (DGBAS 1996; also see Chapter 7).[4] Thus, even if we grant a lag in Taiwan's development in educational opportunities, Taiwan still had more restricted access to higher education than Japan.

Therefore, not only was there a scarcity of low-skilled labor, but the supply of relatively skilled labor was also insufficient in Taiwan. In particular, the transformation of the Taiwanese economy created a considerable demand for skilled labor through the 1980s and 1990s, but it was not until the mid 1990s that the state began to expand its higher education in response to popular demand (Gindling and Sun 2002; Wang 2003).[5] This discrepancy made the supply of educated males insufficient for the increasing demand for skilled labor. Labor shortages, in turn, discouraged employers from implementing practices that would enhance job turnover, such as the policy of firing single women when they marry, also known as the *marriage bar*. In the late 1970s, commercial banks in Taiwan began to abolish the marriage bar, and by the late 1980s, marriage bars became uncommon among private firms in Taiwan (Brinton et al. 1995). All these changes were not mandated by law. In fact, laws for labor protection or equal employment opportunities were virtually absent during this period (Chen 2000). Instead of such laws, shortages of educated labor compelled Taiwanese managers to accommodate married women in the workplace.

Compared with Taiwan, the majority of the population in postwar Japan had at least a senior high school education. Employers generally did not face the problem of an insufficient supply of skilled labor. In turn, there was relatively little economic incentive for workplaces to accommodate women, particularly married women, in the labor market.

### The Japanese Employment System

Although the supply of skilled labor was generally sufficient for Japan for the past half century, this was not always the case historically. Shortages of skilled workers constituted a great impediment for economic development during the early phases of Japan's industrialization at the turn of the past century. The Japanese labor market at that time had two prominent features: an oversupply of unskilled labor and a scarcity of skilled workers (Crawcour 1978). This scarcity enhanced skilled workers' leverage in the market and led to frequent job turnover. The demand for skilled labor rose further with the expansion of heavy industries. By the 1920s, how to retain skilled workers had become one of the most critical concerns for Japanese management.

Similar to the case of Taiwan after the 1970s, the strong demand for skilled workers compelled Japanese workplaces to change. The coping strategy adopted by Japanese managers, however, differed substantially from that of their Taiwanese counterparts. Rather than expanding the labor pool, large-scale Japanese firms jointly developed practices that provided workers with both incentives to stay and disincentives to leave. These practices, first introduced around World War I, later became the core of the "permanent employment system"—one of the best-known institutions of contemporary Japanese society (Cole 1971; Lincoln and McBride 1987; Lincoln and Nakata 1997). Under this system, managers recruit mostly unskilled, new workers and take full responsibility for training them. This preference for young, inexperienced workers at recruitment helps reduce the alternative job opportunities for trained workers. As long as large-scale firms bar experienced workers jointly, trained workers who leave their firms will be penalized: These workers can only find jobs at smaller firms that offer worse career prospects. For this system to be acceptable, large-firm employers also reward trained workers for remaining in the firm. These rewards consist of promotions and wage increases based on a worker's length of service, in addition to long-term job security (Crawcour 1978).

The introduction of the described practices had lasting effects on industrial relations and workplace dynamics in Japan during the second half of the twentieth century. The use of these practices extended to a wider range of companies and occupations after World War II. Mary Brinton (1993) maintains that such factors as job scarcity, rapid economic growth, and a youthful population structure all contributed to this extension in the 1950s and 1960s.[6] What made the system particularly influential and persistent, however, was the cultural flavor added to the system in the process of institutionalization. As Robert Cole (1971) argues, what initially helped institutionalize this employment system was the borrowing and use of cultural ideology in legitimizing the rather innovative practices. Drawing heavily from cultural resources and traditional values, the creators of the system had successfully made it part of the "Japanese tradition." Thus, the institution's inertia came from not only the opposition from the beneficiaries (e.g., senior employees), but also from social forces that strove to preserve traditional cultural values. This strong inertia helps explain why this institution remained unchallenged through the mid 1990s, even though its economic rationale had long disappeared (Lincoln and Nakata 1997).[7]

Many researchers have contended that, in practice, the permanent employment system was not always at work even before the economic crisis in the 1990s. Some small- and medium-size firms failed to keep their permanent employment commitments during economic fluctuations (Cheng and Kalleberg 1997; Koike 1987). Moreover, female workers rarely benefited from the permanent employment system (Brinton 1993; Houseman and Abraham 1993; Ogasawara 1998). If managers rarely offered female workers lifetime employment, why would this practice affect women's working conditions? It is important to keep mind that the permanent employment system nominally applied to all regular full-time employees (*seishain*), regardless of whether most workers remained in their jobs for a long period.[8] This application means that it was generally difficult for managers to terminate employment of regular full-time workers.[9] Moreover, employers had to offer such workers seniority-based wages and fringe benefits as long as they stayed (Houseman and Osawa 1995). Providing long-term employment and age-based wages for noncore workers in a firm was costly, especially since the supply of such workers was plentiful. Therefore, Japanese management had incentives to create a family-irresponsive workplace that encouraged "voluntary" job exits around the time of marriage or childbearing among women. Because women never received much on-the-job training (Brinton 1988, 1989), their job turnover would not waste company resources. Rather, employers benefited from replacing experienced female employees with those fresh out of school who were younger and demanded lower pay. According to a Japanese woman with whom I spoke, the large firm in which she worked before marriage would give a considerable sum as a "wedding gift" to any female worker who left her job for marriage. Although this practice is no longer prevalent among large Japanese firms, this example indicates the need for managers to promote women's voluntary job exits.

The institutionalization of the permanent employment system also affected workplace dynamics by shaping the "implicit contract" between employers and employees in postwar Japan. Sidney Crawcour (1978) points out that what gave the Japanese system its character was "the web of non-material sanctions by which employees and society as a whole have been conditioned to accept the system as both morally good and individually satisfying." For this reason, this system "in principle provides lifetime employment, but in return requires the employee to see himself as a loyal member of the company community on which he and his family are dependent for almost every aspect of their livelihood" (p. 239). This loyalty implies subordinating individual or family interests to those of the corporate family and hence meeting job demands even when they are incompatible with one's family life. Thus, employees nominally covered by the system are expected to work long hours and accept relocation assignments regardless of their families' interests (Yu 2002; also see Chapter 5).

By determining how employees benefiting from lifetime employment should behave, the permanent employment system also defines the conditions under which employees would be deprived of long-term job stability. To be specific, the system prescribes that those who are offered lifetime job security must sacrifice their family lives for job requisites. By the same token, individuals who are not willing to do so would not be employed for a long period. Similarly, such individuals would not be rewarded according to job tenure. For many Japanese managers, this unspoken rule justifies their differential treatment for female and male workers. For instance, a career-minded woman working in a prestigious Japanese firm told me that she once complained about being assigned to the "local" track, which virtually allows no long-term promotion opportunities. The manager's response was, "I don't think you can be relocated anywhere in the country as frequently as a man, can you?" To give another example, several Japanese women with whom I discussed their premarital jobs stated that they were usually not required to spend as much time after hours on either work or social activities as their male coworkers. They were, however, aware that they had to quit their jobs upon marriage or pregnancy in exchange for not being held to the same standards as male employees in the same firm. Because of this quid pro quo logic, the workplace atmosphere generally turns hostile toward a female employee if she does not quit as "timely" as expected. As Yuko Ogasawara (1998) shows in her ethnographic study of clerical work environments, a Japanese woman wanting to stay in the workplace for a long period of time faces not only unfriendly male coworkers but also the possibility of being assigned to a particularly difficult job. It appears that the only way to justify a woman's "overstay" is for her to comply with the norms of long working hours and unconditional commitment.

I therefore argue that the permanent employment system has actually affected workplace norms and job conditions for *all* workers. The existence of such a system has deprived Japanese managers of the option to determine the length of employment based on a worker's performance. Managers thus offer two extreme employment packages with corresponding requirements.[10] Individuals who cannot consistently meet the demands for permanent workers, such as women, must agree to the other extreme: Their employment might be for only a short, limited term, and they are exempt from any of the corporate family's welfare. It is therefore not surprising that most Japanese women with whom I spoke seemed to share the understanding that their premarital jobs were under implicit employment contracts that were supposed to expire by the time they marry or become mothers.

## Industrial Arrangements and Structures of Business Organizations

Taiwan's pattern of exchange between employers and employees has differed from Japan's. An explanation of this difference traces back to the differences in the structures of business organizations between the two countries. To begin, Japan's postwar economy featured two interrelated networks of firms, or two types of *enterprise groups,* as some researchers have called them (Brinton 1993; Clark 1979). Hamilton and Biggart (1988) provide a precise summary of Japan's industrial arrangement:

> One type of enterprise group consists of linkages among large firms. These linkages are usually loosely coupled, basically horizontal connections among a range of large firms. Although such firms differ in terms of size and prestige, the linkages between them are what Dore calls "relational contracting between equals." These groupings of firms are intermarket groups and are spread through industrial sectors. The second type of enterprise group connects small- and medium-sized firms to a large firm, creating what economists call a "dual structure," a situation of "relational contracting between unequals." Both types of enterprise groups make centrally located large firms and associations of large firms the principal actors in the Japanese economy. (p. S57)

Japan's dualist structure that gave power to large firms was partly a continuation of prewar industrial arrangements and partly a result of the state's policy of "creating and promoting strong intermediate powers, each having considerable autonomy, with the state acting as coordinator of activity and mediator of conflicting interest" during the postwar decades (Hamilton and Biggart 1988:S78). The linkages between large Japanese firms, which date back to the prewar period, made it possible for such firms to adopt permanent employment practices jointly when faced the problem of labor shortages. The dominance of large firms in the economy also encouraged the secondary players—that is, small- and medium-size firms—to imitate their employment practices, which helped the permanent employment system expand in postwar Japan.

Facing labor shortages, Taiwanese employers were unable to follow the "Japanese way," because Taiwan's industrial arrangements and organizational structure were very different. The Taiwanese economy has consisted of a large number of small- to medium-size family enterprises dispersed all over the island (Brinton 2001; Shieh 1992; Yu and Su 2004). Two industrial strategies accounted for this dominance of small- to medium-size businesses. First, Taiwan's early focus on exports from light industries encouraged the flourishing of small-scale, family-owned businesses with relatively small capital investments. Second, the Kuomintang regime, which moved to Taiwan after the civil war in 1949, deliberately promoted small-scale establishments, rather than giving business opportunities to a few major players. Not only did this sponsorship of small establishments help secure the regime's dominance, but the strategy of providing opportunities for ordinary citizens also helped legitimize its leader as a benevolent ruler (Hamilton and Biggart 1988; Noble 1998).

To illustrate the difference in the average business scale between Japan and Taiwan, nearly one third of Japan's paid employees were in firms with fewer than thirty workers, whereas more than one half of Taiwan's paid employees worked in such firms in 2000.[11] The difference between Japan and Taiwan in the proportion of small-enterprise participants is even greater if we take into account self-employed and family enterprise workers, whose establishment size is usually small (Ishida 2004; Yu and Su 2004). Compared with Japan, Taiwan has a larger percentage of self-employed workers, whose businesses rely heavily on their family members' labor (Yu 2001b, 2004). Figure 3.4 presents the two countries' percentages of small-business participants, defined as workers who were self-employed, working for their family enterprises, or employed by firms with fewer than 30 employees. Taiwan's proportion of small-business participants has been consistently

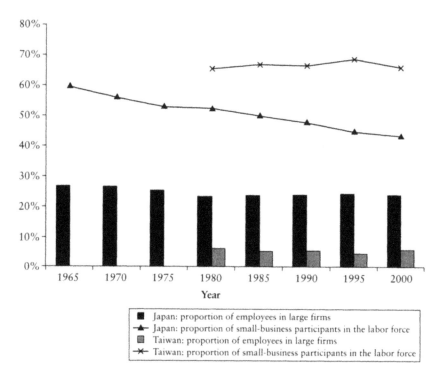

*Figure 3.4.*  Comparisons of the labor force by firm size in Japan and Taiwan.

SOURCE: DGBAS, Executive Yuan, Republic of China, *Yearbook of manpower survey statistics, Taiwan area, Republic of China*, various years; Statistics Bureau, Management and Coordination Agency, Japan, *Annual report on the Labour Force Survey*, various years.

*Note:* The lines represent the percentage of the labor force participating in small-business establishments. Here, small-business participants consist of men and women who are self-employed, employed by family enterprises, or hired by firms with no more than 29 employees. Figures for Japan do not include paid employees in the nonagricultural sector. However, only 0.5 percent of the Japanese labor force belonged to this group during the presented years. The bars represent the percentages of wage employees who work in private firms with 500 employees or more. Data are unavailable for Taiwan in 1975 and earlier.

and significantly greater than that in Japan. Interestingly, despite the rise in capital-intensive industries in the 1990s, Taiwan's percentage of the labor force in small enterprises has remained at almost 70 percent from 1980 to 2000.

The bottom part of Figure 3.4 shows the proportion of paid employees in large-scale firms (those with more than five hundred workers) in selected years in Japan and Taiwan. The percentages were substantially smaller in Taiwan than in Japan in all select years. Therefore, large firms in Taiwan had much less influence on the labor market than those in Japan. Large Taiwanese firms' lack of dominance made it difficult for such firms to institutionalize a system similar to the permanent employment system when faced with labor shortages. Moreover, Taiwan's high proportion of small firms hampered the prevalence of lifetime employment practices, because small firms are generally unable to absorb training costs and to resist hiring experienced workers. Small firms also face difficulty offering long-term job security because the firm's life expectancy is closely tied to economic fluctuations (Yu and Su 2004). In short, the dominance of small enterprises determined that accommodating new groups of workers, such as married women, was the only way to cope with labor shortages.

Taiwan's exceptionally high proportion of small enterprises also has an important effect on workplace norms and atmosphere. Because small firms employ the vast majority of the labor force, the implicit employment contract that the society finds fair has been based on the employer–employee relations in small, family-owned enterprises. Such relations tend to be personal and informal. Lacking formalized rules in the workplace may not always benefit workers, because it allows employers to indulge their discriminatory tastes or deprive workers of proper labor compensation (Reskin and McBrier 2000). However, in the case of Taiwan, employers' underlying concern about labor shortages enables workers to take advantage of an informal workplace atmosphere and to translate this atmosphere into a moderate level of job flexibility. A detailed discussion of job flexibility for working women in Taiwan is provided in the next chapter.

In addition to a relatively high level of job flexibility, Taiwanese employees are less likely to work much longer than regular hours than their Japanese counterparts. Because small-scale enterprises provide relatively little potential for promotion, not to mention poor fringe benefits, Taiwanese employers find that they have an unjustified rationale for demanding overtime work or other sorts of sacrifices from employees. That small businesses in Taiwan have a relatively low "life expectancy" also affords employers little to offer in exchange for more-than-ordinary worker services. Besides, because most large-scale enterprises are owned and managed by family members, employees' long-term mobility is limited even if their firms grant some internal job ladders. The popularity of "becoming bosses" (meaning starting individuals' own businesses) as paid employees' ultimate career aspiration illustrates that most Taiwanese workers are pessimistic about what their employers can offer in the long run (Shieh 1992; Yu and Su 2004). Unable to provide many long-term promises or incentives, Taiwanese employers cannot reasonably demand from their employees the type of loyalty mandated by Japan's permanent employment system.

The prevalent organizational structure in Taiwan also led to a different wage-setting structure than Japan's. Unlike the Japanese system, which granted full-time regular employees considerable wage increases with seniority (Kalleberg and Lincoln 1988; Mincer and Higuchi 1988), the Taiwanese wage structure has been relatively flat. While most Taiwanese firms provide some wage increases with job tenure, the increase is usually small, because most small-scale firms cannot afford high labor costs.[12] Furthermore, low labor costs have been helping Taiwanese export companies secure their niche in the world economy. The need to maintain minimum labor costs makes it difficult for Taiwanese firms to adopt highly hierarchical, seniority-based wage systems like the ones in Japan.

One consequence of this wage-setting structure in Taiwan is that employers lack incentives to keep a youthful workforce. In general, firms with flatter wage structures save less from dismissing older, more experienced workers. Therefore, managers of such firms are less likely to pressure women to quit upon marriage or childbearing. To illustrate this argument from the opposite angle, marriage bars were the most common among Taiwan's credit unions before their abandonment. Credit unions were de facto private banks in Taiwan before the government liberalized the banking sector in 1991. They generally paid better and offered greater wage increases with job tenure among Taiwanese businesses. Credit unions' wage systems provided an incentive for them to ensure female employees' turnover upon marriage. This type of firm, however, is exceptional in the Taiwanese economy. Most Taiwanese firms never had similar wage systems, nor had they ever implemented the marriage bar policy.

Not only has there been little incentive for employers to replace experienced female workers frequently, but Taiwan's average establishment scale also prompts employers to view high job turnover rates as detrimental to business. Job turnover leads to additional training costs, and most Taiwanese enterprises are too small to spend much on training. To give an example of employers' attempt to reduce training costs in Taiwan, most job advertisements ask for applicants who have job experience in the same occupation or require applicants to have a university major in a relevant field. As far as training costs are concerned, keeping the firms' existing employees is the easiest way to keep these costs down. Thus, unlike their Japanese counterparts, Taiwanese employers are likely to find it more economically rational to retain their female employees after marriage or childbearing.[13]

To sum up, because of the differences in the structure of business organizations between Japan and Taiwan, workers in Japan often face greater job demands and less schedule flexibility. For the same reason, Japanese firms generally have more hierarchical wage structures than Taiwanese firms. The prevalent wage-setting structure in Japan creates an incentive for employers to encourage job turnover among female employees. At the same time, Taiwanese employers are likely to benefit from job stability among women workers, given the flat wage structure and small establishment scale in that country. As a result, Japanese women who work continuously after marriage tend to face more hostile work environments compared with their Taiwanese counterparts.

SUMMARY

The differences in married women's employment behavior between Japan and Taiwan constitute an empirical puzzle. In this chapter I discussed the similarities in women's occupational distributions, family norms, and educational systems between the two countries. Such similarities make previous research insufficient to solve this puzzle. I develop my theoretical framework from studies that focus on working conditions and conflict between jobs and family responsibilities for women. I argue that macrolevel economic structures shape the norms and implicit employment contracts prevalent in Japan and Taiwan. Such norms and contracts directly affect workplace dynamics and job demands for individual women. Based on the specific workplace culture and demands they face, women make different decisions regarding whether to continue their jobs following marriage and childbirth. In particular, work environments that are overly incompatible with women's family lives tend to discourage them from remaining in the labor force after marriage and childbearing, regardless of how well their jobs pay.

To reveal why Japan and Taiwan have developed different workplace cultures and norms, I compared labor demands, average firm size, and employment practices in the two countries. The dualist industrial structure in Japan enabled large firms to develop a series of employment practices, jointly known as the permanent employment system, to cope with shortages of skilled labor during the prewar decades. These innovative practices then became a key institution in the labor market with strong inertia. This institution in Japan increased employers' training costs, affected wage-setting structures, and shaped the contents of the implicit contract between employers and employees through the end of the twentieth century. As discussed in this chapter, many of the conditions set by the permanent employment system have led to rather difficult working conditions and to much conflict between work and family for married women. To make matters worse, the labor supply was abundant in Japan during most of the postwar decades. This further allowed employers to demand particularly long working hours and other kinds of personal sacrifices from regular full-time workers.

By contrast, small business scale and high labor demand have made industrial relations in Taiwan different from those in Japan. Given the relatively flat wage structures and shortage of resources for training, Taiwanese employers have little incentive to encourage women's job turnover after marriage and childbearing. They also have relatively little leverage when it comes to demanding after-hours work or other major sacrifices from their employees. Moreover, when encountering labor shortages, Taiwan's structural context does not allow employers to institutionalize Japan's employment practices to resolve such problems. As a result of all these factors, Taiwanese workplaces are compelled to change to become more family-responsive to attract (or retain) married female workers.

The discussion up to this point has dealt with the differing economic structures and labor market conditions between Japan and Taiwan. It is the argument of this chapter that these differences have resulted in divergent workplace climates and working conditions for women in the two countries. However, a microlevel analysis of women's job exits is needed to demonstrate that Japanese and Taiwanese women indeed face different levels of work–family conflict and have diverse patterns of employment exits as a result. The next chapter details this microlevel analysis. Specifically, I will show how women in different occupational and organizational contexts in these two countries respond to the level of work–family conflict they perceive as they step into marriage and motherhood. I will also connect the results from this microlevel analysis with the two countries' divergence in female employment behavior at the aggregate level.

## CHAPTER FOUR

# Patterns of Labor Force Exits Among Women

In the previous chapter I discussed the national labor market conditions in Japan and Taiwan that contributed to the different workplace dynamics for women. I also argued that job conditions and workplace atmosphere play an important role in women's decisions to continue or discontinue their employment careers after marriage and childbearing. To recapitulate, Figure 4.1 illustrates the macrolevel factors discussed in the previous chapter and how they are thought to influence individual women. Because of the aggregate-level differences in labor demand, long-term job security, the wage-setting structure, and firm size between Japan and Taiwan, workplace climate has been more hostile and job conditions less flexible for married women in Japan. In turn, Taiwanese women are argued to have perceived a higher level of compatibility between work and family than their Japanese counterparts.

If working conditions in Japan are less compatible with women's family roles than those in Taiwan, Japanese women will be more likely to be out of the labor force during their childbearing and early child-rearing years than Taiwanese women. Although Chapter 2 demonstrated lower labor force participation rates among Japanese women of childbearing age, a proper comparison of the effects of marriage and child rearing on women's employment must take into account the differences in the two countries' population compositions. In my earlier work (Yu 2005), I estimated the average probabilities that women will be away from the labor force for some time during the period of high family demand in Japan and Taiwan, controlling for the differences between the two female populations in age, education, fertility, family structure, and residential area. I found that the probability is significantly greater in Japan. That is to say, the difference between the two countries remains even after taking into account their population characteristics. This finding is thus consistent with the argument that the degree of difficulty of combining family and work responsibilities is higher in Japan than in Taiwan.

National labor market conditions

Microlevel job context

Individual perception

Overall labor demand

Long-term job security

Wage-setting structure

Firm size

Workplace climate

Time demand and job flexibility

Work–family compatibility

*Figure 4.1.* Explanatory framework.

The overall probability that women will withdraw from the labor force during their child-rearing years, however, is only one indicator that may reflect the differences in workplace dynamics between Japan and Taiwan. We can also expect working conditions in the two countries to manifest in the *patterns* of women's employment exits. Because the barriers to combining motherhood and employment should affect how actively women respond to their labor market opportunities throughout their life course, the factors leading to women's job exits upon marriage and childbirth will differ between countries that are different in such barriers. For example, occupational status and earnings may play the most critical part in women's decisions about working continuously when the context allows them to combine family and job obligations relatively easily. By contrast, married women's rates of employment interruptions are unlikely to be closely tied to their job prospects if balancing work and family demands is very difficult. Instead, the availability of additional help for childcare may be a more crucial factor associated with their employment exits after marriage and childbearing. Thus, the general work climate and job conditions in a country should have an impact on the dynamics of labor force exits among its female population.

In this chapter I use an individual-level analysis to show precisely how the perceived level of job–family compatibility affects women's decisions about continuous employment. This analysis allows me to test rigorously hypotheses that can be derived from the arguments developed thus far. Hypothesis testing, however, is not the only reason to introduce an individual-level analysis. As I show later in this chapter, the differences in women's dynamics of labor force exits between Japan and Taiwan constitute the key to explaining the two countries' divergence in female employment over time. Prior studies comparing women's work in East Asia and elsewhere have paid insufficient attention to the question of which subgroup of women is more likely to leave or stay in the labor force *within* a given country (e.g., Brinton 1993; Brinton et al. 1995; Estevéz-Abe 2007; Schoppa 2006). Moreover, such studies have rarely demonstrated how individual-level dynamics contribute to country-level divergences (or convergences), even when they include a microlevel analysis of women's economic behavior (e.g., Brinton et al. 1995; Shirahase 2007). My analysis nevertheless indicates the need to specify the linkage between microlevel decision-making processes and macrolevel social change.

The organization of this chapter is as follows. I first examine women's decisions to exit the labor force around the time of marriage and first child-birth, as well as at any time throughout their working lives. The data used for the statistical analysis are drawn from the 1995 SSM for Japan and the 1996 TSC for Taiwan. After this analysis I discuss how the individual-level results regarding women's employment exits may be connected to the aggre-gate-level divergence between Japan and Taiwan in women's employment. Last, by linking individuals' employment behaviors with the macroeconomic changes experienced by the two countries, I offer a more comprehensive un-derstanding of the mechanisms through which these two countries diverged in women's economic status relative to men's.

## DYNAMICS OF WOMEN'S LABOR FORCE EXITS

If the labor market differences between Japan and Taiwan have indeed con-tributed to Japan's higher level of conflict between family and job demands for women, then the factors associated with Japanese women's decisions to work continuously will differ from those of Taiwanese women's accordingly. I therefore examine the major job characteristics and personal attributes that may shape women's decisions to exit the labor force in the two coun-tries. Ethnographic notes from in-depth personal interviews are used in the discussions regarding how a given job attribute or personal characteristic can be expected to affect women's exit rates. I rely on a statistical analysis to test systematically the hypotheses derived. To highlight how each job or personal attribute is associated with women's labor force exits, I discuss the expected effects of each predictor separately, and present the corresponding results from the statistical analysis after each discussion. As stated earlier, my focus is on how the effects of the discussed predictors on women's job exit rates differ in Japan and Taiwan. The statistical results, taken together, depict the differences between the two countries in the profiles of women who remain in and leave the labor force after marriage and childbearing.

### Job Characteristics and Women's Decisions
### to Discontinue Employment

The differences in employment practices between Japan and Taiwan may lead to different levels of work–family conflict for women according to their work settings. In the following, I discuss how the context of a woman's job may affect her likelihood of leaving the labor force when she experiences a drastic increase in her family obligations. The job features on which I focus include occupational setting, firm size, and employment sector.

*Occupational setting.* The differing labor market characteristics in Japan and Taiwan might have led to different levels of work–family conflict for women according to their occupational setting. The Taiwanese labor market conditions that help reduce work–family conflict, such as relatively personal employer–employee relations, may generally affect women in office jobs more than their counterparts working in factories because office work allows more room for negotiating job flexibility. The experience of a Taiwanese woman with a bookkeeping job illustrates this negotiation:

> I usually do not need to work overtime, but sometimes we get busy and I have difficulty finishing work by six o'clock. My boss lets me bring the work back home and finish it outside the office. I have worked for him for more than twenty years and he trusts me. . . . Sometimes we older workers, the ones with children, are late for work because of sending children to school. He would not say anything. Last year, during the summer vacation of my daughter's elementary school, for a while I couldn't find anybody to look after her. At the time we had an empty desk in the office, so I took my daughter to the office and asked her to sit there all day while I worked.

The described incident of bringing a child to the workplace was not an isolated or exceptional case in my fieldwork. A woman working in a commercial bank told me that she would sneak out of the office every afternoon to pick up her daughter at a nearby kindergarten. She took her daughter back to the office and had her wait in a less busy area while she finished the last couple hours of her daily work. I have also seen a few other Taiwanese women with office jobs bring their child to work or take a brief break during working hours to handle family emergencies.[1] In contrast, bringing a child to the workplace or changing the work schedule for family matters is much more difficult for women with factory jobs. Because women working in factories are bound by the production lines, they are likely to have less freedom and thus experience greater conflict between their jobs and family responsibilities in Taiwan.

How occupational settings affect the conflict between employment and family obligations can be remarkably different in Japan. To begin, the gap in flexibility between office and factory jobs is not large in Japan because most white-collar workplaces are highly formalized in that country. From work attire to administrative procedures, there are strict protocols for workers to follow (Miller and Kanazawa 2000). The options described earlier for Taiwanese women in white-collar work settings, such as bringing a child to the office for one day, are nearly unheard of in Japan.

In fact, white-collar work environments in Japan are likely to be *less supportive* of women's continuous employment after marriage and child-bearing than blue-collar environments for several reasons. First, the age-based increase in wages has been greater for white-collar than blue-collar occupations (Ishida 1993). Hence, Japanese employers would benefit more from frequent job turnover among women in white-collar occupations than that among women in blue-collar occupations. During my interviews in Japan, a few women who had clerical jobs before marriage stated that there was an implicit pressure for them to leave their jobs upon marriage. This pressure is illustrated by the following statement from a woman who used to hold a clerical job at a medium-size pharmaceutical company: "Of course we were expected to quit our jobs for marriage by men in the company. Who wants to work with lots of *obasan* (middle-age women)? Who doesn't want to see pretty, single girls around every day?"

Another Japanese woman, whose premarital job was at a commercial bank, also described her workplace atmosphere as one that encouraged women to quit as soon as they become married or pregnant. The story of a third informant, who held a clerical job at a bank as well, illustrates this workplace climate even more vividly:

> I quit the job when my father became sick, but I was only using his illness as an excuse for me to quit. I wanted to quit because by then I had been there for five years. It was too long. Many women who came to the bank later had left to get married. I actually had not met my husband then, so I didn't leave for marriage. I just felt that I had to quit because nobody worked there for that long. I felt it was strange for me to stay. The silly thing is that I then started working part-time for the same bank, doing exactly the same kind of work but with much less pay.

The second reason why Japanese managers might be less hostile toward married blue-collar working women than their white-collar counterparts is that they generally presume that women with factory jobs have working-class husbands. Thus, blue-collar working wives and mothers are thought to "need" to continue their jobs for their family's sake. As Glenda Roberts' (1994) ethnographic study shows, married women with factory jobs in Japan frequently justify their employment by expressing concerns about current consumption prices and family income (pp. 27–28). In contrast, the workplace atmosphere described by Yuko Ogasawara (1998) for Japanese clerical workers conveys that marriage is supposed to ensure lifetime financial security for women with office jobs. Hence, there is no justifiable reason for women to retain their white-collar jobs after marriage. Another illustration of such differential attitudes toward women in white- and blue-collar jobs came from a forty-three-year-old Japanese woman whom I interviewed.

Upon marriage she left her job as a fashion show director, a job she really enjoyed, because both her husband and mother-in-law objected to her continuation of employment. She noted:

> At that time, only women working in factories continued their jobs after marriage. People thought that they were from poorer families and they needed the wages. In families like ours—given my husband's job and our financial status—others would consider it abnormal for me to keep working after marriage.

The reasoning regarding how much the family needs the wife's wage also leads to the greater social disapproval experienced by Japanese mothers of young children in white-collar occupations compared with their blue-collar counterparts. The greater amount of social disapproval against mothers with young children in white-collar occupational settings should provide employers additional legitimacy for encouraging women to leave their office jobs upon marriage and childbearing. A detailed discussion of childcare options and child-rearing standards in Japan and Taiwan is provided in the next chapter.

Third, as discussed in the previous chapter, Japan's permanent employment practice has virtually made excessive time demands part of the implicit employment contract for many workers (even after this practice began to decline in recent years). White-collar workers might be more subject than blue-collar workers to such time demands, because their job contents and requirements are less concrete. In comparison, the work hours for blue-collar workers are more likely to be fixed and bound to production schedules. To illustrate, one Japanese woman told me that overtime work was the primary reason why she left her full-time job as a certified dental technician for two part-time, low-skilled, manufacturing jobs. Although her two jobs added up to more hours (and less pay) than her one full-time job, she gained control over her evening time, which she desired to spend with her two school-age children. Her experience suggests that by demanding overtime work more often, white-collar jobs in Japan may be associated with greater work–family conflict than blue-collar ones.

For these reasons, the white-collar work context in Japan can be expected to be more conducive to conflict between work and family than the blue-collar work context. However, the higher wages associated with upper white-collar occupations, such as managerial, professional, and semiprofessional positions, are likely to create an incentive for female workers to remain in their jobs. That is to say, with regard to how an occupation is associated with a woman's decision to leave or remain in the labor force, it is predicted that two opposite effects are at work. The effect of occupation on earnings may offset the disincentive created by white-collar work environments if the monetary incentive provided by the occupation is sufficiently high. By contrast, as discussed earlier, white-collar occupations in Taiwan are likely to provide more job flexibility than blue-collar occupations. White-collar occupations therefore are expected to be associated with both higher earnings and less conflict between work and family for Taiwanese women. Consequently, the higher an occupation's income potential, the less likely Taiwanese women are to leave their jobs, even when experiencing heavy family burdens.

I tested the hypotheses regarding how the association between occupation and women's exit rates may differ between the two countries using logistic regression models on the sample of ever-married women for each country (Appendix B, Tables B.4–B.7).[2] Women who had never married were excluded from the analysis because they were unlikely to have faced the conflict between family and employment. Figure 4.2 shows the effects of occupation on women's decision to leave the labor force at any point during their careers, after marriage, and around the time of first childbirth. I present these effects in the form of an odds ratio against manufacturing occupations.[3] Specifically, the bars in Figure 4.2 indicate the likelihood of employment exits among women in each given occupation compared with those in blue-collar occupations, after controlling for other job characteristics and sociodemographic attributes.

For each country, the occupational effects on women's employment exit rates are similar regardless of whether such exits occurred upon marriage, at the birth of their first child, or at other times. This is because among women who had ever exited the labor force, the majority exited around the time of marriage or first childbirth, and they rarely interrupted their employment careers more than once over their life course. However, occupational effects differ remarkably between Japan and Taiwan. To be specific, Japanese women in clerical occupations were almost twice as likely to discontinue their employment relative to their blue-collar counterparts after marriage and around the time of first childbirth. This finding indicates that Japanese women in lower white-collar occupations tended to find that the conflict between their jobs and family lives outweighed their small gains in earnings relative to their blue-collar counterparts'. In addition, despite their much higher occupational status, Japanese women in professional, managerial, and semiprofessional jobs did not differ from women in factory jobs in their exit rates, indicating that their more hostile work environments constitute a great impediment. This group of women was nevertheless more likely to remain in their jobs than women in clerical occupations as a result of greater rewards associated with their jobs.

By contrast, the results for Taiwan show a negative association between occupational status and women's employment exit rates. Women in managerial

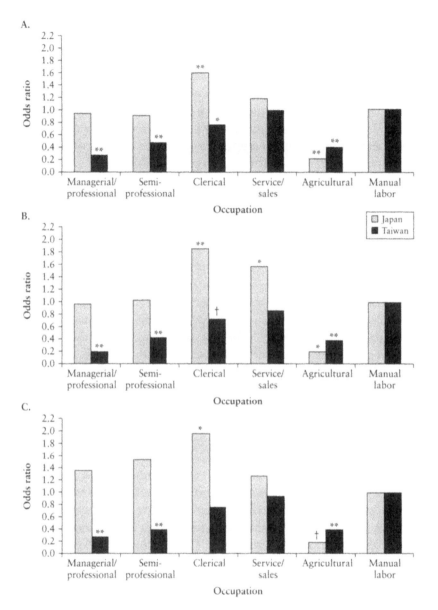

*Figure 4.2.* (A–C) Occupational effects on ever-married women's labor force exits throughout their employment career (A), after marriage (B), and at the birth of their first child (C).

SOURCE: Japan, 1995 SSM, part A; Taiwan, 1996 TSC, part II.

*Notes:* The odds ratios are based on discrete-time logit models predicting women's labor force exits at different points of time (see full models in Appendix B, Tables B.3–B.5). Other predictors in the models include individuals' education, birth cohort, living arrangement, residential location, firm size, employment sector, and the husband's education.

$^\dagger p < .10$, $^* p < .05$, $^{**} p < .01$.

and professional occupations had the lowest exit rates, followed by those in semiprofessional, clerical, and blue-collar occupations, in that order.[4] As argued earlier, white-collar occupations provide women with both higher earnings and less conflict between work and family in Taiwan. Thus, women in white-collar jobs were less likely to leave the labor force at any time during their employment careers, as well as around the times of marriage or first childbirth, than those with factory jobs. Moreover, among women in white-collar occupations, the greater the job returns, the more likely they were to remain in their jobs after marriage and childbearing.

*Firm size.* Workplace dynamics and working conditions for women may also depend on the scale of the firm. In general, larger firms are more formalized and thus less flexible with respect to work schedules. During my conversations with Taiwanese women who had been employed by small firms, I learned about some instances of negotiations between employers and employees regarding time schedules. Although one woman complained that the rather informal atmosphere in small firms allowed her employer to ask her, as a personal favor to him, to postpone her honeymoon trip until the company was less busy, the same atmosphere made it possible for female employees to negotiate for their own benefit. As another woman put it, "In a small firm, as long as the boss likes you, things can usually be flexible."

The lower level of job flexibility is only one of the reasons to expect women employed by larger firms in Japan to find it more difficult to combine their jobs and motherhood. Perhaps more important, managers in larger Japanese firms are likely to have a greater incentive to pressure women to quit their jobs upon marriage or childbearing. To explain this incentive, first, large firms pay significantly more than small firms in Japan (Gao 2001). Second, historically, large firms were particularly committed to a seniority-based wage system, and this commitment is thought to still affect their employment practices today (Ahmadjian and Robbins 2005; Crawcour 1978; Kato 2001; Lincoln and Nakata 1997). The combination of relatively high and seniority-based wages offered by Japan's large firms means that their finances suffer more than small firms when less essential workers remain in the firm until old age. These firms are therefore likely to create a less supportive work environment for married women and mothers to ensure their timely exit. As previous research shows, in addition to indirect pressure and suggestive gestures, large Japanese firms sometimes set institutional barriers to women's career advancement, which discourages women from remaining in their jobs when faced with heavy family obligations (Brinton 1993; Ogasawara 1998). A woman in her early forties, who had worked for more than twenty years in a large Japanese enterprise that manufactured musical instruments, also informed me of such gendered institutions:

Before the Equal Employment Opportunity Act [effective in 1986], men and women who passed the examinations and entered the firm in the same year were assigned to different tracks automatically. Mainly, women were in *ji-mushoku* (clerical track) while men were *eigyoshoku* (sales track). I mean, men and women who were both university graduates. So with equal educational credentials, I was four levels down [in the job ranking system] compared to my male *doki* (workers who enter a firm in the same year). Within this firm, we can switch to a different track, but one has to arrive at a certain level first. It took me a long time just to get to the point where my male *doki* were assigned to immediately after they entered the firm.

Another reason why women in large Japanese firms might find their working conditions less compatible with marriage and motherhood is the more frequent use of job rotation in those firms. Job rotation was an important part of the Japanese employment system, and many companies still require it. Large, multifunction firms are particularly likely to adopt this practice to equip their core workers with a broad range of skills and knowledge (Koike 1987). Because job rotation in large firms often involves geographical mobility, it serves as a source of conflict between women's family and employment. A woman in the *sōgōushoku* (managerial track) in a large Japanese firm explained to me why the resignation rate among her female coworkers in this career track seemed higher than that among women in the less promising *yippanshoku* (general track): "Because they cannot move to a different area in the country easily." Although a job in the general track limits one's chance of career advancement, it does not require job rotation either. However, even before Japanese employers began to include women in the managerial track,[5] the practice of job rotation used in large firms made it difficult for female employees, who had a high probability of marrying their coworkers, to maintain job continuity. The experience of a middle-age Japanese woman illustrates this fact:

I met my husband in the company when he was assigned to my branch because of *tenkin* [job rotation]. Our firm is a huge insurance company with many branches. I quit when we got married because we worked in the same firm, and I knew that job rotation was common and frequent for our male employees. Had I stayed in the same job, he would have been transferred to other regions and I would have stayed in Kyushu. Women generally had no opportunity of job rotation. Hence, we would not have been able to have a family life. We would have needed to live separately. My husband has told me stories about couples who both remain in the firm and live apart due to job rotation.

In contrast, working in larger firms may not lead to much greater conflict between family and work for Taiwanese women, even though larger establishments in that country are still likely to provide less job flexibility. One reason for this expectation is that the employment practices just discussed for Japan are virtually absent in Taiwan. Therefore, unlike in Japan, large and small firms in Taiwan do not differ in their interest in retaining or replacing female employees. In addition, we should keep in mind that the vast majority of Taiwan's labor force is either currently employed by small-scale firms or has experience working in such environments. The pervasiveness of this small-enterprise experience, plus the fact that large Taiwanese enterprises were never as dominant in the economy as their counterparts in Japan, leads to the high popularity of rather informal workplace atmospheres across firms of different scales. The examples provided earlier regarding women sneaking out of the office or bringing children to the workplace are only possible because of the rather casual workplace dynamics in Taiwan. Moreover, Taiwan's high labor demand has compelled employers in firms of all sizes to provide friendlier work environments for women. All these structural conditions suggest that, in the statistical analysis of the survey responses, the contrast between the exit rates of women employed in larger and smaller firms will be less sharp in Taiwan than in Japan.

In fact, the statistical analysis does corroborate that Japanese women employed in larger firms were more likely to leave their jobs than those in smaller firms. Figure 4.3 presents the relative likelihood that a woman will leave her job if employed by a firm with 10 to 99, 100 to 499, or more than 500 employees than if working at a very small firm with less than 10 employees. The increase in the odds ratio with firm size for Japan indicates that larger firms were associated with greater labor force exit rates among ever-married women, regardless of the timing of their exits.[6] In particular, being employed by a firm with more than 100 workers rather than by one with less than 10 workers largely increased a woman's likelihood to discontinue employment upon marriage in Japan. This finding is consistent with my argument that working conditions in larger Japanese firms are less compatible with women's family roles.

Figure 4.3 also shows that the differences in exit rates between women employed by firms of various sizes were smaller in Taiwan than in Japan. Although, as in Japan, women employed by medium-size firms (i.e., those with 10–499 employees) were more likely to discontinue employment than those working at very small establishments in Taiwan, the contrast in their exit rates was much sharper in Japan. The only exception is in Figure 4.3C, which shows the effects of firm size on the decision to leave the labor force around the time of first birth. To explain the closer effects of firm size on women's exits around first childbirth, I note that previous studies and my own findings from ethnographic research both suggest that until quite recently, the workplace atmosphere in large firms in Japan tended to pressure female workers out upon marriage (e.g., Ogasawara 1998).[7] The large-firm employees who remained in the labor force until the time of first childbirth

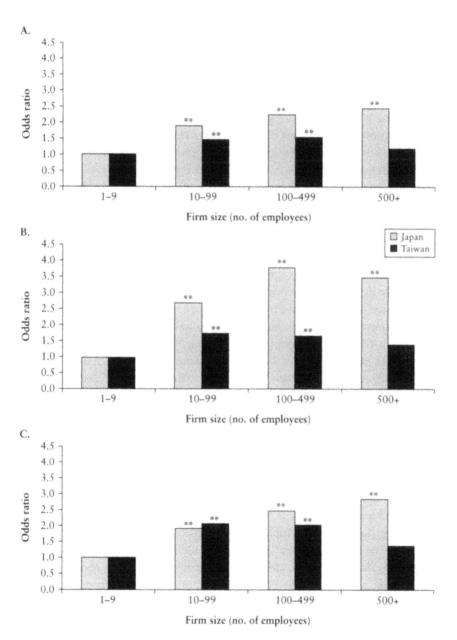

*Figure 4.3.* (A–C) Effects of firm size on ever-married women's labor force exits throughout their employment career (A), after marriage (B), and around the birth of their first child (C).

SOURCE: Japan, 1995 SSM, part A; Taiwan, 1996 TSC, part II.

*Note:* The odds ratios are based on results from the same models described in Figure 4.2.

$^\dagger p < .10$, $^* p < .05$, $^{**} p < .01$.

were likely to have been either particularly committed to work or in relatively supportive work environments. Because the analysis of the decision to leave the labor force for motherhood excluded women who had already been pressured out of large firms by marriage, the effects of organizational settings become rather similar for Japan and Taiwan.

Not only did Taiwanese women's exit rates increase less with firm size than Japanese women's, but how their exit rates were associated with organizational settings also differed. The relation between firm size and exit rates for Taiwanese women is nonlinear. Female workers in relatively large and very small firms were both more likely to remain in their jobs than those in medium-size firms in Taiwan. As discussed, the work environments in large firms are neither as formalized nor as hostile toward married women in Taiwan as in Japan, not to mention that Taiwan's higher labor demands generally prevent managers from making excessive demands on their employees. In addition, the smaller wage increases with seniority in Taiwanese firms create less incentive for maintaining a young, female workforce. Thus, the higher wages generally paid by larger Taiwanese firms are enough to offset the disincentive created by their organizational settings. Besides, firms with more than five hundred employees offer exceptionally good opportunities for upward mobility in Taiwan, where most enterprises are small and family owned. The nonlinear relation between firm size and women's exit rates also has to do with these mobility opportunities permitted by large firms in Taiwan. In other words, women employed in medium-size firms were the most likely to exit the labor force in Taiwan because these firms offer only moderate job rewards while imposing less job flexibility than smaller firms.

*Employment sector.* The extent to which a woman's working conditions enable her to combine job and family responsibilities may also depend on her sector of employment. To be specific, the public sector is more likely than the private sector to implement workplace policies that are compatible with women's family obligations (Brinton 2001; Rosenfeld and Birkelund 1995; Shirahase 2007). In the cases of Japan and Taiwan, the differences in working conditions between the public and private sectors begin with their level of support for workers' basic rights mandated by law. The legal environments in these two countries allow some leeway for employers in the private sector not to comply with the regulations regarding the rights of their female employees. Laws for promoting gender equality or family-responsive workplaces in both countries specify few penalties for noncompliance. In addition, the legal systems in both countries discourage litigation (Chen 2000; Upham 1987). Because lawsuits are uncommon, private-sector management can afford to discourage their workers directly or indirectly from asserting their legal rights. For example, though it is a worker's right, "Taking maternity leave in a private firm is like asking for the employer's mercy," as put by a Taiwanese woman whom I interviewed. Yuko Ogasawara (1998) also finds such discouragement in the private Japanese bank she studied. According to her ethnographic notes, although maternity leave of fourteen weeks and childcare leave up to one year were supposed to be available for female workers, those who attempted to utilize such benefits were either criticized or harassed by their supervisors, or were transferred to more difficult jobs within the firm (Ogasawara 1998:66–67).

Not only must the public sector support policies that aim to ease the difficulties experienced by working wives and mothers, but the general conditions in this sector also tend to be more compatible with married women's family responsibilities than those in the private sector. In particular, because public-sector officials are less concerned about labor cost reduction and profit maximization compared with employers in the private sector, they are less likely to demand overtime work or deprive their employees of personal leave. This difference in time demands may affect the level of conflict between work and family experienced by married women. To illustrate, a single woman working in a ward office in Tokyo explained to me why women in her office often continued their full-time jobs after marriage and childbearing:

> Women in the ward office seem to all work through marriage and childbearing. I asked them, particularly those with kids, why they are able to continue their work for so many years. They said that it is because they are always able to get as many days of annual leave as the law regulates. You know, in many Japanese firms, you don't get annual leave regularly, even though you are entitled to. You are too busy to take any time off. That type of scenario is uncommon in the public sector.

For the reasons discussed here, we should expect the statistical analysis to show that women working in the public sector have encountered fewer obstacles toward combining their roles as workers, mothers, and wives than those in the private sector in both Japan and Taiwan. Nevertheless, the relative advantage of public-sector employment over private employment might not be equivalent in the two countries. To be specific, the more reasonable job demands or more family-friendly working conditions associated with public work settings can be expected to benefit women more in Japan, where private workplaces tend to less compatible with wives' and mothers' family responsibilities than those in Taiwan.

The statistical results confirm that the different working conditions that women in the public and private sectors experience affect their rates of exiting the labor market. Figure 4.4 shows the likelihood that a woman with a public-sector job will exit the labor force after marriage and first pregnancy

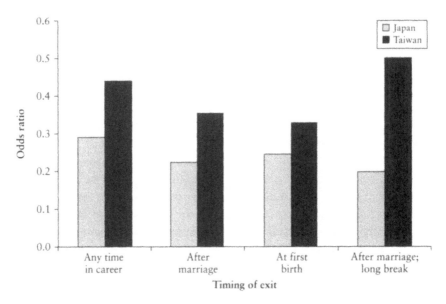

*Figure 4.4.*    Relative odds of labor force exit of public- to private-sector employees.

SOURCE: Japan, 1995 SSM, part A; Taiwan, 1996 TSC, part II.

*Note:* The odds ratios are based on results from the same models described in Figure 4.2. Here, the reference group works in the private sector. Each bar indicates the ratio of the odds of labor force exit for public-sector employees to the odds for private-sector workers. All odds ratios are statistically significant at the 0.05 level.

compared with a woman holding a private-sector job. Figure 4.4 also shows the effects of public-sector employment from an additional analysis of women's postmarital retreats that led to at least five years of absence from the labor force. The analysis of major work interruptions (greater than or equal to five years) enables me to exclude brief employment interruptions among private-sector workers resulting from firm bankruptcies or layoffs. Such exits are particularly plausible in Taiwan, where most firms are small and their average life expectancy is short (Yu and Su 2004). By focusing on major work interruptions, I am able to tell how women employed in the public and private sectors might have differed in their tendencies to leave the labor force for family reasons.[8]

As seen in Figure 4.4, the probabilities of leaving the labor force for women employed in the public sector compared with their counterparts in the private sector were from one fourth to one half, depending on the country and the timing of exit. These results indicate that women working in the public sector were much less likely to exit the labor force around the time of marriage or childbearing. Thus, the work environments of the public sector encouraged women to participate continuously in the labor force in both countries.

The results also reveal that public-sector employment reduced women's likelihood of exiting employment more in Japan than in Taiwan. The gap between the two countries is particularly large when examining only women's major work interruptions ("long break") after marriage. This large gap has to do with the fact that the difference in exit rates between Taiwanese women working in the public and private sectors narrows (i.e., odds ratio closer to one) when short interruptions that were related to economic fluctuations were not taken into account. Conversely, excluding short breaks from the labor force hardly affects the effect of public-sector employment in Japan, suggesting that economic fluctuations were not responsible for the greater exit rate of women employed in the private sector. Overall, the cross-national differences are consistent with the argument that the differences in working conditions between public- and private-sector employees were greater in Japan. Because juggling job and family duties is generally more difficult for married women working in Japan's private sector than their counterparts in Taiwan, the benefit of public-sector employment is also greater for Japanese women. Thus, holding public-sector rather than private-sector jobs decreased Japanese women's exit rates more than it did Taiwanese women's.

### Other Individual Characteristics

In addition to job features, a woman's likelihood of exiting the labor force for motherhood may also depend on her own work orientations, family finances, and whether she has easy access to childcare support (Gerson 1985; Glass 1992; Goldin 1990; Leibowitz and Klerman 1995). Independent of her job opportunities, a woman with more education may be more prone to participating in the labor force. Moreover, a woman's likelihood of remaining in the labor force after marriage may be associated with her husband's income. Because marriage often enables women to gain access to their husband's income, those whose husbands earn more may find less incentive to remain in their jobs during a period of heavy family responsibilities. Nevertheless, women also participate in the labor force for reasons other than their family's financial needs. Some may work to ensure economic independence; others work for self-realization. How sensitive women's decisions to participate in the labor force are to their husbands' earnings, rather than their own preferences, should depend on how difficult it is to combine employment and motherhood. That is to say, in a society in which work environments are generally harsh and unsupportive of working mothers and wives, women are likely to be unmotivated to continue their employment and only do so out of necessity. We can therefore expect women's participation in the labor force to be closely tied to their husband's earnings within that society. By contrast, in a context where combining employment and motherhood is quite feasible, women's own interests and gains from work may play a more important role than their husband's income. Since Japanese women are argued to face greater difficulty combining family responsibilities and their jobs than Taiwanese women, their husbands' earnings can be expected to affect their decision to leave the labor force to a larger extent.

In addition to a woman's own education and her husband's income potential, living with extended family members may allow a mother to receive additional help for childcare from kin (Morgan and Hirosima 1983). Such access to childcare support is likely to increase a woman's likelihood to remain in her job after marriage and childbirth. While an extended family structure normally reduces childcare demands on the mother in both Japan and Taiwan, how much it affects women's likelihood of exiting the labor force may differ between the two countries. A decrease in family demands means more to a working mother whose job conditions are in greater conflict with her family roles. For example, for a woman whose job often requires overtime work, childcare assistance from her parents or parents-in-law critically determines the feasibility of continuing her job after childbearing, whereas such assistance is beneficial but not necessary for one whose job grants schedule flexibility. Thus, if working conditions are in greater conflict with women's roles as wives and mothers in Japan, whether women have coresiding kin would affect the compatibility between employment and motherhood more critically in that country.

I tested the hypotheses regarding the individual characteristics just discussed in statistical models. Figure 4.5 shows the effects of a woman's own education, her husband's education, and extended family support on her likelihood of leaving the labor force upon marriage and at the time of her first birth, after controlling for her job characteristics. I used husband's education as a proxy for his income in the analysis, since the data do not include information on husband's income throughout a woman's working life (which is required for fitting the regression models with an event–history approach).[9] Education serves as a valid proxy for earnings because the wage systems in both labor markets correspond closely to workers' educational credentials (Appendix B, Table B.2). I also used coresidence with any extended family member as a proxy for the additional childcare support women receive from relatives.[10] Unlike in earlier figures, here I present the corresponding coefficients from the logistic regression models on employment exits, rather than the odds ratios. Because women's own education and their husbands' education are both continuous measures, a presentation of the regression coefficients, rather than the odds ratios, is more intuitively understandable. The values presented indicate the net effects on the log odds ratios.

According to the figure, one additional year of schooling was associated with a small yet significant decrease in Japanese women's probabil-

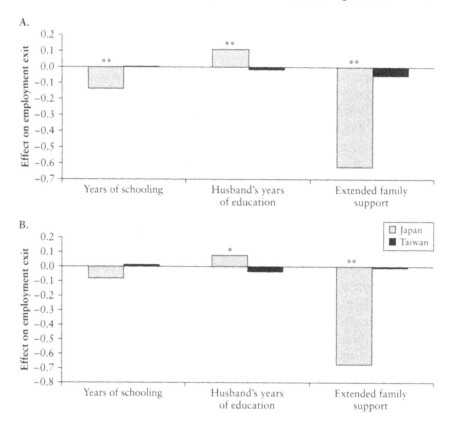

*Figure 4.5.* (A, B) Effects of individual characteristics on the likelihood of exiting the labor force after marriage (A) and around first childbirth (B).

SOURCE: Japan, 1995 SSM, part A; Taiwan, 1996 TSC, part II.

*Notes:* The effects presented here are based on the coefficients from the same models described in Figure 4.2. A negative effect indicates an odds ratio less than one, whereas a positive effect indicates one larger than one.

$^{\dagger}p < .10$, $^{*}p < .05$, $^{**}p < .01$.

ity of leaving the labor force upon marriage (about a 3% decrease in the probability). This finding is consistent with the expectation that a woman's higher educational attainment increases her commitment to work. Nonetheless, education does not have the same effect in Taiwan, perhaps because women's employment decisions were more closely tied to their occupational opportunities than education per se in that country. A husband's education was positively associated with his wife's probability of discontinuing employment in Japan, but not in Taiwan. I have argued that married women working in unfriendly environments are particularly likely to make decisions to withdraw from the labor force based on their husbands' earnings. The difference in the effects of the husband's education between Japan and Taiwan is consistent with the argument that working conditions and job demands are less compatible with married women's family roles in Japan.[11]

Living with parents, parents-in-law, or other extended kin who may serve as alternative childcare providers decreased Japanese women's odds of job discontinuity after marriage by nearly half (the effect of extended family support in the figure, –.625, is in log odds ratio and represents a reduction of the odds by 53.5%). My ethnographic notes collaborate this finding: Most Japanese women with whom I spoke enlisted some help from their parents or parents-in-law with childcare if they participated in the labor force before their children entered school. One woman interrupted her employment career after the birth of her second child because her mother-in-law became ill and could no longer provide help.

Compared with Japan, the effects of coresidence with extended family members are much smaller (and nonsignificant) in Taiwan. This result is consistent with the argument that the more difficult working conditions in Japan make the benefit of having a live-in relative (parent) greater than in Taiwan. Part of the explanation for the small benefit of extended family structures on Taiwanese women's employment is also that childcare assistance from those other than coresiding kin is generally more accessible in that country than in Japan. As mentioned, a detailed comparison of childcare options between the two countries is presented in the following chapter.

## LONG-TERM CHANGES IN WOMEN'S EMPLOYMENT CONTINUITY

The cross-national differences in women's postmarital employment exit patterns presented thus far help explain the broader divergence in women's employment behavior between Japan and Taiwan in recent decades. An increase in single women's participation in jobs that are typically associated with lower exit rates upon marriage will naturally lead to an overall rise in women's job continuity. In Japan, clerical jobs were associated with higher exit rates than manufacturing jobs. The increase in the proportion of single women in clerical jobs during this period therefore led to a greater number of labor force exits following marriage and childbearing among the female population. The decline of the number of Japanese women employed in small-scale, family-based enterprises similarly contributed to an increase in labor force exits. Other prominent changes in postwar Japanese society, including a decrease in extended family residence and an increase in husbands' educational attainment, also worked against women's continuous labor force participation.

In contrast, the improvement of single women's occupational opportunities over time led to an overall increase in married women's continuous employment in Taiwan. The fact that higher occupational status was associated with lower postmarital exit rates among Taiwanese women accounts for this relationship. Other trends in postwar Taiwan, including an increase in the size of firms where single women worked, a rise in men's education, and a decline in extended family structure, all had weaker effects on women's job discontinuity than in Japan. These demographic changes have therefore deterred growth in Taiwanese women's continuous employment to a lesser extent.

To demonstrate the effects of women's changing job and demographic profiles on the aggregate trend regarding female labor force participation, I estimated the average probabilities of exiting the labor force in the year of marriage for Japanese and Taiwanese women born in the periods 1946 to 1955 and 1956 to 1965.[12] The estimated probabilities are based on the results from the logistic regression models predicting a labor force exit upon marriage (Appendix B, Table B.4). I also estimated the probabilities of leaving the labor force for these two cohorts of women based on the coefficients from the regression model for the other country. Such probabilities tell us what the average exit rate of the Japanese women would have been if they had lived in Taiwan and vice versa. In other words, this exercise allows us to separate the effect of the composition of the female labor force from the effect of the characteristics of the two employment systems.

Figure 4.6 presents the predicted probabilities just described. The average probability of labor force exit upon marriage increased slightly for Japanese women born in later years as a result of their changing demographic composition, whereas the probability decreased for Taiwanese women of later birth years for the same reason. Thus, although the average probability of leaving their jobs upon marriage for women born in 1956 to 1965 was only slightly lower in Taiwan than in Japan, the gap widened for women born a decade later. More interestingly, had women with the same jobs and demographic characteristics as the Japanese women in the sample been subject to the same workplace dynamics as those in Taiwan, they would have had considerably lower labor force exit rates in the year of marriage. Moreover, the trend in such women's postmarital employment continuity would have been reversed (as shown by the arrows in Figure 4.6). At the same time, the probability of labor force exits upon marriage would have increased over time for Taiwanese women had they lived in Japan. In other words, women in these two countries would have converged in their labor force behavior if their exit rates by occupation, firm size, employment sector, and other individual and family characteristics had been similar. The reversal of the trends also indicates that the differences in single women's job and demographic profiles between the two countries cannot explain women's higher probability of interrupting employment in Japan. Rather,

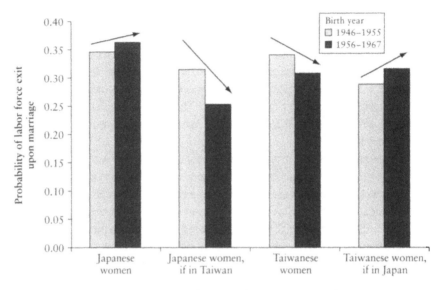

*Figure 4.6.*    Predicted probabilities for labor force exit during the marriage year.

SOURCE: Japan, 1995 SSM, part A; Taiwan, 1996 TSC, part II.

*Note:* The probabilities for Japanese and Taiwanese women were estimated directly from the logistic regression results in the any-break model for their own country in Appendix B, Table B.4. The probability for "Japanese women, if in Taiwan" was estimated for Japanese women in the sample using regression coefficients from the model for Taiwan, and vice versa regarding the estimated probability for "Taiwanese women, if in Japan."

because women working in similar occupational and organizational settings in the two countries experienced different levels of conflict between work and family, we observe the cross-national divergence in female employment over time.

SUMMARY AND CONCLUSION

The results of the individual-level analysis presented in this chapter are consistent with the argument that the characteristics of the Japanese labor market led to a lower degree of compatibility between work and family responsibilities than in Taiwan. While the statistical analysis does not directly measure the workplace dynamics that pressure Japanese women to withdraw from the labor force, the effects of occupations and organizational settings corroborate the ethnographic findings on women's working conditions and perceived conflict between their jobs and family roles. Specifically, the results support the argument that unfriendly work environments outweigh women's incentive to continue their well-paying jobs during child-rearing years in Japan. By contrast, relatively low role conflict enables their

Taiwanese counterparts to make employment decisions based primarily on economic returns.

Using individual-level data, this chapter demonstrates the linkage between the macrolevel economic changes and microlevel decisions that women make regarding their employment. The effects of economic development on women's employment decisions are mediated by the degree of conflict between work and family. Although historical changes in women's occupational options increase their earnings opportunities, they do not always bring about increases in women's job continuity after marriage and childbearing. Contextual constraints affect how women decide on the timing of labor force participation during their life cycles. When women face severe constraints, economic development, even when accompanied by improved occupational opportunities for women, may not necessarily result in their greater employment continuity after marriage and childbearing.

In conclusion, this chapter, along with the previous one, has shown that aggregate labor demand, prevalent organizational structures, and institutionalized employment practices account for the different effects of occupational and demographic changes on women's postmarital employment between Japan and Taiwan. Had job characteristics and family structure been associated with women's employment exit rates in similar patterns in Japan and Taiwan, their long-term trends in female employment behavior would be in the same direction. Specifically, because of the work environments they face, Japanese women with clerical jobs or those employed by medium- to large-size firms are more likely than those with other jobs to exit the labor force upon marriage or childbearing. The relatively high conflict between work and family for Japanese women also led to a relatively large gap in exit rates between those with and without easy access to the assistance of extended family members. Consequently, the overall increase in the proportion of single women in white-collar occupations or working for medium- to large-size enterprises, along with the declining prevalence of extended family residence, has contributed to a greater number of labor force exits among Japan's female population over time.

By contrast, the growth of single women's white-collar occupational opportunities has largely increased Taiwanese women's tendency toward continuous employment, because such opportunities are generally associated with lower exit rates. Other similar changes that Taiwan has experienced, including the increase in women employed by medium to large establishments and the decrease in extended family living arrangements, have deterred the growth of women's job retention rates only to a small extent because the effects of these factors on women's labor force exit rates are relatively small in that country. The different effects of occupation, firm size, and family structure essentially explain why Taiwanese women's job continuity increased from one generation to the next, whereas the same demographic trends hardly deterred their Japanese counterparts' rate of labor force withdrawal.

The analysis presented in this chapter therefore reveals the importance for comparative gender research to ask two questions: Which subgroup of women within each country is more likely to make a certain employment decision? How do long-term economic and social changes affect the relative share of each subgroup within the female population? As demonstrated in this chapter, without knowing how Japanese women's patterns of labor force exits have differed from Taiwanese women's, or tying such patterns to country-level sociodemographic changes, we would not be able to explicate the dramatically different trends in women's employment continuity between these two countries. Only by linking microlevel decision-making dynamics to changes in population characteristics can we fully understand the mechanisms behind broader shifts in women's economic behaviors.

Although this and previous chapters have provided a large amount of evidence supporting the differences in labor market structures and working environments between Japan and Taiwan, the attention I have paid to women's family responsibilities in these countries may seem insufficient. After all, the differing levels of conflict between work and family I have argued for Japan and Taiwan might also result from a discrepancy in wives' and mothers' obligations at home. I therefore turn to the family part of the story in the next chapter, which addresses the societal conditions that shape childcare options and domestic demands on women in the two countries.

## CHAPTER FIVE

# Challenges from the Home Front

The analysis presented so far has centered on women's working environments and the labor market structures that shape them. An incompatibility between women's work and family, however, may arise not only from higher work demands, but also from their greater responsibilities at home. To provide a complete explanation of how female employment patterns differ between Japan and Taiwan, I examine the effects of women's family roles and obligations in this chapter.

During the decades after World War II, both Japan and Taiwan experienced rapid declines in fertility rates, accompanied by decreases in extended family residence. Although these demographic trends began at different times—in the 1930s in Japan and in the 1950s in Taiwan—the patterns and rates of change were similar (Feeney and Mason 2001). One major impact of the shrinking family size in both societies is that it freed up more of women's time, which in turn encouraged female participation in the labor market. Nevertheless, Japanese women have continued to interrupt their employment careers for motherhood. By contrast, their Taiwanese counterparts have increasingly chosen both employment and motherhood, rather than one or the other.

Earlier I argued that Japan's greater job demands have continuously discouraged women from remaining in the labor force after marriage or childbearing. This argument, however, does not deny the possibility that the roles and responsibilities of Japanese mothers and wives may differ from those of their Taiwanese counterparts. Across industrialized societies, mothers' "caring burden" often varies substantially because of cross-national differences in the level of institutional support for childcare (Esping-Anderson 1999; Gornick and Meyers 2003; Stier et al. 2001). Furthermore, cultural differences may lead to variation in mothers' family responsibilities across societies. Although in Chapter 1 I briefly compared gender attitudes and state policies in the two countries, that comparison by no means exhausted the factors that may lead to cross-national differences in women's roles and responsibilities at home. For instance, while Taiwanese men and women appear to agree with the separate sphere ideology more than their Japanese counterparts, this does not necessarily suggest that the general expectations of mothers' involvement in child rearing are also higher in Taiwan. In fact, previous research on Japan finds an overly strong emphasis on mothers' roles in child rearing, despite a declining belief that the domestic world is for wives and the external world is for husbands (Fujita 1989; Hirao 2001; Retherford, Ogawa, and Sakamoto 1996). Therefore, this chapter is devoted to providing a more comprehensive analysis of the family demands women face in Japan and Taiwan.

One may wonder: If women's family roles have also contributed to Japan's greater tension between women's job and family demands, are the labor market factors discussed in earlier chapters really that important in explaining the divergence in women's postmarital employment trajectories between these countries? Is it possible that, instead, the cultural differences between Japan and Taiwan explain most of this divergence? Before addressing these questions, I should note that the demands women face at home are not always independent of their labor market opportunities. To give an example, research shows that broader changes in the U.S. economy have led to better and more job opportunities for married women, resulting in increasing female employment rates (Goldin 1990). As women's participation in the labor force increased, attitudinal support for traditional gender roles that prescribe women as full-time mothers and homemakers declined (Gerson 1985; Glass 1992). Because of this value change, succeeding generations of U.S. women became much more likely to envision combining employment and motherhood (Goldin 1995, 1997). In the scenario just described, although the change in U.S. women's family roles helped shape their employment behavior in recent decades, this change cannot be considered as the primary reason for the initial increase in female employment. Rather, the formation and change of cultural values that are supportive of female employment resulted from women's improving job opportunities (Goldin 1990). Nevertheless, once cultural values become prevalent in a society, they are likely to generate their own momentum, thereby affecting future generations.

In light of the complex relations between women's labor market opportunities and family roles, this chapter has two objectives. One is to examine how differences in family demands and women's gender roles between Japan and Taiwan shape their employment careers at *present*. The other is to determine whether the labor market conditions described in the previous chapters *preceded* the differences in the culturally prescribed roles for Japanese and Taiwanese women that affect their employment behaviors. Hence, I first compare the challenges that married women in the two societies face because of the normative expectations and structural constraints they experience at home. The discussion centers on how the different family conditions between the two countries shape married women's employment decisions. Second, I examine long-term trends related to the different family demands on women in the two countries to establish the sequential order of changes in female employment behavior and modifications of women's culturally or structurally determined family responsibilities. In doing so, I aim to provide an understanding of the dynamic process of change in women's employment careers in each society.

## A COMPARISON OF FAMILY DEMANDS

A family requires input from its members to function. Roughly speaking, the family demands that shape married women's employment decisions fall into two categories: demands for financial resources and demands for caring labor, including the labor put into domestic chores. When a household demands more domestic labor than financial resources from the wife, she is likely to be out of the labor force. Conversely, a married woman is highly likely to participate in market activities if her family has a sufficient amount of caring labor, but lacks financial inputs.

I argue that the demand for married women's time and labor at home is generally higher in Japan than in Taiwan. At the same time, Taiwanese families tend to demand a greater financial contribution from wives than Japanese families. These cross-national differences aggravate the already greater level of incompatibility between work and family that Japanese women have experienced as a result of Japan's workplace culture. To demonstrate this argument, I compare the availability of the husband's labor at home, the commuting distance between home and work, the accessibility of alternative childcare providers, and the culturally defined norms regarding child rearing in these two countries. I also examine the need for the wife's financial input among Taiwanese and Japanese households.

### Demand for the Mother's Time at Home

In previous chapters I have argued that the time demands placed on regular Japanese employees tend to be greater than those placed on their Taiwanese counterparts. Hence, more women in Japan than in Taiwan are likely to find their jobs incompatible with their family responsibilities. In addition to affecting female employment directly, the relatively great time demands placed on Japanese workers are also likely to have an indirect effect on the feasibility of combining motherhood and employment. To be specific, assuming a family requires a fixed amount of time from its members to maintain its normal functioning, the demand for the wife's time at home should be expected to increase with the time her husband spends away from home. The greater this time demand, the more difficult it is for the wife to participate in the labor force. In Japan, most employed men are expected to devote long hours at work, whereas this is not the case in Taiwan. Consequently, even if Japanese wives are able to find jobs that require little overtime work, they are still likely to face greater time demands from their families than their Taiwanese counterparts because of their husbands' longer working hours.[1]

To illustrate the demands for Japanese wives' time at home, I present in Figure 5.1 the trends of men's presence at home during weekday nights in that country. I show the percentage of men present at home, rather than their actual working hours, because it is common for Japanese men to spend after-hours on work-related social activities; hence, statistics indicating husbands' hours spent in the workplace may not provide an accurate picture of their families' need for their wives' time and labor. Figure 5.1 indicates that Japanese men have been increasingly likely to return home at late hours on workdays. In the 1990s, only slightly more than 50 percent of the male employees in Japan reported being home at 8 PM on weekdays. The percentages were similar among men in their thirties and forties (i.e., those who were likely to have young children at home). In fact, a national survey reported that only 12.3 percent of Japanese fathers of preschool children returned

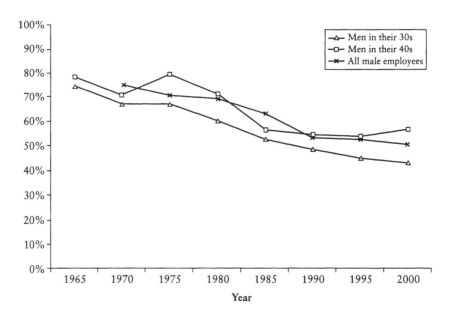

*Figure 5.1.*    Percentage of Japanese men at home by eight o'clock on weekdays.

SOURCE: Nippon Hōsō Kyōkai, *National Time Utilization Survey*, various years.

home before 7 PM on a typical workday, whereas almost half of them did not arrive home until after 9 PM in 2003 (Ministry of Health, Labour, and Welfare, Japan 2003). Japanese men's frequent absence at night makes it highly difficult for their wives to hold jobs that require any overtime work during the years when young children are present.

Statistically speaking, Taiwanese workers spend no less time at work than their Japanese counterparts. Until relatively recently, workers were required to spend eight hours a day, Monday through Friday, and at least four hours on Saturday in the workplace, which adds up to at least 44 hours of work per week. Manufacturing jobs sometimes require 48 hours of work per week. However, overtime work at night is less common in Taiwan than in Japan. During my interviews with married women in the two countries, a few Japanese women brought up their husbands' frequent absence at night as the reason why they had to be responsible for nearly all the domestic chores. Conversely, the Taiwanese women with whom I spoke almost never mentioned overworking as a reason for their husbands' lack of participation in household work. Although there are no similar data regarding the time when Taiwanese men return home, time–use statistics collected by the government from 1987 to 2000 indicate that male workers, on average, spent no more than eight hours at work on a weekday (DGBAS 1988, 1995, 2001b). Such statistics suggest that overtime work is uncommon among Taiwanese men.[2] Thus, while the average working hours among Taiwanese employees are not exactly short, their work schedules tend to allow them to care for family needs at night. Having time for the family at night is important because childcare arrangements available through the market do not tend to provide services after regular working hours. (I revisit this issue in a later section regarding childcare arrangements in the two countries.)

In addition to the time demand from jobs, Japan and Taiwan differ in workers' average commuting time. The commuting time to work adds to the time demand, and therefore exacerbates the time conflict between work and family for married women. Population density and city size both affect commuting time to work. Both Japan and Taiwan have high population densities, particularly in major cities. Nevertheless, urban residents tend to spend more time commuting in Japan than in Taiwan because Japanese cities, on average, are larger in geographical size. There are two reasons for this difference in city size. First, Japan is more able to expand its cities simply because the total land area of the country is greater. Second, earlier and better development of mass transportation systems in metropolitan areas allowed cities in Japan to expand outward. As high population density in metropolitan areas increased the price of land, city residents in Japan moved to suburban areas for less expensive housing. Lacking equivalently convenient means of transportation, major Taiwanese cities have been dealing with population growth by constructing taller residential buildings, rather than expanding the metropolitan areas outward.

According to the 2000 census, the average size of Japan's seven major metropolitan areas was 7,067 sq. km (Statistics Bureau, Ministry of Internal Affairs and Communications, Japan 2001). In contrast, Taiwan's largest metropolitan area, including Taipei City, Taipei County, and Keelung City, was 2,457 sq. km in the same year (Department of Statistics, Ministry of Interior, Republic of China 2001). Not only are cities smaller in Taiwan than in Japan, but urban residents in Taiwan also concentrate more in city centers. To illustrate, the population densities in the two major cities in Taiwan (Taipei and Kaohsiung) were 9,737 and 9,704 people per sq. km, respectively, as of 2000 (ibid.). In comparison, the densities in the central cities within Japan's two largest metropolitan areas (Kantō and Keihanshin), were 8,995 and 4,025 people per sq. km, respectively (Statistics Bureau, Ministry of Internal Affairs and Communications, Japan 2001). The higher population density in Taiwan's cities is consistent with the observation that residential buildings in its major urban areas are generally taller than those in Japan. The difference in population density also suggests that Japan's urban residents are likely to travel a longer distance to work compared with their Taiwanese counterparts.

To give a more precise idea, according to a national survey of time use conducted in 1995 (Nippon Hōsō Kyōkai 1996), the average commuting time for Japanese workers was one hour 15 minutes a day. The same source reported that residents in the 13 largest Japanese cities spent about 10 minutes more than the national average—that is, near 90 minutes total—on their daily, roundtrip commute. By contrast, in 1994, the average Taiwanese worker spent 50 minutes per working day commuting to and from work (DGBAS 1995). The average commuting time for workers reduced to 44 minutes in Taiwan in 2000, perhaps because Taipei initiated the subway system (i.e., the "mass rapid transportation system") during the 1990s (DGBAS 2001b).

The issue of having a long commuting time was brought up frequently in my conversations with working women in Japan. For example, a woman who had left her job as a pharmacist at a hospital in Tokyo a few weeks before we met told me that she left her job because of the long commute. Upon marriage, she and her husband moved to Saitama, an adjacent prefecture to Tokyo, where many young couples can afford to buy a house. The moving substantially increased the distance from her home to work. She described her experience to me:

> I felt so tired when I was working. I needed to spend three hours a day on commuting. There was never any seat on the train. Besides, after a full-time

job, I still need to do housework. My husband doesn't do any. He comes home too late. I did that for a while and I became really tired. So I quit my job. When I worked, we both were so tired and we rarely talked to each other. . . . Yes, I am looking for a new job. I want to find a job closer to home but it is really difficult.

Commuting times also came up in a conversation I had with a young Japanese mother who worked at a private daycare center. She noted that she might quit her job soon for her daughter, who was a little more than one year old at the time. She then explained:

I live in Kamakura and work in Yokohama. It's a long distance for commuting. Right now I put my daughter in a daycare center near home, and my parents-in-law, who live next door, pick her up in the afternoon before I get home. They have to send her to the daycare in the morning for me, too, because I leave home early. If I leave here [the office] at 6 PM, it is almost 8 PM when I arrive at home. My daughter is usually already asleep by the time I return home. With the help from my in-laws, it works out okay. But I feel that I do not spend enough time with my daughter. When she is older, I want to be able to spend more time with her. If I have to spend so much time on transportation, I hardly have time to talk to her. That is why I am thinking about quitting this job and finding something closer. I am not sure whether I can, though. . . . I've commuted for this long for several years, ever since I was single, but it didn't bother me before. Now I have a child. It's different.

As this woman's statement reveals, having a long commute, while tolerable for single women (and men), is a major problem for Japanese mothers who try to handle the dual roles of wage earner and caregiver.

The commuting time also makes the time cost of holding a job greater for urban than rural residents. This gap is likely to be wider in Japan than in Taiwan, not only because Japanese cities are larger, but also because the business and residential areas are closer in Taiwanese cities. One major feature of Taiwan's initial industrialization is the lack of geographical concentration of businesses (Brinton et al. 1995; Hamilton and Biggart 1988). Despite the government's recent efforts to implement industrial zoning, earlier policies that encouraged a dispersed distribution of small enterprises throughout the island have led to a considerable mixing of business and residential districts in most of Taiwan's cities. As a result, Taiwanese women residing in urban areas are likely to spend only slightly more time than those in rural areas on commuting to work. By contrast, urban Japanese mothers are likely to find continuous employment much more difficult than their rural counterparts because of their greater commuting time and effort. Results from my statistical analysis of women's employment exits (Appendix B, Table B.3) are consistent with this assertion. All else being equal, urban Japanese women were 1.4 times as likely as rural ones to exit the labor market at one point in their careers. Conversely, Taiwanese women residing in urban and rural areas were not significantly different in their rates of labor force withdrawal. As argued, Taiwan's differences in urban and rural commuting times are relatively small, such that the greater job opportunities in urban areas offset the inconvenience of long commutes.

In sum, the evidence suggests that Japanese women face greater schedule conflict than Taiwanese women when continuing their jobs after marriage and childbirth. Because Japanese management is more likely to demand overtime work from their employees, it is likely that working mothers in that country find it more difficult to combine job demands with family roles than in Taiwan. To make matters worse, Japanese workers' commuting time is generally longer than Taiwanese workers', particularly in urban areas. In addition, because men in Japan are more likely to spend their evening hours at work or work-related social events, the demand for their wives' time (and effort) at home is also greater than that in Taiwan. Altogether, these differences lead to a greater time crunch for working mothers in Japan.

### Childcare Support and Caregiving Norms

In addition to schedule conflict, the accessibility of childcare facilities has a crucial impact on women's labor supply during the early stage of child rearing. I begin the comparison of childcare options with the situation in Japan. Providing childcare facilities is primarily the responsibility of local governments in that country. In general, there are two types of childcare facilities managed by local governments: kindergartens (*yōchien*) and daycare centers (*hoikuen*). Kindergartens accept older children, whose mothers are likely to be full-time homemakers, because children only stay there for a short amount of time (e.g., from 10 AM to 1 or 2 PM). In contrast, daycare centers provide care for all children up to 6 years of age through 5 or 6 PM on weekdays, since they are designed for full-time employed mothers. Local governments also subsidize privately owned childcare facilities under the condition that they will operate in the way public ones do. All government-affiliated daycare centers charge according to the parents' income level.[3] Private, nongovernment-subsidized childcare facilities also exist in Japan, but they cost considerably more than public ones; hence, most working mothers rely on public or government-sponsored daycare centers. There are also some nannies and baby-sitters, but not many because licenses are often required if they work through agencies.

My interviews with Japanese mothers and caregivers at daycare centers suggest that there has been and is still a shortage of public childcare centers in almost all urban areas. A 45-year-old woman told me her story:

I had my mother-in-law take care of my first child. At the time, we lived with my parents-in-law. I was able to work because of their help. Then my mother-in-law was sick, so we moved out of their house and they could not help us anymore. I did not want to quit, but it was extremely difficult to find a day-care center. I tried all possibilities, but I was told that I had to be on the waiting list for several months to a year before I could put my child into a daycare center. So I had no choice. I had to quit.

Another Japanese woman in her forties, who worked as a hairdresser, experienced a similar situation. She intended to return to her job immediately after her first childbirth, but had to wait for two years for her daughter to be accepted by a public daycare center. She told me: "During the two years I kept going back to the ward office and asking the man in charge to find a spot at a daycare center for my daughter. I remember that man was really annoyed by my frequent visits and questioned me several times about why I had to go back to work."

Although the declining fertility rate has reduced the shortage of public childcare facilities, vacancies for children younger than the age of three at public daycare centers have remained scarce (Boling 2007). According to a caregiver with whom I spoke, new mothers still find it difficult to have their babies admitted to public daycare centers. A caregiver from a public childcare center in Tokyo commented on how this difficulty impedes women's job retention after childbearing:

> We do not have enough facilities to take all children under three years old. There is always a long waiting list for babies between birth and three years old to enter our center. After age three it becomes easier, because older children require fewer caretakers around and hence we can accommodate more of them. I know many young mothers on the waiting list are really worried. They can take unpaid childcare leave (*ikuji kyūgyō*) for up to one year from the birth, according to the law, but some of them still could not get in after waiting for nearly one year. They tell me they are worried that they will not be able to go back to work if they don't find a place for their babies before the leave ends. People like us, who work in a daycare center, know how difficult it is to get in. So we will apply to the ward office—it is the ward office, not us, that decides which children to accept—as early as possible. But many women don't know that. They have a whole year of leave but they do not apply until the seventh month or so. By then it is too late. Not enough waiting time. Moreover, the ward office releases vacancies every April, so the timing of childbearing also affects how soon the child could be admitted.

The other problem with Japan's government-managed childcare facilities is that few operate according to the schedule of many employed mothers. Most daycare centers are open from 8 AM to 6 PM at the latest. For a working mother to meet this schedule, she has to hold a job that requires no overtime work at all. Even if she finds such a job, she still needs to live relatively close to the workplace because commuting can be time-consuming.

Frequent overtime work and a long commute together make it extremely difficult for working parents to arrive at daycare centers for their children by 6 PM. The example provided earlier, of the Japanese mother of a one-year-old daughter living in Kamakura, helps illustrate this scheduling difficulty. She relied on assistance from her parents-in-law, in addition to using a daycare center, because the daycare schedule did not accommodate her working hours plus commuting time. One possible way for working mothers to meet daycare centers' operating schedules is to have the child attend one near their workplace. In the case of the Japanese woman just mentioned, she herself worked at a daycare center. I asked her whether she considered bringing her daughter to the daycare center where she worked. I thought by doing so she might be able to continue her job and spend time with her daughter at the same time. She answered, "I don't think so. Can you imagine bringing a young child onto a crowded train for two hours, without a place to sit? It is too difficult for children." Recalling my experience with rush-hour trains in Tokyo, I realized that she was correct that taking a preschool child to work by train is nearly impossible. For many urban residents in Japan, driving a child or taking a taxi to a daycare center on a work day is simply too costly, however. Their only means of transportation to workplaces are trains or buses, which are extremely crowded during rush hour. Given the difficulty of transporting their children, mothers generally use childcare facilities near the home instead of the workplace. Thus, for Japanese mothers to hold full-time jobs, the schedules of daycare centers must take into account their commuting times, particularly in large cities.

In a conversation with a *kachō* (section manager) responsible for women's welfare in a ward office in Tokyo, I asked whether the local government considered extending the operating hours of public daycare centers to accommodate working mothers' schedules. She replied, "We don't have any plan like that. I don't think it is right for Japanese corporations to make employees work this late. Shouldn't corporations shorten employees' working hours, rather than have us extend daycare centers' hours?" Her reply was consistent with the Japanese government's effort to promote leisure and shorten working hours in recent years. Nevertheless, as I was told, Japanese employees generally view the upper limit of working hours set by the Labour Standard Law as *tatemae* (a "principle" that does not necessarily reflect the underlying reality). The trends shown in Figure 5.1 further support that Japanese employees' tendency of overworking has not decreased with the government's effort to shorten working hours. Without a real change in the system, childcare support in Japan is far from sufficient for working mothers.

Unlike in Japan, working mothers in Taiwan make childcare arrangements primarily through kin networks or the market, given that the state provides hardly any daycare facilities (Chen 2000; Yi 1994). According to my calculations from the data provided by the Taiwanese government (DGBAS 1979, 2003), in 1979, 84 percent of married mothers age 15 to 64 who were not the primary caregiver before their first child turned 3 years old relied on care from relatives, whereas 14 percent of them hired a nanny. Those employing a nanny increased to 24 percent in 2003, whereas those having kin provide childcare remained the majority at 74 percent. These statistics indicate that institutional care was highly uncommon. Relatives, in most cases grandmothers, and nannies constitute major sources of childcare assistance for Taiwan's dual-earner families.

Despite the relatively high percentage of Taiwanese women who rely on kin's childcare assistance, the statistical analysis presented in Chapter 4 shows that having a live-in parent or parent-in-law failed to increase married women's participation in the labor force significantly in Taiwan (Figure 4.5). These seemingly contradictory results can be explained by the fact that Taiwanese mothers have relatively easy access to childcare provided by relatives who do not live under the same roof, or by hired nannies. In other words, because there are other viable childcare options, along with relatively family-friendly work environments, Taiwanese women do not have to live with their parents or parents-in-law to be able to balance work and family responsibilities.

Paradoxically, while childcare support from extended kin substantially increases Japanese women's ability to combine employment and motherhood (Figure 4.5), the grandmother's help is less accessible for them than for Taiwanese women. To elaborate, first, the percentage of nonemployed grandmothers is greater in Taiwan than in Japan. In one conversation I had with a Japanese mother about her childcare options she noted, "I cannot ask my mother to quit *her job* to take care of my baby just because I want to stay with my job!" This statement is less likely to be heard among Taiwanese mothers, because women older than 50 years are much less active in the labor market in Taiwan than in Japan (Figure 1.2). Second, the elderly in Taiwan continue to live close to their married children, despite the decline of the three-generation family residence (Biddlecom, Chayovan, and Ofstedal 2002; Hermalin and Yang 2004; Lin, Goldman, Weinsten, Lin, Gorrindo, and Seeman 2003). This type of living arrangement makes it easy for a grandmother to care for the preschool grandchild during her daughter's or daughter-in-law's working hours. In fact, several Taiwanese women with whom I spoke admitted that they chose to live within walking distance of their parents' or parents-in-law's residence precisely for the purpose of having the parents' help with childcare. Young Japanese couples may want to do the same, but can barely afford the freedom to choose where to live, especially in large cities. High housing costs in Japan's metropolitan areas make it extremely difficult for those about to start a family to purchase a place close to their parents'. As a result, only those living under the same roof with their parents-in-law or their parents can benefit from relatives' childcare support in Japan.

The third reason why grandmothers' childcare assistance is less accessible for Japanese couples than for Taiwanese couples is associated with their somewhat different attitudes regarding seeking help from relatives outside the nuclear family. Based on my interviews, Taiwanese women appeared to be more comfortable with asking their parents or parents-in-law to provide childcare, whereas Japanese women more frequently expressed hesitation and worry about causing trouble to their parents or parents-in-laws by doing so.[4] The belief that it is inappropriate to bother the grandparents with childcare responsibilities is also stronger among the younger generations of Japanese women. The woman living in Kamakura, whom I described earlier, primarily used a daycare center for looking after her one-year-old daughter. The help from the grandparents was only secondary, when there was a void to fill. This type of childcare arrangement is highly unusual in Taiwan; a mother who has access to childcare from her parents or parents-in-law tends to rely on them for the entire time she spends at work.

Perhaps the different degrees of financial dependence of the elderly on their children between the two countries help explain the different attitudes just described. Taiwan's lack of retirement pensions and welfare programs has made it necessary for many older people to depend on children in addition to their own savings. Research shows that the elderly in Taiwan receive a substantial amount of financial support from their children (Biddlecom et al. 2002; Lee, Parish, and Willis 1994; Lin et al. 2003). The financial dependence of older Taiwanese people justifies the childcare assistance they offer to their children as part of the exchange between generations. Although Japan's welfare provision has been limited compared with that of other advanced industrial countries (Brinton 1988; Gao 2001; Schoppa 2006), the existence of retirement and public pension programs enables the elderly to depend less on their children than they do in Taiwan. Parents' financial dependence on their children is also weaker among more recent generations in Japan, because the parents of those who are in their thirties or forties tend to have gained from Japan's high economic growth and have accumulated sufficient wealth on their own. When the *Yomiuri Shimbun* (*Yomiuri Daily Newspaper*) asked respondents in a 1990 national poll to list multiple sources of old-age financial support, only 9 percent of respondents cited children as one of their sources (The Japanese Public Opinion Database). Research also shows that there has been a drastic change in the norms regarding filial care for elderly parents since the 1980s. By 1994, more than half the Japanese no longer considered children's care for their elderly parents a "good custom" or a "natural duty" (Retherford et al. 1996). Overall, the greater independence of Japanese grandparents in comparison with their Taiwanese counterparts makes it less appropriate for their working children to enlist their help for caregiving.

Another common childcare option for employed mothers in Taiwan is to hire a nanny or baby-sitter. In most neighborhoods, there are a few women who run informal, tiny-scale daycare centers in their own homes. Rather than holding jobs outside the home, they contribute to family income by looking after preschool children for dual-earner families in the neighborhood. One such "nanny" usually cares for two or three children, sometimes including her own, at her residence at the same time. The match of a baby-sitter with a working mother with a young child often occurs through word of mouth among acquaintances and neighbors.

Hiring a neighborhood nanny has been the second most popular childcare option for employed mothers in Taiwan, next to kin care (Yi 1994). This type of childcare arrangement tends to be informal and unregulated by the state; thus, the supply is plentiful. Until recently, certification for caregiving was neither required nor offered by any institution. This lack of regulation greatly encouraged the supply of caregivers in Taiwan. As one Taiwanese woman put it, "If one is not picky—I mean, if one does not care too much about the quality of a nanny—it's pretty easy to find one. Any woman who does not have a job can do it." Compared with Japan, Taiwan's lower level of state intervention in childcare activities, though risking the quality of care, has led to more childcare options for mothers.

By having grandmothers or housewives in the neighborhood provide childcare, Taiwanese mothers have relatively high schedule flexibility, unlike their Japanese counterparts, who rely primarily on daycare centers. The greater schedule flexibility increases the feasibility for Taiwanese mothers to balance their job and childcare schedules. To elaborate, when grandmothers or nannies provide childcare, the location of caregiving is often the caregiver's home. Therefore, the schedule arrangements can be more personal, rather than institutional. For example, a few working women in Taiwan whom I interviewed mentioned that it was possible for them to leave their children overnight at the grandparents' or the nanny's home when they had particularly high workloads. To give another example, one Taiwanese woman told me that the nanny she hired was thrilled that the mother promised to pick up her child by 6 PM, which suggests just how often Taiwanese nannies have to extend their childcare services to nighttime hours.

In addition to schedule flexibility, the common childcare arrangements in the two countries differ in their costs in relation to the mother's earnings.

Japanese working mothers tend to rely on public childcare facilities that charge based on the household income level, whereas Taiwanese mothers of all household income levels pay similar fees for childcare when hiring a nanny. Under the Japanese system, a woman with higher earnings pays more for childcare if she decides to remain in her job after childbirth. Conversely, when childcare expenses are relatively fixed, as in Taiwan, women with better paying jobs have a greater financial incentive to continue their careers after childbearing. In the previous chapter, we observed that women in higher status occupations were less likely to leave their jobs after marriage and childbearing in Taiwan, whereas those with blue-collar jobs were particularly likely to stay in the labor market in Japan. The difference in childcare expenses for working mothers between the two countries in part accounts for such observed discrepancies in women's labor force exit patterns.

Japan and Taiwan have also differed in their norms concerning motherhood and child rearing, leading to the varying childcare options for mothers. Specifically, the normative expectations for full-time maternal care during a child's early years are stronger in Japan than in Taiwan. In both cultures, there exists an expression that conveys that the first three years of development shapes one's personality and capability for the rest of one's life, but only in Japan did I hear women reciting this saying repeatedly to emphasize the importance of being with their children full-time until the children turn 3 years old. In addition, aggregate statistics on time use in the two countries are consistent with Japan's greater expectations for maternal involvement in raising children. In Taiwan, women reported spending nearly 2 hours 55 minutes, on average, each weekday on child rearing and household chores in 1994 (DGBAS 1995). On average, Japanese women spent two hours more each day than their Taiwanese counterparts on the same tasks in 1995 (Nippon Hōsō Kyōkai 1996), despite Japan's smaller family size (please look ahead to Figure 5.3). Even when comparing Japanese women with nonemployed Taiwanese women only, the former still spent 1 hour 15 minutes more each day than the latter on child rearing and domestic work.

Previous research has documented the great social pressure for Japanese mothers to be the full-time caregiver and educator of their preschool children (Fujita 1989; Hirao 2001). According to the 1994 data from the ISSP, 63 percent of Japanese respondents believed that women with preschool children should stay at home, rather than take a part- or full-time job. By contrast, 55 percent of the U.S. respondents and 42 percent of Canadian respondents felt the same way.[5] The ISSP conducted eight years later reported relatively little change in attitude toward the employment of mothers with young children in Japan. Only about 40 percent of Japanese respondents approved of the mothers of preschool children being employed full- or part-time, whereas the same survey found a 67 percent approval rate among

Taiwanese respondents.[6] The following statement from a woman whom I interviewed further illustrates the general sentiment toward working mothers with young children in Japan:

> A job is important for a woman, but family is important, too. Sometimes I look at those women who spend the entire day in the office and leave their children at daycare centers from eight o'clock in the morning to six or seven o'clock at night, and I really wonder what kind of people their children will grow up to be!

Interestingly, despite her disapproval of employed mothers of young children, this woman actually believed that "women ought to participate in the labor market." I also observed a similar sentiment of disapproval toward mothers who use daycare centers from, ironically, a daycare center director in Kyoto. The woman with whom I spoke was assigned to the job as the center's director by the local government. As a public-sector employee, her job performance is independent of the amount of business that working mothers bring to the center. Thus, rather than trying to satisfy her "clients," she appeared to criticize the mothers who sent children to the center for failing to fulfill their caring responsibilities. For example, she mentioned that she would always give "homework assignments" to the mothers, such as having them write about their children's activities at home. She explained, "I have to remind those mothers about their roles as mothers. Some mothers simply send their children to daycare centers and then forget about their maternal responsibilities!"

The strong social norms concerning mothers' direct care of young children can sometimes sway mothers who intend to continue employment after childbirth. A young mother who just gave birth and went back to her *sōgōshoku* (managerial track) job in a prestigious Japanese firm shared with me her own experience of such social pressure:

> I have been told by many people that staying at work may hurt my relationship with my child. They also say it can hurt my daughter psychologically without a mother around her 24 hours a day. People kept telling me that I should quit my job when I was pregnant. Everybody says things like, "What a poor baby (*kawaisō*)!" when they know I put my daughter in a daycare center until 8 PM each day. . . . I know women who quit because other people keep saying things like that.

By contrast, while Taiwanese families generally prefer childcare provided by family members to that provided by hired individuals (Yi 1994), their emphasis on maternal care is weaker than in Japan. For instance, the Taiwanese women with whom I discussed childcare issues never expressed any sentiment that the mother would necessarily provide better childcare than the grandmother, although some did feel hesitant about using nonkin baby-sitters. An extreme example of the extent to which the Taiwanese so-ciety accepts caregivers other than mothers is the existence of "weekend parents" in metropolitan areas. Weekend parents are those who leave their infants or toddlers in the grandparents' or nannies' care throughout the workweek. The parents take their children home only on weekends. Al-though most Taiwanese parents do not fall into the category of weekend parents, I observed surprisingly little criticism toward weekend parenting in that society. The low involvement in childcare among weekend mothers in Taiwan is unimaginable in Japan.

To summarize, mothers have more childcare options in Taiwan than in Japan because of their greater accessibility to grandparents' help and Taiwan's low level of state intervention in childcare activities. Moreover, Taiwan's prevalent childcare arrangements, such as depending on grandpar-ents and nannies, enable greater time flexibility for working mothers than Japan's. Consequently, it is easier for Taiwanese mothers to combine their jobs and family responsibilities. In addition, the culturally defined norms for Japanese mothers focus on their full-time involvement in children's early development, whereas mothers' direct care of their young children is not as strongly emphasized in Taiwanese society. The differences in childcare arrangements and norms, taken together, lead to Japanese women's greater burden of caring responsibilities compared with Taiwanese women.

I also note the greater incentive for Taiwanese women with better pay-ing jobs to remain in the labor market upon childbearing because childcare costs tend to be fixed for families of different incomes. In contrast, Japan's government-sponsored childcare centers tend to charge families based on their income levels. Women with higher paying jobs must pay more for childcare in that country; thus, they have no monetary incentive to keep working during their early child-rearing years. This incentive structure is likely to account in part for the relatively high labor force exit rates among Japanese women with white-collar jobs. As discussed in the previous chap-ter, the consistently high exit rates among these women explain Japan's small change in female employment patterns throughout the second half of the twentieth century.

While pointing out the consequences of the different childcare systems between Japan and Taiwan on women's continuous employment, I by no means imply that a welfare state approach to childcare provision (i.e., de-termining childcare cost based on the family's income levels) will always impede increases in women's likelihood to continue employment after child-birth. Comparative studies on welfare regimes and women's employment have clearly demonstrated this is not the case (e.g., Esping-Anderson 1999; Stier et al. 2001). It is when workplaces are overly family unfriendly and the prevalent social norms are against the employment of mothers with young children, as in Japan, that the greater childcare expenses for women with higher earnings might constitute "the last straw." In other words, Japan's household income-based childcare expenses were not the *only* reason why women holding better paying jobs were reluctant to continue their employment careers upon childbearing. Along with other difficulties combining family and work, however, this system helps tip women's decisions about employment.

### Family Wage and Demand for Wives' Financial Contribution

Women's rising participation in the labor market has increased their potential as providers of family income across industrial societies, even though they have continued to bear the responsibility for housework and childcare (Fuwa 2004; Hochschild 1989). In societies where the gender ideology supports the male breadwinning model, whether the husband brings in sufficient income determines the wife's financial responsibility to the family. In both Japan and Taiwan, there are relatively high levels of support for traditional gender roles, which prescribe the husband as the primary breadwinner for the family. The two countries nevertheless differ in the average wage of married men in relation to the prevailing living standard. As a result, married women in the two societies are subject to different family needs for financial resources.

I use statistics from government reports to illustrate the likelihood for a married man to receive a "family wage"—that is, a wage that is sufficient for providing for the entire family—in the two countries. In 1995, a Japanese man received a monthly wage of ¥361,000 on average (Ministry of Labour, Japan 1996). The average household consumption expenditure in the same year was ¥329,092 each month (Statistics Bureau, Management and Coordination Agency, Japan 1997). In addition, Japanese employees usually receive an annual bonus equal to three to six months of wages, which makes an average man's wage substantially surpass his family's expenditure. By contrast, the average annual consumption expenditure among Taiwanese households was NT$591,035, which makes the monthly average NT$49,253. Meanwhile, the average of men's monthly wages was NT$40,602, including bonuses and overtime payments (DGBAS 1996). Based on these numbers, an average male employee in Taiwan can pay for only 82 percent of his household's consumption expenditure. Thus, an average Japanese man has sufficient wages to provide for his entire family, whereas Taiwanese families are likely to need more than one earner to afford the average lifestyle. Insufficient family income in Taiwanese households raises the demand for wives' financial contribution. The following statement from a Taiwanese woman in her late forties, who had worked at various textile factories since age 13, illustrates the situation:

Why did I choose to continue working after marriage and childbearing? I did not choose it. I didn't have a choice. You young kids have no idea how difficult it was in the old times (laughs). We were so poor. If I didn't work, where did the money come from? We couldn't live solely on my husband's wage.

This woman's experience reflects the situation among working-class families. Even among middle-class Taiwanese families, however, wives' contribution to family income has become increasingly desirable. To illustrate, a report from the *United Evening News* on September 26, 1998, cited a poll indicating that more than 90 percent of urban middle-class men prefer their wives to work for pay, rather than being stay-at-home mothers. According to this report, the reason for this preference is that "housing is really expensive in Taiwan, and it is helpful to have another earner in the household to pay back the mortgage."

The demand for wives' financial contribution is greater in Taiwan also because families in that country are likely to benefit more from wives' employment than Japanese families. This greater benefit results from the fact that Taiwanese women's relative earning potential is higher than Japanese women's. Yoshio Okunishi (2001) shows that Taiwan's gender wage gap has been constantly smaller than that of Japan for the past several decades. The difference between the two countries is more pronounced when comparing the gender wage gaps for white-collar occupations. Data from 1995, for instance, indicate that female employees in nearly all white-collar occupations earned more than 80 percent of their male counterparts' wages in Taiwan, whereas Japanese women made less than 70 percent of their male counterparts' wages in these occupations (Yu 1999).

In summary, not only are Japanese husbands more likely to earn a family wage than their Taiwanese counterparts, but wives also have greater income potential in relation to their husbands in Taiwan. Taken together, these cross-national differences lead to a higher expectation for married women in Taiwan to shoulder their families' financial demands. In the meantime, married women in Taiwan generally face lower demands for their time and caring labor at home compared with those in Japan. In turn, Taiwanese mothers are likely to prioritize their family's demand for financial resources over that for caring labor, whereas their Japanese counterparts are likely to set their priorities in the opposite way.

## WHAT TRIGGERED THE CHANGE?

The comparison so far has demonstrated that, in addition to differences in job demands and workplace cultures, the differing family demands married women face also contribute to a higher level of conflict between work and family in Japan than in Taiwan. One reason why married women in the two countries encounter different challenges at home is the divergent normative expectations regarding mothers' direct involvement in raising children. It is therefore reasonable to suspect that differences in cultural preferences, rather than those in labor market conditions, play an essential role in the divergence in female employment behaviors between the two societies. If this is the case, then the discussion in the previous two chapters on workplace practices has overemphasized the importance of national labor market structures. For this reason, it is important to clarify what really triggered changes in women's employment behaviors in the two countries. Thus, in the remainder of this chapter I examine several long-term trends related to female employment behaviors to reveal the ultimate driving force behind the development of women's postmarital employment patterns in these countries.

I begin with a discussion of social norms regarding mothers' roles in Taiwan. Research on Taiwanese women in the 1970s revealed that they were generally expected to leave their premarital jobs to raise and educate their children (e.g., Diamond 1979; Kung 1994). In particular, Norma Diamond (1973) found a rising ideology that prescribed women's place to be at home as educators of their children among middle-class families as Taiwan became increasingly industrialized. The ideology Diamond described is rather similar to the prevailing norms for Japanese mothers currently. Such norms, however, did not prevent increases in Taiwanese women's continuous employment since the 1970s. In other words, the research evidence from the 1970s suggests that the increase in married women's employment preceded, rather than followed, the easing of expectations surrounding motherhood in Taiwan.

To illustrate further the changes in the norms regarding full-time maternal care in Taiwan, Figure 5.2 shows the proportion of ever-married women who expressed approval of working mothers with young children by their educational levels in various years. Because the surveys used to estimate the trends presented here contain samples of different age ranges, I only show the approval rate among a demographic group that exists in all these surveys: ever-married women between the ages of 20 and 40. Figure 5.2 reveals that, through 1996, the overall rates of approval of employed mothers with young children were around 20 to 30 percent among ever-married women within the given age range, with those with higher education expressing greater support. In addition, there was relatively little change in the percentage from the mid 1970s to the mid 1990s. Nevertheless, Taiwanese women's employment rates after marriage and childbearing increased continuously from the 1970s to the 1990s, as shown in previous chapters. Apparently, the norms concerning full-time maternal care did not preclude the growth of women's postmarital employment. Figure 5.2 also indicates that the level

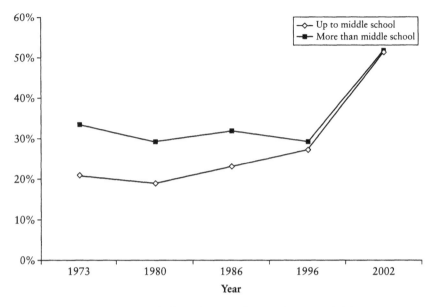

*Figure 5.2.*    Percent approval of working mothers with young children among Taiwanese women, by education.

SOURCE: The Knowledge, Attitude, and Practice of Contraception (KAP) Survey, 1973, 1980, and 1986; TSC 1996, part I, and 2002, part II.

*Note:* The percentages were calculated among ever-married women age 20 to 40. The KAP survey asked respondents to answer whether they agree with the following statement: "It is perfectly all right for women to be active in organizations or work or other outside activities when the children are still small." The TSC asked respondents to report whether they think that "preschool children will suffer if the mother has a job." The percentages shown here include those who answered "agree" or "strongly agree" for the KAP survey question, and those who answered "strongly disagree," "disagree," or "it depends" for the TSC survey question.

of acceptance of employed mothers with young children increased sharply from 1996 to 2002. This trend suggests that once women who continue their employment careers upon childbirth became the majority, as they did in the past decade, the overall social approval of employed mothers would rise as a *result*.

Just like in Taiwan, the change in childcare standards has not exactly coincided with trends of women's postmarital employment in Japan. I use women's time spent on child rearing, from caring for an infant to helping a school-age child with homework, as an indicator of childcare standards. Data from the time–use surveys conducted by Nippon Hōsō Kyōkai (Japan Broadcasting Corporation, also known as NHK) indicate only a small increase in the average amount of time Japanese women spent on child rearing from 1970 to 1990. Namely, the amount of time on a weekday shifted from 116 minutes in 1970 to 129 minutes in 1990.[7] The more drastic change occurred after 1990. The total amount of time women reported spending on raising children each day increased from around two hours in the 1980s to about three and a half hours in the 1990s (216 and 208 minutes in 1995 and 2000, respectively), on average. Also worth highlighting is that this increase partially coincided with Japan's resumption of a fertility decline among married couples since 1985 (Ogawa and Retherford 1993; Retherford et al. 1996). Therefore, the average time Japanese mothers spent on each child rose far more than 50 percent in the 1990s.

The time–use trend just described suggests that the normative expectations for Japanese mothers' involvement in child rearing have become stronger over time, with the key change occurring in the 1990s. This tendency does not exactly correspond to the fact that there has been little change in Japanese women's employment after marriage and childbirth. In particular, there was no dramatic decrease in women's postmarital employment in response to the considerable increase in mothers' involvement in child rearing since 1990. Rather, the emphasis on mothers' roles in raising children appears to have strengthened *after* a substantial number of highly educated Japanese women were pushed out of the labor force for full-time mothering. I showed in Chapter 4 that Japanese women with white-collar jobs were more likely than their blue-collar counterparts to leave their jobs upon marriage or childbearing. Therefore, women who become "professional housewives," as they are called in Japan, are likely to be relatively educated. This group of women has become even more educated over time with the overall improvement of women's schooling during the postwar era (Brinton and Lee 2001; also see Chapter 7). I argue that this particular demographic characteristic of homemaking women in Japan is conducive to the society's strong emphasis on maternal involvement in raising children. This emphasis intensifies as the educational levels of homemaking women increase.

To elaborate, more educated mothers tend to want to be more involved in child rearing (Even 1987). In addition, women with more schooling are better equipped to be the educators of their children. Hence, having highly educated women at home is conducive to a popular discourse that advocates a great amount of maternal participation in child development. Perhaps more important, highlighting the benefits of maternal involvement on the child helps justify highly educated women's inability to utilize their human capital in the workplace. The more important the popular discourse makes a mother to the child, the more likely the society and the homemaking women themselves can accept that their human capital is not "wasted." This discourse thus enables highly educated homemaking women to cope with their frustration from giving up a career for the family.[8]

The change in childcare standards also seems to have coincided with macroeconomic shifts in Japan. Keiko Hirao (2001) shows that since the mid 1970s, publications stressing early education and maternal roles have proliferated. The mid 1970s was also a time when Japan's high economic growth period ended and women's long-term job prospects deteriorated (Brinton 1989, 1993). This economic context, along with the increasing educational levels of homemaking women, appeared to have contributed to the immediate and ever-rising popularity of books and magazines on maternal roles in child development since the mid 1970s. Interestingly, the 1990s, during which we observe a considerable increase in mothers' child-rearing time, was also Japan's recessionary period. These trends suggest a correlation between worsening job opportunities for women and an increasing focus on maternal involvement in raising children.

In addition to child-rearing norms, in an earlier section I also discussed how the demands for financial resources from wives differed between Japanese and Taiwanese families. The family's need for income certainly plays a role in a wife's decision about whether to participate in the labor market, particularly during her early child-rearing years. However, did Taiwanese men's lower likelihood of receiving family wages per se lead to the long-term divergence in married women's employment behaviors between the two countries? To answer this question, Figure 5.3 presents trends in the ratio of average male wages to mean household expenditures over time. Figure 5.3 also includes trends regarding average family size, because family size affects expenditures. The ratio of one man's wage to one household's expenditure is smaller when the family has more members.

As Figure 5.3 reveals, the ratio of an average man's wage to the mean household spending has been greater than one for Japan since the 1970s. Perhaps because of the further decline of family size in Japan, the ratio has even increased steadily since the late 1980s. What this trend indicates is that a single-earner family with a male breadwinner has generally been able to maintain an average level of consumption in Japan for the past several decades. Conversely, the ratio of an average man's wage to family expenditures in Taiwan is less than one for each year shown in the figure. That is to say, Taiwanese families have been unable to keep up with the average living standard with the husband's earnings alone.

At first glance, Figure 5.3 seems to support the argument that the difference in men's capacity to make family wages between Japan and Taiwan was the driving force behind the different paces of change in married women's employment behavior. Nevertheless, a closer look at Taiwan's trends suggests that the family's need for the wife's earnings is unlikely to explain why women of earlier generations began to change their employment behaviors in that country. It is true that the mean of Taiwanese men's wages has never surpassed the average family expenses. Hence, during Taiwan's early industrialization, families commonly sent older children, particularly daughters,

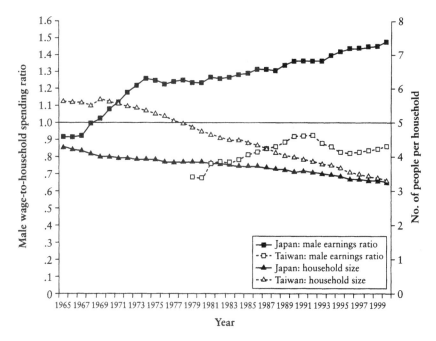

*Figure 5.3.*    Trends of male-wage-to-household-spending ratio and family size, 1965 to 2000.

SOURCE: DGBAS, Executive Yuan, Republic of China, *Social indicators, Taiwan area, Republic of China,* various years, *Yearbook of manpower survey statistics, Taiwan area, Republic of China,* various years; Ministry of Labour, Japan, *Yearbook of labour statistics,* various years; Statistics Bureau, Management and Coordination Agency, Japan, *Historical statistics of Japan,* 1987, *Statistics of Japan,* various years.

Note: The ratio of male earnings to household spending is calculated as the average monthly earnings of male employees, including annual bonuses and special compensations, divided by the average monthly household expenditures.

to work for pay to fill the gap between the father's earnings and the family's financial need (Greenhalgh 1985; Kung 1994). As family size shrank in Taiwan, the ratio of a man's wage to household expenditures increased to close to one from the late 1970s to the early 1990s. This increase indicates Taiwanese men's rising capacity to take on the role of the family's sole breadwinner. Yet, despite men's increased capacity, married women's employment continued to grow during this period. For this reason, whether men received wages that could support the family could not have been what triggered the change in married women's participation in the labor force in Taiwan.

In addition, Taiwan's trend regarding the ratio of men's average wage to household expenditures reversed in the early 1990s, despite the continuing decline in family size. This reversal suggests that whether a male earner alone is sufficient for providing for the family is the *result*, rather than the *cause*, of married women's changing employment behaviors in the society. That is to say, as married Taiwanese women become increasingly likely to participate in the labor force, the possibility that a husband can support the entire family with his own wage decreases in that country. To explain this relation, we need to pay attention to how the composition of the female labor force in Taiwan has changed over time. In Chapter 4 I showed that the increase in Taiwanese women's postmarital employment was more rapid among those with higher occupational status. Such women tend to marry men with relatively high socioeconomic status. Consequently, in Taiwan, families with relatively well-paid husbands are also the ones that are more likely to have employed wives, whereas husbands in single-earner families tend to hold lower status jobs. This tendency generally leads to greater income inequality across households, as well-off families become wealthier after the addition of the wife's earnings.

Previous research has corroborated the trend of increasing economic inequality across Taiwanese families. Bourguignon, Fournier, and Gurgand (2004) show a rise in Taiwan's household income inequality from 1979 to 1994, notwithstanding its declining earnings inequality among individuals. Also supporting my argument, their analysis finds that the greater increase in female entrants into the labor force among households with higher income levels is the key factor explaining this evolution of household income inequality.

Since married women from relatively well-off families were more likely to be employed, insufficient family income apparently was not the initial reason why most Taiwanese women participated in the labor market after marriage. The consequence of these women's increasing employment, however, makes it more a necessity for women of the following generations to continue their jobs after marriage and childbirth. To elaborate, as wealthy families became wealthier and spent more, Taiwan's commodity prices increased and the average household expenditures rose as a result. This increase explains why the ratio of men's average wage to mean household spending reversed its course and began to decline in the 1990s, when dual-earner families became the majority. With a rising number of upper- and middle-class families with dual earnings, the average household expenditures became relatively close to the consumption level of dual-earner, upper middle-class families. Having two white-collar earners therefore becomes a requirement for the next generation to maintain a middle-class standard of living. This financial need adds to the reasons for women of later generations to remain in the labor market during their child-rearing years, particularly if their jobs pay well.

In contrast, Japanese women in blue-collar occupations have been more likely to continue their employment careers after marriage and childbearing than their white-collar counterparts, as shown in the previous chapter. Given that women in blue-collar occupations are likely to marry men with relatively low-wage jobs, Japan's pattern of female employment should help equalize family income. In fact, Bai Gao (2001) argues that the fact that Japanese women with husbands holding higher status jobs tend to stay away from the labor market, and that those with husbands receiving lower earnings tend to participate in part-time or full-time jobs, is precisely the key to the country's highly equalized distribution of household income. Thus, unlike in Taiwan, "keeping up with the Joneses" is not too difficult a goal for Japanese families with a husband as a white-collar employee and a stay-at-home wife. For this reason, Japanese women with higher paying jobs are very unlikely to be persuaded by their family's financial demand to continue their employment careers.

The increasing prevalence of dual-earner, middle-class families' consumption levels also helps justify the grandparents' replacement of the mother as the primary childcare provider in many Taiwanese families. After all, the mother *must* work to provide for the family. Besides, without the earnings from both the husband and the wife, a family may not have spare resources to support the grandparents. Thus, it makes economic sense for Taiwanese families to adopt the new household division of labor: a division of labor *between generations*.[9] With this type of household division, the grandparents are the primary caregivers, whereas the middle generation, including both the husband and the wife, "brings home the bacon" (or rice, in this case). A young professional woman with whom I spoke offered a rather interesting comment about this new household division of labor:

> All my married female friends' mothers-in-law tell them not to quit their jobs after childbearing. The mothers-in-law are like: "Don't worry. All you need to do is give birth and I will take care of everything else from then on. I will help raise your children and you should continue to work. We need you to make money so my son doesn't need to work unusually hard in order to provide for the family. . . ." Of course, all these female friends of mine are professionals and really good at making money (laughs).

CONCLUSION

The analysis in this chapter has revealed a dynamic model for explaining long-term changes in women's employment behaviors in society. Neither the culturally defined maternal roles nor men's likelihood of obtaining family wages was the initial reason for Taiwanese women to be more likely to continue their employment careers than their Japanese counterparts. Rather, as argued in the previous two chapters, the different labor market conditions between the two countries led Taiwan to have family-friendlier work environments than Japan. Facing less conflict between family and work, Taiwanese women were more likely to make decisions about postmarital employment according to the returns to their jobs than their Japanese counterparts. As the occupational opportunities for women improved over time, Taiwan's overall rate of female employment upon marriage and childbearing increased. This change in women's employment behaviors has nevertheless altered the normative expectations for Taiwanese wives and mothers. Not only have employed mothers of young children become more acceptable in Taiwan, but making a financial contribution to the family has also grown to be part of the normative expectations for married women, particularly if they hold reasonably well-paid jobs. In other words, because the change in women's postmarital employment raised the average standard of living, having a dual income gradually became a necessity as well as a norm for middle-class families in Taiwan. This norm shift further affects Taiwanese women of current generations when they face decisions to leave or remain in their jobs after marriage or childbirth. A comment made by a woman who had a one-year-old daughter and worked in a large commercial bank illustrates how these recently developed norms affect young mothers with white-collar jobs:

> I actually don't mind quitting my job and becoming a stay-at-home mother. I think it's important to spend time with my daughter when she is young. But the fact is, these days there is hardly anyone [around me] who quits upon childbearing. Most people left for a better job, but not for giving birth. I've seen one woman who used childbirth as the reason to quit—three months later I found her working at another bank. If you quit, your coworkers may wonder: Why? What's wrong? Why are you leaving a job if nothing goes terribly wrong? It's like quitting a job to raise a child is not acceptable.

In contrast, the greater tendency for those with white-collar occupations to leave for motherhood in Japan is conducive to a strong emphasis on mothers' involvement in child development and education. The trends shown in this chapter suggest that the normative expectations for Japanese mothers have intensified over time, and they were particularly strong when the economy worsened and women were less needed in the labor market. At the same time, the development of Japan's child-rearing norms has not fully coincided with its slow pace of change in women's postmarital employment behaviors. Hence, the child-rearing norms per se cannot account for the lack of change in Japanese women's employment patterns. Rather, I argue that the increase in the number of highly educated women who leave their jobs to be full-time homemakers has contributed to the strengthening of such norms over time. The rising expectations for mothers then become an important impediment for women of current generations who attempt to combine family and work.

In this chapter I also discussed a few other differences between Japan and Taiwan that currently contribute to Japan's lower level of compatibility between family and work for women. Some factors are related to the differing labor market conditions between the two countries, such as the husbands' long working hours and the distance to work. Another factor adding to Japan's greater job–family conflict involves the difference in the predominant types of childcare arrangements for working mothers. In addition to greater schedule flexibility, Taiwan's prevalent childcare arrangements encourage mothers with a high income potential to remain in the labor force because the cost is relatively fixed. Conversely, by charging parents for childcare according to their household income level, Japan's design of institutional care for young children reduces the incentive for women with a relatively high earnings potential to utilize it. Nevertheless, it is important not to exaggerate how decisive these different childcare arrangements are in shaping women's employment decisions in the two countries. After all, neither Japan nor Taiwan has had sufficient institutional support for employed mothers of young children. Moreover, the childcare options adopted by Taiwanese women are not entirely absent in the Japanese context, despite differences in accessibility. Finally, as shown in earlier chapters, workplace cultures in Japan often pressure women to leave even before they face the issue of childcare arrangements. Had workplace dynamics been more encouraging for women who attempted to combine employment and motherhood in Japan, these women might have been willing to try alternative childcare options to suit their needs, rather than be constrained by the limited options the state has provided for them.

# Returning to the Labor Force

In previous chapters I focused on women's exits from the labor force upon marriage and childbirth. Like in other industrial societies, however, women's employment careers often do not end with their postmarital job exits in Japan and Taiwan. Many married women in these countries return to the labor force later in their lives. The transition back into employment is important because the economic consequences of women's decisions to leave the labor market largely depend on whether they can locate suitable jobs upon labor force reentry. Thus, examining homemaking women's decisions to reenter the labor force is critical for providing a comprehensive picture of how the socio-institutional context shapes women's employment opportunities over the life course in Japan and Taiwan.

In this chapter I analyze married women's decisions to resume employment using life and work history data from the 1995 SSM and 1996 TSC surveys. As I showed at the beginning of this book, the female participation rate in the labor force typically reaches another peak among Japanese women age 45 to 55 (refer back to Figure 1.2). The proportion of older Taiwanese women in the labor force has been smaller. Are women in Taiwan less likely to reenter the labor force after the early stage of child rearing than in Japan? What accounts for the lower employment rate among older Taiwanese women compared with their Japanese counterparts? Do similar factors affect homemaking women's decisions to return to the labor force in both countries? In other words, do the dynamics of labor force participation in the later stage of women's life course differ between the two countries? More specifically, do the contextual differences that contribute to the level of compatibility between work and family for married women, discussed in previous chapters, also account for the differences, if any, in employment patterns for women in later life course stages? These questions guide the analysis to be presented in this chapter.

## A COHORT ANALYSIS OF WOMEN'S
## LIFETIME EMPLOYMENT RATES

The lower employment rate among middle-age women in Taiwan hints that Taiwanese women who have left the labor force are less likely to reenter the labor force after their child-rearing responsibilities decline than women in Japan. That the employment rates decline among older age groups also seems to indicate that Taiwanese women begin to retire in their mid forties— a relatively early stage in their lives. To verify these impressions, I compare the labor force participation of women of different birth cohorts over the life course to show how their work trajectories changed over time. Figure 6.1

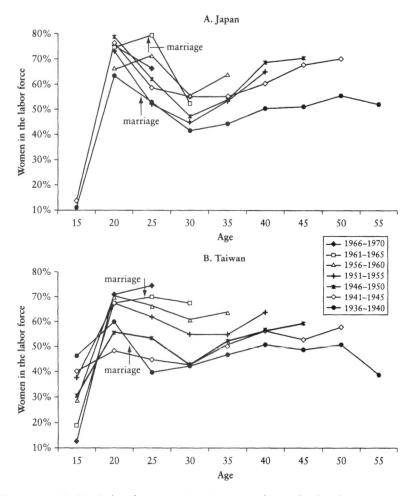

*Figure 6.1.* (A, B)   Labor force participation rates of seven birth cohorts at various ages for Japanese (A) and Taiwanese (B) women.

SOURCE: Japan, 1995 SSM, part A; Taiwan, 1996 TSC, part II.

presents the employment rates of women born 1936 to 1970 at different ages. I eliminated the percentages for birth cohorts born after 1956 at 15 years of age for Japan in the figure because less than 10 percent of Japanese women in the later cohorts began to work at such an early age.

According to Figure 6.1, women born 1936 to 1940, who entered working ages in the 1950s, had remarkably similar work patterns in Japan and Taiwan. About 60 percent of them were in the labor force at age 20. The employment of this birth cohort of women decreased by 20 percent at age 30 in Japan and age 25 in Taiwan, corresponding to their respective average age of first childbirth.[1] After these points in time, the employment rates among these women increased slowly with age, suggesting that some returned to the labor force after their childbearing years. Women born in the following decades still participated in the labor force in a similar fashion in these countries, with relatively large proportions of them leaving the labor force by age 30 and returning afterward. Nevertheless, consistent with what previous chapters have shown, over time, the proportion of women exiting the labor force around age 30 has significantly decreased in Taiwan, but not so much in Japan.

Quite contrary to what the cross-sectional trend suggests, the cohort analysis of female employment indicates that there was no tendency toward early retirement among Taiwanese women. Rather, for each cohort, the employment rate increased as their child-rearing responsibilities declined. Moreover, a comparison of cohort experiences reveals that the gap in middle-age women's likelihood of returning to the labor force between the two societies may not be as large as we would have expected based on cross-sectional information (e.g., Figure 1.2). Specifically, Figure 6.1 shows that Taiwanese women's work patterns after age 35 were similar to their Japanese counterparts'; their employment rate increased and reached another peak in their mid forties.

The magnitude of the cohort change in Taiwanese women's lifetime employment explains why its aggregate-level female labor force participation rate by age does *not* form an M-shaped pattern, which is typical in countries where many women return to the labor force after early child rearing. Taiwanese women nearly always had higher labor force participation rates than those of an earlier cohort at a comparable age. The increase in female employment rates from one cohort to the next was so substantial that the rate for a later cohort, even at its lowest point, still surpassed the rates for earlier cohorts at their relatively high points. For example, the participation rate of Taiwanese women born in 1946 to 1950 in the labor market at age 45 was almost the same as their rate at ages 20 to 25. It is therefore possible that nearly all women of that cohort who had been in the labor force before marriage returned to work after some child rearing. Women of that cohort, however, participated in the labor market much less in their twenties than those born a decade later. Thus, even with all the labor force returns, the employment rate of those born in 1946 to 1950 at age 40 was lower than that among women born in 1956 to 1960 at age 30, a typical age for many women to be out of the labor force. Consequently, when we analyze female labor force participation by age in a cross-sectional fashion, the second employment peak in the life course of older cohorts becomes unnoticeable in Taiwan. By contrast, the two-peak, M-shaped female employment pattern is apparent in a cross-sectional figure for Japan because cohort differences in lifetime employment patterns have not been very dramatic.

Needless to say, some of the cohort differences shown in Figure 6.1, such as increases in the tendency to reenter employment, reflect postwar demographic changes in the two countries. Among other changes, the drastic fertility declines during the postwar decades should have increased married women's frequency of labor force reentry in both societies (Feeney and Mason 2001; Retherford et al. 1996; Yu and Su 2006). Having fewer children generally allows women who had once left the labor force for maternal obligations to return to work sooner. The descriptive analysis presented here, however, does not indicate the exact child-rearing stage during which married women decided to return to the labor market, nor does it show cohort differences in this regard. More generally, we do not know whether the factors accounting for the reentry patterns observed are similar in Japan and Taiwan. These issues are left to a later section in which I present a multivariate analysis of women's postmarital labor force reentry among women in the two countries.

## STRUCTURAL CONTEXTS AND TRANSITION BACK INTO THE LABOR FORCE

Do Japan and Taiwan differ in the rates and dynamics of married women's employment reentry? If so, why? One way to answer these questions is by considering what motivates women's return to the labor force in general. Economic research addressing this issue largely centers on two factors. The first one is the opportunity cost of a woman's time allocated to domestic work and child rearing (Mammen and Paxson 2000). Both women's education and premarital work experience increase with economic development. This growth of women's human capital raises their prevailing wage rate and hence the opportunity cost of choosing home production over employment. The increasing opportunity cost of homemaking eventually accelerates married women's rate of return to the labor force (Goldin 1990). The second factor pertaining to married women's employment is their potential earnings in relation to their husbands' (e.g., Becker 1981). The shrinking gap between men's and women's wages in industrial societies makes the husband's income less able to compensate for the wife's income lost from a long period of nonemployment. Married women therefore become more likely to reenter employment (Leibowitz and Klerman 1995).

Sociologists commonly argue that these economic explanations alone are insufficient to explain married women's employment decisions. As discussed earlier in this book, structural conditions that are conducive to creating conflicts between work and family for married women often affect their choices regarding labor force participation. A higher level of work–family conflict tends to persuade more women in society to adopt a strategy of sequencing their roles as workers and mothers over their life course (Rindfuss and Brewster 1996). Following this strategy, a woman will take on the responsibility of a worker before marriage, become a stay-at-home mother upon childbirth, and resume the worker role only after a decline in her maternal obligations. Thus, married women's employment reentry should be more closely associated with their decreasing child-rearing responsibilities in societies where women encounter greater conflict between work and family.

Despite its impact on female employment, incompatibility between family and job responsibilities is not always the reason why a woman becomes a full-time homemaker. Some women prefer homemaking to market work. Others become homemakers with an intention to take a "time-out" from their employment careers. In the latter situation, a woman's opportunity cost of nonemployment is likely to affect the amount of time that she is willing to remain out of the labor force. The long-term economic cost of a work interruption should also influence the rate of labor force return among women whose choice of homemaking reflects primarily a work–family conflict. A married woman is likely to resume employment sooner, despite enduring more job–family conflict, if a slower return will be highly detrimental to her long-term occupational attainment.

The structural context shapes how the cost of labor force withdrawal varies with its duration, in addition to the role conflict that working mothers experience. This cost affects the dynamics of homemaking women's employment reentry. According to human capital theory, a worker's occupational skills depreciate, and the cost of an interruption increases, with more time away from the labor force (Polachek 1979). It is therefore rational for a woman to return to the labor force as soon as possible, unless she intends never to work again. Nevertheless, this formula for calculating the cost of homemaking has failed to take into account firms' use of internal labor markets (Doeringer and Piore 1971). The existence of firm-internal labor markets causes firm-specific skills to be more highly valued than occupation-specific skills (Koike 1987). A preference for firm-specific skills, on the one hand, leads to particularly great rewards for workers who remain in the same firm. On the other hand, it limits job opportunities for individuals in the open external labor market. Following this logic, in a context where firm-internal labor markets are prevalent, leaving a firm will devastate a woman's career opportunities over the long run. In addition, for any woman who has left the labor market, the additional cost incurred with the depreciation of her occupational skills will be relatively small. This reduces the urgency of returning to the labor market. Thus, the prevalence of firm-internal labor markets in the economy lessens the incentive for women's timely return.

A country in which firms often utilize internal labor markets is also likely to feature a high degree of labor market segmentation. The labor market segmentation perspective argues that different sectors in the labor market provide uneven monetary rewards and advancement opportunities for workers, and the barriers to each sector are set according to relative return (Kalleberg and Sørensen 1979). In a dual labor market that facilitates high barriers to the primary sector, individuals without preferable profiles, such as women who have interrupted their employment careers, can only expect to find jobs in the secondary sector (DeSoto 1989). A greater length of non-employment hardly affects such individuals' market opportunities because the secondary sector neither requires nor rewards the occupational skills that may depreciate during that time (Hodson and Kaufman 1982). Thus, in this type of labor market, women who have exited the labor force tend to remain out of it until their family responsibilities decline substantially.

The theoretical perspectives concerning married women's employment returns, taken together, suggest that the national context will affect the relative importance of two time measures related to married women's return to the labor force: (1) the family time that determines a woman's family roles and child-rearing responsibilities and (2) the personal time away from the labor force that shapes her long-term job opportunities. In a context characterized by immense work–family conflict, the association between married women's labor force returns and their family time tends to be strong. By contrast, married women's employment returns should correlate more closely with their personal time out of the labor force, reflecting their economic concerns, if their market opportunities decrease more rapidly with the duration of nonemployment.

I have shown in previous chapters that the divergent labor market practices and family demands between Japan and Taiwan have led to different contextual constraints on women's employment options. Specifically, as a result of prevalent workplace cultures and norms regarding mother–child relations, the role conflict that working mothers experienced in Japan was substantially greater than that in Taiwan. The two countries also differ in how a woman's cost of work interruption varied with her time away from the labor force. The widespread use of internal labor markets among Japanese firms (Brinton 1989; Kalleberg and Lincoln 1988; Koike 1987), a central part of the Japanese employment system, has undermined the effect of the depreciation of occupational skills with the time spent away from the labor force on a woman's long-term career prospect. In addition, since the 1970s, Japanese employers have increasingly used part-time and contingent workers at the expense of regular full-time employees (Houseman 1998; Houseman and Osawa 1995; Schoppa 2006), resulting in higher barriers to the standard employment sector. This growing economic dualism had largely decreased married women's likelihood of reentering the labor market into jobs that would reward their occupational skills appropriately. A detailed discussion of the destinations of women's labor force reentry is provided in a later section.

In contrast to Japan, the benefit and wage structures in Taiwan have been similar across employment sectors, with the exception of the public sector (Yu and Su 2004; also see Chapter 4). This lower degree of labor market segmentation has generated a wider range of job options for married women upon labor force reentry in Taiwan. Even more important, the small-firm-based Taiwanese economy does not generally allow internal labor markets within firms, but instead encourages interfirm job turnovers, since individuals' opportunities are easily blocked in small firms. Occupational skills are crucial when small firms recruit new workers because they cannot afford much in training costs. As one's occupational skills depreciate with more time away from the labor market, the training costs for one's reemployment increase. Following this rationale, the longer a married Taiwanese woman has been out of the labor force, the less likely a Taiwanese employer will hire her. Thus, a Taiwanese woman's opportunity cost of nonemployment can be expected to increase considerably with the duration of her work interruption.

In summary, Japan exemplifies a national context in which combining employment and motherhood is relatively difficult, and the cost of labor force withdrawal for married women is hardly contingent on the duration of their time away from the labor market. Conversely, the Taiwanese context features a relatively low level of work–family conflict and highly time-relevant costs associated with work interruption. These contextual differences are likely to play an important role in shaping the two countries' respective dynamics of women's postmarital returns to the labor force.

## ANALYZING MARRIED WOMEN'S EMPLOYMENT REENTRY

In this section I examine the timing of labor force return among married women in the two countries. I expect the contextual differences discussed earlier to affect homemaking women's decisions about when to resume employment. My analysis specifically focuses on how women's rates of labor force reentry vary over the family life cycle and across the duration of homemaking, and whether the patterns differ significantly between Japan and Taiwan.

### Profiles of Homemaking Women in Japan and Taiwan

Before comparing married women's transitions back to work in Japan and Taiwan, I should note that the profiles of women who are eligible for making such transitions are likely to differ between these countries. Only those who have left the labor force to become full-time homemakers face the decision of whether to return to the labor force. As shown in Chapter 4, during the past several decades, the dynamics of women's postmarital employment exits differed considerably between Japan and Taiwan. In Japan, women's decisions about leaving the labor force largely depended on whether work environments were compatible with their family roles and whether they had easy access to childcare assistance, rather than their earnings potential or work orientations. Conversely, because combining family and job obligations was relatively feasible in Taiwan, women's decisions to interrupt their employment careers were more closely tied to their own income potential. Specifically, Taiwanese women with more schooling and better job opportunities were more likely to work continuously after marriage and childbirth. Thus, women with lower career prospects or weaker preferences for market work are likely to be overrepresented among homemaking women in Taiwan, whereas this is not the case in Japan.[2]

Despite the different profiles of homemaking women between the two countries, Table 6.1 shows a number of similarities in their employment trajectories. Nearly 60 percent of women who had once entered homemaking did so during the year of or the year before marriage in both countries. A relatively small proportion of the women left the labor force upon first childbirth in each country. Moreover, notwithstanding their discontinuous work patterns, most women who had become full-time homemakers experienced labor force exit no more than once. More interestingly, the proportions of homemaking women who later returned to the labor force were strikingly similar—close to 50 percent—in the Japanese and Taiwanese samples. Table 6.1 nonetheless reveals cross-national differences in the percentages of employment reentry by age group, indicating possible discrepancies between these countries in homemaking women's timing of returning to the labor force.

To understand further how these two groups differ in the timing of resuming employment, I estimated the cumulative probability of a married woman reentering the labor force by the duration of her nonemployment period using the Kaplan–Meier method of estimation (Blossfeld, Hamerle, and

TABLE 6.1

*Description of work trajectories of homemaking women,
ages 25 to 60.*

| Variable | Japan, % | Taiwan, % |
|---|---|---|
| No. of labor force exits in work history* | | |
| 1 | 87.7 | 82.2 |
| 2 | 10.6 | 16.0 |
| 3+ | 1.6 | 1.7 |
| Timing of shift into homemaking[†] | | |
| Upon marriage | 58.8 | 57.6 |
| Upon the first childbirth | 18.7 | 14.6 |
| Other | 22.5 | 27.8 |
| Returning to the labor force | 49.6 | 49.2 |
| Reentry within age group | | |
| 25–34 | 17.8 | 35.4 |
| 35–44 | 54.4 | 54.0 |
| 45–54 | 64.6 | 55.2 |
| 55–60 | 47.4 | 50.0 |

SOURCE: Japan: 1995 SSM, part A; Taiwan: 1996 TSC, part II.

*Labor force exits ended before the most recent marriage are also included.

[†]Exit upon marriage/childbirth is defined as leaving the labor force in the year of or the year before the event occurred. When the year of marriage is also the year of or the year before the first childbirth, I use marriage rather than childbirth to define the timing.

Mayer 1989). The estimation indicates that most of the labor force returns for married women in both societies occur during the first twenty years of the homemaking period.[3] Despite their differences in levels of development and women's education, Japan and Taiwan display nearly equivalent probabilities that married women will return to the labor force in the long run. There are, however, differences between the two countries with respect to how the probability of labor force reentry changes with duration. Among Japanese women, the rate of labor force return is relatively slow during the first several years of homemaking. It then increases after the seventh year of the homemaking period and decelerates again after seventeen years elapse. Among Taiwanese women, the rate of return declines steadily with time. Nevertheless, the cumulative probability that Taiwanese women will return to work after marriage is greater than for their Japanese counterparts throughout almost the entire twenty-year period.

### Dynamics of Women's Labor Force Reentry

I used a multivariate event–history analysis to test whether married women's rates of returning to work indeed reflect the differing job and family conditions between Japan and Taiwan. Specifically, I estimated the likelihood that homemaking women will reenter the labor force at different family stages, after taking into account their own income potential, previous employment experience, and the macrolevel labor demand of each year. In the same models I also estimated how this likelihood will change with women's duration of nonemployment (Appendix B, Table B.6).

The results indicate that child rearing plays a more important role in Japanese homemaking women's decisions to reenter the labor force than in the decisions of their Taiwanese counterparts. Japanese women with children younger than age 3 were about one fourth as likely to return to market work as mothers with children in school (i.e., the youngest child was age 7 or older). Their Taiwanese counterparts were about one half as likely as those with older children to return. Furthermore, Japanese women whose youngest children were 3 to 6 years of age were significantly less likely to resume employment than those with older children, whereas that was not the case for Taiwanese women. The contrast between childless women and women with school-age children also reveals different employment reentry dynamics between Japan and Taiwan. Women without children were almost twice as likely as those in a later child-rearing stage to return to work in Taiwan, but the difference between the two groups of women is not statistically significant in Japan. This finding suggests that married women in Japan are quite unlikely to resume their worker roles while anticipating motherhood— that is, during the time period after marriage and before the birth of their first child. The same cannot be said for Taiwanese women.

The two countries also differ in how married women's likelihood of labor force return varies with their duration of homemaking. The time away from the labor force is relatively important for Taiwanese women's processes of labor force returns, but not Japanese women's (the duration effects are not statistically significant). Married women in Taiwan were more likely to return to the labor force within the first couple of years of homemaking than at later times. Their rate of return also declined with increasing time out of the labor force. Taken together, these results suggest that Taiwanese women tend to reenter the labor market before their occupational skills depreciate too much with time. This pattern of duration dependence is consistent with the argument that occupational skills accumulated from past work experiences are key to one's job opportunities in that small-firm-based economy.

Figure 6.2 illustrates the different probabilities of labor force reentry estimated for Japanese and Taiwanese women across family stages and durations of nonemployment, while controlling for their differences in other characteristics.[4] Specifically, these probabilities are for hypothetical women who had their first and their last children after three and five years in the homemaking period, respectively. Based on Figure 6.2, the probability of a woman with children older than age 3 returning to the labor force is higher in Japan than in Taiwan. This cross-national difference is particularly noticeable if the woman's children are old enough to be in school (i.e., after

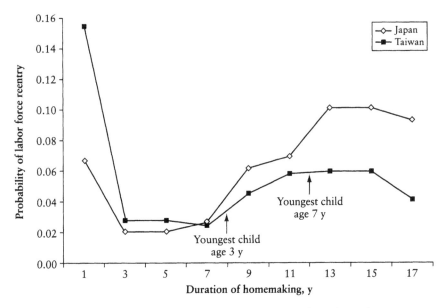

*Figure 6.2.* Estimated probability of labor force reentry, hypothetical cases.

SOURCE: Japan, 1995 SSM, part A; Taiwan, 1996 TSC, part II.

*Note:* The estimates indicate the probability of returning to the labor force within a time unit for each hypothetical case.

twelve years in the homemaking period for the hypothetical case). However, without a child, a Taiwanese woman is more likely to resume employment than her Japanese counterpart. In particular, a childless woman who has exited the labor force relatively recently (within two years from the exit) has a much higher probability of returning to work in Taiwan than in Japan. Therefore, even though Japan and Taiwan have similar percentages of women returning to the labor force after marriage (Table 6.1), the timing differs along both the nonemployment duration and family cycle dimensions.

As stated earlier, Japanese women are generally unlikely to return to work during the period after marriage and before the birth of their first child. That the anticipation of child-rearing responsibilities is sufficient to keep Japanese women away from the labor force suggests that they follow more frequently the strategy of sequencing mother and worker roles across time than Taiwanese women. To provide more evidence, I tested additional regression models with variables related to women's sense of having completed their maternal obligations. I replaced the variables measuring actual child-rearing responsibilities with a dummy variable indicating whether the last child in the respondent's fertility history was beyond school age (at least

7 years old), while controlling for other individual characteristics and the duration of homemaking.[5] The reason for introducing this variable is that the timing of the labor force return for a woman who sequences her mother and worker roles could reflect whether she has completed the crucial part of rearing her *last child*, rather than whether she has any preschool children at the time. The results indicate that the sense of having completed maternal obligations has significantly different effects on homemaking women's decisions about employment between the two countries. Japanese women are almost twice as likely to return to work after they have completed the early stage of child rearing, whereas Taiwanese women's likelihood of reentering the labor force barely differs before and after their last child enters school.

Another analysis of changes in the mother's probability of returning to work, presented in my earlier work (Yu 2006), also shows that this probability increases much more rapidly in Japan than in Taiwan as the last child ages. That is to say, married women's likelihood of resuming worker roles increases more markedly with their sense of having completed maternal responsibilities in Japan. This finding suggests that the difficulty of combining work and family responsibilities lead Japanese women to follow a life plan that clearly sequences motherhood and employment across time. Married women in that country are hence unlikely to enter the phase of employment until they no longer expect to raise a young child. In comparison, Taiwanese women's labor force reentry seems to be more responsive to fluctuations in their child-rearing responsibilities over time, rather than their sense of having completed a particular life course phase. Thus, although family obligations also affect Taiwanese women's decisions to return to the labor force, the mechanism appears to be more closely tied to the actual time involvement in child rearing.

To summarize, the dynamics of married women's labor force reentry in Japan and Taiwan reflect their respective national contexts. Even though these countries have comparable percentages of women returning to the labor force after marriage, the timing differs along both nonemployment duration and family cycle dimensions. Because of the relatively high level of conflict between work and family that Japanese women perceive, their timing for returning to market work generally reflects their strategy of sequencing worker and mother roles over their life course. By contrast, changes in women's family roles affect their employment returns less in Taiwan. At the same time, the rate of married women's labor force reentry changes with the duration of work interruption more in Taiwan than in Japan because the labor market structure provides incentives for timely returns in the former country.

Taiwanese women's probability of returning to the labor force is particularly high when they have not been out of the labor force for long, usually before having their first child. This pattern suggests that it is rather common for married women in Taiwan to take short breaks from their employment careers, even without having the intention of being full-time homemakers in the long term. That is to say, whereas a large proportion of Japanese women exit the labor force upon marriage because of their anticipation of motherhood, many Taiwanese women do the same for a different reason: an increased access to additional income. To be specific, in addition to family obligations, marriage can also bring women access to their husband's earnings. Taiwanese women are likely to leave the labor force around the time of marriage because taking a break from employment becomes affordable at that time.

Similar to the comparison of women's employment exits presented in the previous chapters, the analysis of women's employment returns has demonstrated that women's employment decisions are more often tied to their family roles and caring responsibilities in Japan than in Taiwan. The structural context appears to have restricted Japanese women's employment options at various points of their life cycles. In comparison, among Taiwanese women, the constraints brought by their family obligations have interfered less often with their participation in the labor force. In Taiwan, individual preferences and economic utilities play relatively important parts in women's decisions to participate in the labor force over their life course.

## DESTINATIONS OF LABOR FORCE REENTRY

So far this chapter has centered on married women's timing of their labor force return. Yet another important question related to this life course transition is the types of jobs married women obtain when reentering the labor force. This is also to ask whether the labor markets in Japan and Taiwan present married women who intend to resume employment with equivalent job opportunities. The short answer to this question seems obvious. I have argued that the Japanese labor market has become increasingly segmented and restrictive against those with discontinuous work experience. Thus, it might not be surprising to find that the job prospects of female reentrants are relatively poor in that country. The analysis I have presented so far, however, offers few empirical details about women's exact job opportunities at the time of labor force reentry. In the following pages, I provide comprehensive comparisons of the destinations of women's postmarital employment returns between the two countries.

I first examine women's occupational opportunities upon labor force reentry. A comparison of the distribution of occupations held by women upon their first postmarital employment return with that for all women in the labor market provides some evidence that female reentrants tend to have worse occupational options. For example, among currently working women ages 25 to 60, about 45 percent of them were in white-collar occupations, including clerical, semiprofessional, professional, and managerial occupations. Only 40 percent and 28 percent of those who returned to work in Japan and Taiwan, respectively, were in such occupations. That is to say, in both countries, more than half the reentrants were in occupations with relatively low status, such as blue-collar or service and sales jobs. These occupations are also likely to pay by piece rate, hourly wage, or commission. As put by one Taiwanese woman with whom I spoke, "The employer does not care about one's job turnover history or marital status as long as one is paid by piece rate." Therefore, factory work and service or sales jobs are often the last resort for reentrants who have difficulty finding adequate jobs.

Rather surprisingly, the occupational distribution among female reentrants was more akin to that among all female workers in Japan than in Taiwan. More than 70 percent of the Taiwanese reentrants ended up in manual labor, service, or sales occupations, which was 20 percent more than the percentage for the general female labor force. In Japan, the difference was only about 10 percent. Do these results mean that Taiwanese women are more likely to move downward when returning to the labor force than their Japanese counterparts? To answer this, we should keep in mind that, in Taiwan, women who tend to have discontinuous career trajectories are those with less education and blue-collar jobs. By contrast, clerical workers constitute the most probable occupational group to follow such work patterns in Japan. Hence, that Taiwanese reentrants on average have lower occupational status might be a consequence of the overrepresentation of those among them who held factory or service and sales jobs before marriage.

To assess more accurately the impact of a work interruption on occupational opportunities, I compare the occupations before and after a work interruption among those who have returned to the labor force between the two countries and present a summary of the comparisons in Figure 6.3. The first pair of bars in the figure shows the percentages of those formerly in office jobs, including managerial, professional, associate professional, and clerical jobs, reentering one of these white-collar occupations. The probability that a woman with a white-collar job will reenter one is generally higher in Taiwan. The next two pairs of bars present the percentages of women previously holding white-collar occupations who shifted to blue-collar and service or sales jobs upon labor force reentry. These percentages indicate that Japanese women are more likely to move from office jobs to factory jobs or service and sales jobs after their labor force withdrawal than Taiwanese women. Thus, the occupational opportunities for labor force reentrants are actually worse in Japan than in Taiwan.[6]

Another way to assess the job opportunities for labor force reentrants is by examining the types of firms in which reentrants work. Research has

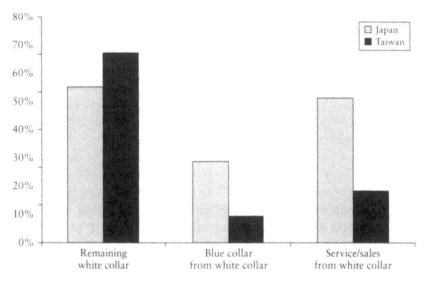

*Figure 6.3.* Comparison of occupations before and after a work interruption.
SOURCE: Japan, 1995 SSM, part A; Taiwan, 1996 TSC, part II.

shown that a Japanese woman's chance of working at a large-size firm decreases with her age (Brinton 1993; Roberts 1994). This tendency is thought
to account in part for the relatively poor economic conditions of older
women in the Japanese labor market. It is nonetheless unclear whether the
association between women' age and firm size has to do with the obstacles
faced by female reentrants in that country. Hence, I ask: Are married women
returning to the labor market particularly likely to find jobs in small firms in
Japan? Are the two countries similar or different in this regard?

Figure 6.4 presents the distributions of labor force reentrants and
working women ages 25 to 60 by firm size in both countries. In Japan,
the percentage of labor force reentrants in firms of 29 or fewer employees
was actually smaller than that of the overall female labor force in firms of
equivalent size. This difference means that Japanese women returning to the
labor force are prone to work in firms that, on average, are larger than those
that employ women without any work interruption. Therefore, although
older Japanese women tend to work in small- to medium-size firms, those
who are in such firms are more likely to be those with continuous employment careers, rather than labor force reentrants. By contrast, Figure 6.4
shows that Taiwanese women with discontinuous work experience were
somewhat underrepresented in large-size firms. This underrepresentation is
mostly related to the barriers to Taiwan's public sector, which I discuss later.
Because I grouped the public sector with large-size firms in Figure 6.4, the

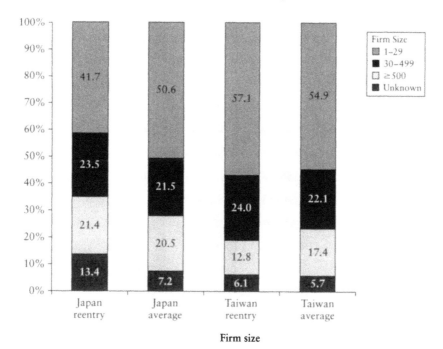

*Figure 6.4.* Comparison of firm size between the female labor force and women reentrants.

SOURCE: Japan, 1995 SSM, part A; Taiwan, 1996 TSC, part II.

female reentrants' particularly low likelihood of holding government jobs leads to their underrepresentation in firms or organizations with more than 500 employees. After excluding public-sector workers, my finding suggests that labor force reentrants do not face unusually great difficulty obtaining jobs in medium- to large-size firms in either country.

While there is little indication that labor force reentrants experience a severe disadvantage in terms of firm size, the story is completely different when their employment status is concerned. Figure 6.5 compares the employment status of the labor force reentrants with those of the female labor force in the two countries. There were substantial discrepancies in the percentages of public-sector employees between labor force reentrants and all working women in both countries, suggesting that obtaining a job in the public sector after a work interruption is particularly difficult. A major reason for this difficulty is that the public sectors of both countries typically recruit employees through standardized examinations that are based on school materials rather than actual occupational skills. The public-sector examinations are usually competitive because government jobs are considered relatively secure and prestigious in both societies. The Taiwanese government, in particular, is

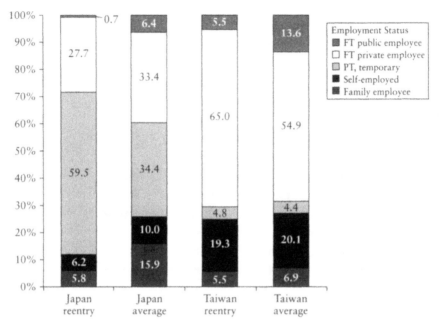

*Figure 6.5.* Comparison of employment status between the female labor force and women reentrants.

SOURCE: Japan, 1995 SSM, part A; Taiwan, 1996 TSC, part II.

*Note:* FT, full time; PT, part time.

among the few employers in the economy that are capable of offering long-term job security and fringe benefits, as well as steady wage advancement and promotions.[7] The competitive entrance examinations greatly obstruct labor force reentrants' access to the public sector, since they tend to have finished school a long time ago and bear other responsibilities that distract them from studying.

Accompanied by their lower level of participation in the public sector was a greater proportion in full-time private-sector employment among Taiwanese women who had reentered the labor force. The two bars for Taiwan presented in Figure 6.5 are otherwise similar, which is not the case for Japan. Near 60 percent of the labor force reentrants in Japan held part-time jobs. This percentage is almost twice as large as that among average female workers. A further exploration shows that more than 80 percent of the Japanese reentrants in part-time employment held full-time regular jobs before their work interruptions. Furthermore, whereas 57 percent of these reentrants were in managerial, professional, semiprofessional, or clerical occupations before labor force withdrawal, only 41 percent of them returned to a white-collar occupation. In fact, Japanese women obtaining part-time jobs upon labor force reentry are more likely than those reentering other types of employment to descend in occupational status. Thus, Japanese women's shifting to part-time employment after work interruptions largely accounts for their downward occupational mobility shown in Figure 6.3.

The analysis of labor force reentrants' job destinations has shown that Japanese women have a much greater probability of changing employment status after a work interruption compared with Taiwanese women. This difference also leads to the greater downward mobility in occupational status that Japanese women experience upon labor force reentry. Hence, Japanese reentrants' frequent movement to part-time and temporary employment is essentially what makes the economic consequences of women's work interruptions differ between Japan and Taiwan. Given this, it is important to ask why female labor force reentrants concentrate on part-time and contingent employment in Japan. Heavy family burdens for married women do not appear to explain this inclination completely, because labor force reentrants in Japan tend to be past the early stage of child rearing.[8] Besides, previous research has found that Japanese women with preschool-age children are more likely to hold full-time rather than part-time jobs if they are in the labor force at all (Nagase 1997; Yu 2002). That part-time employment is not the choice of women with the most child-rearing responsibilities suggests that Japanese reentrants' participation in such employment is unlikely to merely reflect their concerns about family demands.

Another possible explanation for the concentration of female reentrants in part-time jobs is individual preferences. Some women may prioritize non-market activities and prefer not to work full time (Hakim 1995). The fact that a part-time job is associated with declining occupational status in Japan, however, should make us suspicious that the "choice" of part-time employment is entirely voluntary. Furthermore, using government statistics in 1995, for example, the total number of new applicants for part-time jobs throughout the year was 13,300, whereas 114,120 part-time job placements were arranged by all public job-matching services in Japan during that year (Ministry of Labour, Japan 1997). The number of part-time jobs available apparently outnumbered applicants, suggesting that a substantial number of those placed were originally seeking full-time regular jobs.

Since neither family responsibilities nor individual tastes sufficiently explain Japanese women's high probability of taking part-time jobs upon labor force reentry, perhaps we need to turn our attention to employers' behaviors. Japanese firms have increasingly used part-time and temporary jobs to adjust for the large labor cost necessitated by the permanent employment system. Firms' intention to save labor costs is therefore thought to account for the concentration of female labor force reentrants in part-time and contingent jobs (Houseman and Osawa 1995, 2003). Nevertheless, if saving labor costs is the main concern, the corporate strategy of replacing regular workers with contingent workers should affect men more than women. Because men with regular full-time jobs are compensated more than women of the same status, a cost-conscious employer should try to place more men than women in part-time temporary jobs. Interestingly, the increase in nonstandard jobs in Japan had little impact on men at least through the late 1990s. Thus, even though firms' concerns about labor costs led to the expansion of Japan's nonstandard employment sector, they do not explain why this sector ends up absorbing most of the married women reentering the labor market. How exactly does the market sort labor force reentrants into part-time employment in Japan? I address this question in the following section.

## LABOR FORCE REENTRY AND NONSTANDARD EMPLOYMENT IN JAPAN

To explain why Japan's labor force reentrants are predominantly part-time employees, first I need to discuss the particular meaning of part-time work in that country. What I have referred to as part-time work in Japan in fact contains both part-time and temporary types of employment, including *paato, arubaito, rinjikoyō, haken, keiyaku*, and *shokutaku*. Generally speaking, *paato* (or *paato taimu*), the dominant form of employment for nonregular Japanese employees, refers to part-time employment. In reality, however, *paato* reveals the status of a job rather than the amount of time spent at work (Gottfried and Hayashi-Kato 1998; Japan Institute of Labour 1991). Working as many hours as a full-time employee at a job designated as *paato* will *not* make one a full-time worker in Japan. In fact, Houseman and Os- awa (1995) show that a sizable proportion of part-time employees work just as many hours as their full-time counterparts. An *arubaito* job is a part-time and side job for the job holder, who is likely to be primarily devoted to study or a full-time job. Hence, students who work part-time are usually considered *arubaito* workers, rather than *paato* workers. *Rinjikoyō* literally means temporary employment, and the work terms and durations can vary to a great extent. *Haken, keiyaku*, or *shokutaku* workers are mostly hired from a dispatching agency for temporary help. The hours and job content of *haken, keiyaku*, and *shokutaku* jobs are usually quite close to those of full-time employees' work, but the former are under fixed, short-term contracts and are likely to be exempt from firm subsidies and fringe benefits.

The definitions of the forms of employment just described are fluid. Not only do the uses of the terms vary from employer to employer, but also the line between these types of employment may not be drawn based on the total hours of work. Therefore, part-time and temporary jobs indeed belong to the same category in Japan. They all share the status of nonregular, nonstandard employment. As I argued in Chapter 3, one major impact of the lifetime employment system on Japanese workers during the past half century was that it had, paradoxically, normalized the terms and conditions for those excluded from the system. That is to say, the existence of the lifetime employment system and its beneficiaries—regular full-time employees—helped define *hiseishain*, a Japanese term inclusive of all types of nonstandard employees.

Under this broader dichotomy, workers with nonstandard employment status do not belong to the regular system, nor are they entitled to the package for standard full-time employees. To illustrate this exclusion, I noticed at one company I visited that the seating chart outside each office never included any part-time workers, regardless of how frequently they appeared in the office. More substantially, whereas regular employees are supposed to have lifetime employment in Japan, nonstandard employees are always under renewable term contracts.[9] Part-time and temporary employees are also likely to receive wages below the market rate (as shown in Chapter 2), not to mention that they usually are exempt from fringe benefits, promotions, and wage increases.

Japan's dual employment system is analogous to the formal and informal economies observed in many developing countries (Portes 1994). The persistence of the informal economy is thought to be a response to an overly rigid formal economy that implements numerous rules and regulations for employment activity. In a highly regulated economy, the established practices in the formal sector are often not designed to accommodate new groups of participants in the labor market, such as immigrants. Consequently, it can be extremely difficult for new participants to enter the formal employment sector. In turn, newcomers in the labor market tend to be absorbed by the informal sector, which has lower entering barriers (DeSoto 1989; Piore and Sabel 1984; Portes and Benton 1984).

My earlier research (Yu 2002, 2004) suggests unequal accessibility to the standard and nonstandard employment sectors in Japan, similar to those to the formal and informal sectors described in the literature. Among Japanese individuals, job changes from full-time regular employment to any other type of employment, including part-time (temporary) employment, self-employment, or family enterprise employment, are much more common than movement in the opposition direction. Such asymmetrical tendencies of job movement are especially apparent among women. If entering the standard employment sector is difficult in general, doing so should be particularly challenging for women resuming employment after some years of child rearing. The rationale is that, in Japan, married women older than their mid thirties, as a demographic group, began to participate in the labor force relatively recently. At the same time, many employment practices in Japan's standard employment sector have been strictly designed for the "usual" labor force, which consists of men before the mandatory retirement age and young, single women. Newcomers in the labor force, like older married women, are likely to find their qualifications or needs incompatible with the existing practices and rules. The rigidity of the standard employment sector thus compels many newcomers to enter the nonstandard sector.

One example of Japanese employers' negligence of labor force reentrants as potential candidates for full-time standard jobs is that they often equate the seniority-based wage system with an age-based system. The justification for equating the two is that seniority is highly correlated with age for men and single women who join the company soon after school graduation. As reported by Japan's Ministry of Labour (1997), in 1995, age—rather than work experience, qualifications, education, ability, or previous job positions—was the second-most important determinant for the wage of a midcareer person (i.e., a person who has prior work experience elsewhere before entering the job) across all sizes of firms. Age was less important only than a "balance with the wages of those who have been serving." In the case of married women with discontinuous work patterns, age and work experience do not match. They hence present a dilemma for management: It is nearly impossible to fit them into the age-based reward system without jeopardizing the balance with existing employees' wages. This difficulty of incorporating labor force reentrants to the existing system explains why Japanese companies often set upper age limits when recruiting regular full-time employees.[10] The existence of *nenrei seigen* (upper age limits) was brought up by a few middle-age Japanese women I interviewed as the reason why they did not seek full-time jobs.

Many of Japan's workplace norms and conditions discussed in previous chapters, such as the primacy given to the workplace over the family, were also developed for the more typical labor supply: men and single women. The implicit assumption was that a regular employee, either a male or a single female, could sacrifice his or her other responsibilities relatively easily for job demands. Knowing that the established norms and practices are unable to accommodate newcomers, Japanese management tends to be hesitant about recruiting those from atypical demographic groups. The job-searching experience of one woman whom I interviewed exemplifies this tendency. She had a university degree and relatively continuous work experience, and was looking for a full-time job shortly after having left her premarital job:

> I went to a Belgian bank in Tokyo for a job interview. The middle-level manager, who was a Japanese middle-aged man, kept asking me questions about my family, how I was going to take care of my kids since they were too young to be at school, whether I had anybody to help me if my kids got sick, etc. He went on and on. Finally, the top-level manager, a foreign man, who was also

interviewing me, stopped the Japanese man and said, "Well, since she is here to apply for the job, she must have solved all these family issues." I almost laughed. That was really funny.

In addition to employers' preferences, the implicit rules and norms for the standard employment sector that fail to adapt to the needs of newcomers have discouraged married women from returning to that sector. A few Japanese women with full-time jobs mentioned to me that they felt compelled to attend after-hours company functions that may even require them to be away from home overnight. It is not difficult to imagine that such an implicit rule could dissuade married women, particularly those with children, from seeking full-time jobs. The common practice of overtime work also pushes married women away from standard employment. A Japanese woman described the situation to me as a genuine dilemma: "Most women prefer to have full-time jobs, but do not want to do overtime work." Another woman's story further illustrates the role that the standard employment sector's practices play in matching married women with part-time and temporary jobs:

> When I first returned to work, I tried to find a full-time job. I had obtained my license for denture making then, so I tried to get a job in those medium-sized firms that made dental materials. I told every employer during my job interviews that I could only work until seven o'clock in the evening, because I needed to be home by then to cook dinner and take care of my kids. I told them that I didn't mind getting less pay but I couldn't to do overtime work. The firm I went to said yes to me. So I started to work there. Then right after I went to work, I found it impossible for me to stay away from overtime work. I wanted to leave by seven, but they always kept me late. There was so much work to do. I went to tell the manager that I couldn't stay that late, and he got really upset and said it was my responsibility. He expected me to finish my job as a worker, no matter how late it took me. I was angry and told him that he lied to me about the work condition. I only worked there for a month and I resigned. Then I thought, "That's it. Full-time jobs don't work. I would have to do overtime work anyway—they always lie about it." So I didn't try to look for full-time jobs any more.

Thus, to understand the concentration of labor force reentrants in the nonstandard employment sector, we need to pay particular attention to Japan's standard employment system. Conventional recruitment practices and workplace demands in the standard employment system have been designed for men and single women. Such practices and demands were never meant to accommodate older married women—a new source of labor. Nonregular nonstandard employment, on the other hand, is largely exempt from the prevalent norms and practices in the standard employment sector. For example, part-time and temporary workers may excuse themselves from after-hours *tukiai* (informal social functions, which are customary among coworkers as a way of reinforcing social ties), given that they do not officially belong to the "corporate family." My observation from brief participation in a regular Japanese office setting also helps illustrate how expectations for workers vary with employment status in the workplace. The section where my seat was had one male and five female employees, who nearly always left the office in the same order. The man frequently continued his work at night, so he left the last. Among the women, I realized later, the one who often stayed until around eight o'clock was the only regular full-time employee. The woman who usually left around six o'clock was a "temporary" employee whose contract had been renewed annually for seven years by that time. The woman who left slightly earlier than the temporary worker was on a six-month contract; the others, who left at four or five o'clock, were part-timers. The different expectations and requirements for part-time and irregular employees, as just described, make nonstandard jobs comparatively appealing to Japanese women reentering the labor market.[11]

In addition to the working conditions, nonstandard jobs are relatively easy to obtain because management offers neither a long-term commitment nor high labor compensation to employees with such jobs. Unlike those for regular job openings, advertisements for part-time positions frequently announce that "*shufu* [housewives] are welcome," as I noticed during fieldwork in Japan. Some employers even make an extra effort to attract mothers to part-time work. When I visited an enterprise union for a large textile firm, which regularly hires part-time workers in many of its factories, a male official in the union proudly spoke to me about what the firm had done for female workers:

> In our factories in Chiba, we have childcare centers for part-timers. So those mothers can bring their children to work and put them in the daycare. I think it is rare in Japan. . . . No, we don't provide any daycare service for regular employees. They don't need it.

The reason regular employees are assumed not to need the firm's daycare service is that incumbents of standard full-time jobs are supposed to be either married men or single women. Once again, the union official's statement corroborates that full-time regular jobs are designed for the groups that traditionally make up the labor force. Thus, newcomers in the labor market, such as married women, can only be matched with newly created, nonstandard jobs, for which the rules and requirements are more flexible.

Earlier in this chapter I showed that married women return to the labor force relatively slowly in Japan. One may suspect that this rate of return has obstructed reentrants' access to full-time standard employment. An employer is likely to consider a woman as a less serious worker if she has been out of the labor force for a long time. A further analysis of married women's work status helps clarify whether merely being a married, female job seeker reduces one's chance of obtaining a full-time regular job in Japan, regardless of the time spent not being employed. Using the SSM data from 1995, I conducted a multinomial regression analysis of the effects of entering their current employment status in the year of marriage or later on women's chances of being in nonemployment, part-time and temporary employment, full-time standard employment, or other nonemployee status (i.e., self-employment and family enterprise employment). If the hypothesized discrimination against married women in job searches does exist, then the timing of a woman's job entry—before or after marriage—will affect her likelihood of obtaining a full-time rather than a part-time job, all else being equal. In addition to the timing of entering the current status, the model controlled for individual qualifications, family conditions, gender attitudes, the length of work experience, and the age at which the respondent entered her current status.

Figure 6.6 shows the main results from the multinomial logit model (see Appendix B, Table B.7 for details). Japanese women who had entered their current status around the time of marriage or later were more than four times as likely to be in part-time rather than full-time employment. The same analysis also indicates that women entering their current jobs at age 45 or older were more likely to hold part-time or temporary jobs rather than full-time jobs. Age discrimination, however, does not fully account for the fact that married women, as job seekers, were largely excluded from full-time jobs.[12] Regardless of her total work experience and the age at which she sought her current job, a Japanese woman's probability of moving into part-time and temporary employment increased considerably if she had ever left her premarital job. Women who had withdrawn from their jobs upon marriage or childbearing were also more likely to participate in the labor force in the status of self- or family employment ("other" status) rather than in full-time regular employment. These findings support that there are systematic barriers that obstruct married female job seekers' access to standard full-time employment.

These barriers help explain a seemingly surprising finding from previous research: Working mothers of preschool children are more likely to participate in full-time rather than part-time or temporary employment in Japan (Nagase 1997; Yu 2002). Being employed part-time during child-rearing years will not remove the impediment of reentering full-time employment later on, because a woman with such an experience still has to present herself as a wife and mother when seeking regular full-time jobs. Given this, there is little incentive for a new mother in Japan to consider part-time employment as a third option apart from leaving or remaining in her full-time job obtained before marriage.

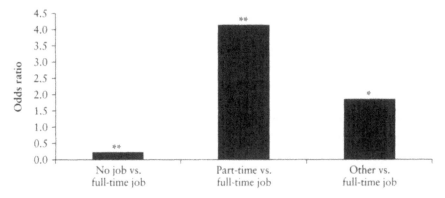

*Figure 6.6.*    Effects of postmarital entry on women's current work status in Japan.

SOURCE: 1995 SSM, part A.

*Note:* The effects are based on coefficients from a multinomial logit regression of current work status among all women who had ever married and worked in the SSM sample, controlling for education, work experience, presence of preschool children, living arrangement, husband's employment status, husband's income, urban residence, gender attitudes, and age of entering current work status (see Appendix B, Table B.7). "Other" refers to nonemployee status, such as self-employment and family enterprise employment.

$^{\dagger}p < .10$, $^{*}p < .05$, $^{**}p < .01$.

In summary, part-time or temporary employment is not the means for Japanese mothers with young children to *remain* in the labor force. Rather, this employment status serves as the channel for older married women to *reenter* the labor force. As a result of the declining fertility rate and prolonged life expectancy, women from their late thirties to mid fifties, mostly married, have contributed to much of the growth of the Japanese labor force since the 1960s (Yu 2002). The standard Japanese employment system, however, did not change to accommodate these newcomers. A mismatch between oversupplied older married women and overly rigid standard employment thus results in Japan's high concentration of labor force reentrants in nonstandard employment. Although the rising labor costs resulting from the aging workforce has raised Japan's demand for part-time and temporary workers, this increasing demand cannot fully account for the sector's great absorption of married women returning to the labor force. Instead, the fact that the standard employment sector has never been ready for these reentrants explains why they are particularly likely to be pushed to part-time or temporary jobs.

CONCLUSION: GETTING THE SECOND CHANCE

One reason to examine married women's transition back into the labor force is to reveal their likelihood of obtaining a second chance in the labor market after leaving their premarital jobs for child rearing. Between Japan and

Taiwan, ironically, the country in which women experience greater difficulty combining motherhood and employment is also the one that provides them with worse job opportunities the second time around. As discussed in this chapter, the labor market structures that account for the different employment exit patterns between Japanese and Taiwanese women also shape their career dynamics in a later stage of their life course. Results from my analysis demonstrated that sequencing worker and mother roles over the life course is a more popular strategy for women in Japan than in Taiwan. The reason why Japanese women are more likely to adopt this strategy is not that the penalty of interrupting employment for motherhood is smaller in that country. On the contrary, Japan's labor market is highly unforgiving. In this chapter I showed that what waits for Japanese women after the completion of child rearing are usually part-time or temporary job opportunities that are associated with low occupational status and low economic returns. In fact, a Japanese woman's chance of holding a regular full-time job that properly rewards her qualifications diminishes as soon as she decides not to continue her premarital job. Also, regardless of how soon a woman resumes employment, the penalty associated with leaving her premarital job remains.

Notes from my interviews suggest that most Japanese women recognize the detrimental effects of work interruptions on their employment careers but see no other option, given that they often find their job requirements and family responsibilities incompatible. Two women who were contemplating changing their jobs at the time I spoke with them both acknowledged that they might have to take a part-time job, against their preference, if they decide to leave the full-time jobs they have held since before marriage. Among other women I interviewed in Japan, almost all those who had reentered the labor market held part-time jobs if they were not self-employed. Few of these women preferred part-time or temporary jobs to full-time standard jobs.

Acknowledging their restricted opportunities, homemaking women in Japan are likely to take time to raise their children and return to work only after they have completed the major part of their maternal obligations. Even though this pattern of labor return does not fully account for married women's likelihood of becoming part-timers upon labor force reentry, it does increase this likelihood because discrimination against older job seekers also exists. Moreover, the tight connection between married women's family status and their timing of resuming employment reinforces Japanese employers' notion that married women's child-rearing obligations make them suboptimal workers. Employers' prejudice further obstructs women's opportunities of receiving standard jobs upon labor force reentry. Thus, a vicious cycle is formed.

In comparison with women in Japan, women in Taiwan are more likely to be given a second chance in the labor market. This does not mean that it is never too late for Taiwanese women to grab their second chance. On the contrary, the economic structure in Taiwan leads to a relatively positive association between married women's market opportunities and their speed of returning to the labor force. Therefore, unlike in Japan, women who eventually resume employment in Taiwan tend to do so before much time has passed since their job exit. In this sense, the quality of a Taiwanese woman's second chance depends on the timing of her employment reentry. On the whole, however, Taiwanese reentrants' market opportunities are almost comparable with those of general workers. Rather than concluding that Taiwanese employers treat married, female job seekers more fairly, I argue that the country's relatively flat rewarding system reduces the incentive to penalize those having taken time-outs. The lack of hierarchical wage and promotion structures that are strictly based on age makes it unnecessary to screen job applicants carefully, and taking in newcomers presents little threat to established practices. Besides, the labor shortage in the Taiwanese economy has discouraged employers from barring labor force reentrants to the extent that Japanese employers have. Thus, Taiwan's labor market conditions give married women a second chance as long as they return to work in a timely fashion, whereas Japanese women typically face great disadvantages in the labor market even the second time around.

## CHAPTER SEVEN

# Higher Education and Gender Inequality

Highly educated Japanese and Taiwanese women's different tendencies of continuing employment around childbirth largely contributed to the two countries' divergence in married women's postmarital employment behaviors. Similar to the U.S. experience, Taiwanese women with higher education and enhanced occupational prospects were the first to work continuously after their marriage and during childbearing years (Chapter 4; Goldin 1997). The increase in Japanese women's educational attainment nonetheless coincided with the popular discourse's stronger emphasis on mothers' roles as children's educators, rather than changes in women's economic roles (Chapter 5; Hirao 2001). Why did women's improved educational opportunities have different effects on changes in women's long-term employment opportunities between the two countries? In previous chapters I argued that Japan's lifetime employment system and abundant supply of educated men encouraged the prevalence of family-unfriendly working conditions, resulting in a relatively low employment rate of highly educated women. By contrast, Taiwan's restricted number of college students contributed to a shortage of highly qualified male labor. To cope with this shortage, Taiwanese employers had to utilize highly educated women and increasingly accommodate married women in the workplace. Facing a relatively high level of compatibility between work and family obligations, Taiwanese women became more attached to the labor force as their opportunities for high-status jobs improved.

The story about the development of women's employment opportunities in the two countries, however, is incomplete without addressing another key factor affecting employers' willingness to hire and retain highly educated women in the workplace: the level of gender equality in educational attainment. One major reason why Taiwanese employers were likely to encounter difficulties filling their job openings with highly educated men is that, in addition to that country's limited number of university graduates each year, there had been relatively equal shares of male and female students in universities, especially in the prestigious ones (Luoh 2002). This equality means that only about half of the highly educated labor supply was male. Facing an insufficient supply of highly educated male labor, Taiwanese employers could hardly afford to maintain their preferences for highly qualified labor and male workers at the same time. Giving up the preference for male workers seemed rational.

Japanese women's experience with higher education was substantially different. In particular, the shares of male and female students have been highly unequal in Japan's prestigious universities. To illustrate the difference between Japan and Taiwan, female students constituted more than 45 percent of the students at National Taiwan University, Taiwan's most prestigious university, as early as the 1960s. Throughout the past four decades, this university's percentage of female students has been relatively stable, about 42 to 47 percent (Luoh 2002). Such figures contrast sharply with the percentage of female students at its Japanese counterpart, the University of Tokyo. During the 1960s, only slightly more than 3 percent of the students admitted to the University of Tokyo was female. Even as late as 2001, after the steady growth of female university enrollment (Schoppa 2006), women made up only 18 percent of the students admitted to the University of Tokyo (Komaba-50-Year-History Editorial Committee 2001).

I turn my attention to educational inequality between genders in this chapter because the differences in women's relative educational opportunities between Japan and Taiwan play an important part in explaining the two countries' divergence in women's economic roles. My objective is to illuminate the conditions that led the two countries to offer women different opportunities for receiving a high-quality university education. It is noteworthy that Taiwan actually had a long history of gender inequality in educational attainment (Greenhalgh 1985; Parish and Willis 1993; Yu and Su 2006). As a later section in this chapter shows, Taiwanese women's educational opportunities have trailed behind men's until recent years, even though the shares of male and female students at National Taiwan University have been relatively equal since the 1960s. That is to say, for many years Taiwanese women's chance of entering the most elite university relative to men's, paradoxically, was higher than that of entering any university. Conversely, in Japan, the more prestigious a university, the more likely women were underrepresented within its student body (Fujimura-Fanselow and Imamura 1991). Explaining these puzzling differences between the two countries is crucial to our understanding of the divergence in women's economic opportunities.

EDUCATIONAL SYSTEMS IN JAPAN AND TAIWAN

What makes Japan and Taiwan's different patterns of educational inequality so striking is perhaps the similarity of their school systems. It is not surprising that these countries share many features in this regard. Both countries have been heavily influenced by the Confucian tradition, which gives primacy to educational achievement and emphasizes standardized examinations as the primary method of screening students (Berger and Hsiao 1988; Broaded 1997; Rohlen 1983). More important, Japan set the foundation of a modern educational system during its colonial rule of Taiwan from 1895 to 1945 (Cumings 1987; Gold 1988; Woo 1991). Although the goals of Japan's colonial education were to enhance Japanese proficiency among the Taiwanese people and to produce loyalty toward the imperial state, the early and wide establishment of common schools, as means to these ends, provided abundant opportunities for Taiwanese children, particularly girls, to receive primary education (Tsurumi 1977). By 1944, the elementary school enrollment rate for Taiwanese children age 6 to 14 reached 71 percent, which was higher than most Asian countries (Woo 1991). Japan also established a limited number of secondary and tertiary educational institutions, including today's National Taiwan University, during its colonial period in Taiwan. Most of these institutions became Taiwan's most prestigious public high schools and universities after Japan's colonial rule ended with its World War II defeat.

The early postwar years were associated with major educational reforms in both societies. Figure 7.1 illustrates the products of these reforms: the postwar school systems in Japan and Taiwan. Under the occupation of the allies, Japan began its current educational system, which features six years of primary school, three years of middle school, three years of high school, and four years of university education, with nine-year compulsory schooling. The new system modified the prewar system by abandoning the separation between boys and girls upon the completion of primary education. The new system also allows a greater proportion of students to pursue upper secondary education. Nonetheless, not all students in upper secondary educational institutions are enrolled in the same type of program. About one fourth of Japanese high school students are enrolled in vocational, rather than academic, high schools (Okano and Tsuchiya 1999). Students of vocational high schools are expected to seek employment, rather than to attend universities, after graduation (Rohlen 1983; Rosenbaum and Kariya 1989).

Upon completing their high school education, Japanese girls and boys may choose to attend a two-year junior college (*tanki daigaku*) or a four-year university. Special training courses are also available for high school graduates to gain additional vocational skills, but such education is usually not considered part of formal tertiary education.[1] Whereas Japanese universities offer a relatively wide range of majors, most of Japan's junior colleges only offer study in the liberal arts. Junior college students therefore rarely have opportunities to study the sciences or receive other specialist training. In addition to universities and general junior colleges, there are

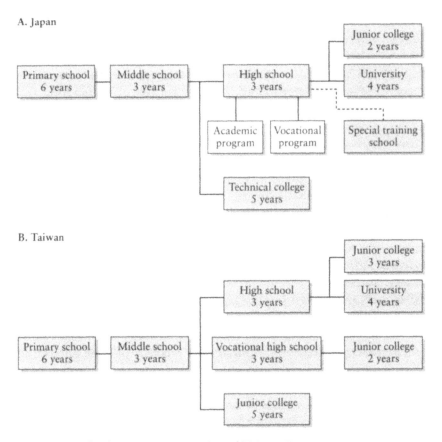

*Figure 7.1.*    School systems in Japan (A) and Taiwan (B).

also a small number of technical colleges (*kōtō senmongakkō*), which admit middle school graduates and offer five years of training, usually in the applied sciences. However, relatively few Japanese boys and girls take this route. In 2003, less than 1 percent of middle school graduates decided to attend a five-year technical college (Ministry of Education, Culture, Sports, Science, and Technology [MEXT], Japan 2004). Both regular junior colleges and technical colleges have lower status than four-year universities, since their graduates tend to have worse job prospects.

Taiwan's postwar educational system is more complex than Japan's. After taking over the island, the Kuomintang regime established a 6-3-3-4 school system, similar to Japan's, as the core segment. Attending six years of formal schooling was mandatory until 1968, when compulsory education was extended to nine years. Unlike Japan's, Taiwan's 6-3-3-4 system only applies to a relatively small group of students. The Taiwanese government considered the development of vocational education as part of its broader economic plans. To this end, the state enthusiastically introduced additional vocational tracks to the school system as the economy became industrialized (Woo 1991), resulting in Taiwan's multitrack educational system.

As Figure 7.1 illustrates, Taiwanese students generally face three possibilities after completing nine years of compulsory education, if not seeking employment right away. The first option is to attend a general high school, from which individuals are expected to advance to universities. Less commonly, a general high school graduate would attend a three-year junior college (*sanzhuan*), which orients toward high-level vocational education.[2] The seats in general high schools are very limited. Until the late 1990s, when higher education began to expand, most middle school graduates who wished to continue their study could not be admitted to general high schools. Many of them thus turned to the next best option: a five-year junior college (*wuzhuan*) (Broaded 1997). This type of college is similar to technical colleges in Japan, and its programs aim to prepare mid- to high-level technicians for the economy. Students in five-year junior colleges generally would miss getting a general high school education and thus rarely advance to universities. However, because the sophisticated vocational training provided by these colleges tends to promise decent job prospects, many parents and students regard the top-ranked five-year junior colleges, usually the public ones, more highly than general high schools with relatively low advancement rates.[3] The third and often least desirable option for middle school graduates is vocational high school. Graduates from vocational high schools may advance to a two-year junior college (*erzhuan*), but they are highly unlikely to attend universities because their vocation-specific education does not equip them sufficiently for university entrance exams.[4]

Thus, just like in Japan, students are divided into general and vocational tracks from middle school onward in Taiwan. One major difference between the two countries, however, is that vocational high schools actually constitute the majority of Taiwanese high schools.[5] Eager to prepare human resources for its rapid economic development, the Taiwanese government strongly promoted the growth of private vocational high schools, while restricting the number of general high schools. Consequently, the student enrollment in vocational high schools surpassed that in general high schools in 1970, and the number of students in vocational high schools continued to grow during the following years. By 1980, the ratio of vocational to general high school enrollment was 66:34 (Woo 1991).

Although Japan and Taiwan differ in how much they have focused on vocational education, their educational systems share several important features. First, tracking starts early in both countries. Those who enter the vocational track upon the completion of compulsory education, such as Japanese students in vocational high schools and Taiwanese students in five-year junior colleges, rarely receive a second chance for academic study and a university education (Brinton 1993; Rohlen 1983). Second, the selection of students at every level beyond compulsory education is strictly based on their performance on school entrance exams. That is to say, to be admitted to an upper secondary or tertiary educational institution, individuals must take comprehensive, curriculum-based achievement tests (Broaded 1997; Okano and Tsuchiya 1999). Both countries' highly regulated curricula and reliance on standardized textbooks are conducive to the adoption of national or regional entrance exams.[6]

The exam-based screening process in part contributes to the third common feature of the two schooling systems: strict age grading. There are minimal age differences among the students attending every grade at each level of schooling, including the university. This feature in part has to do with the intense study required for passing entrance exams. It is difficult for those who are no longer students to pass the exams to return to school. Institutional barriers such as upper age limits for each educational level also existed until recently (Brinton 1993).

Fourth, schools are highly stratified in both countries. A school's ranking generally corresponds to its advancement or job placement rate, depending on whether its graduates are expected to study further. Because many schools hold entrance exams jointly and admit students based solely on examination scores, the minimum score required for entering each school explicitly reveals its relative desirability. Therefore, school hierarchies are more unequivocally defined in both countries than in societies that do not rely on standardized exams as much, such as the United States. In addition, knowledge about the school hierarchies is pervasive in the two societies. Even those without school-age children or relevant educational experiences can learn about the school rankings every year from the intensive media reports on major entrance exams and the performance of graduates from various schools on those exams (Broaded 1997; Rohlen 1983).

Fifth, public schools tend to be ranked higher than private ones in the school hierarchy in both countries. For example, Japan's University of Tokyo and Taiwan's National Taiwan University, the most selective university in each respective country, are both public institutions.[7] Other than a few exceptions, most elite universities are national in both countries. Taiwan's top-ranked academic high schools, particularly those in major cities, are also mostly public. In Japan, public high schools were ranked higher historically. Students from elite private schools, however, began to outperform top public high school students in the 1970s, when Japan's educational reform led to more even distributions of students of different achievement levels across public high schools. Kariya and Rosenbaum (1999) argue that the rising performance of private high schools resulted from the flight of high-achieving students from public schools after the reform weakened the prestige of elite public schools. Nevertheless, Japan's public high schools on the whole are still well regarded.

Last, although both countries provide relatively high-quality public education, the road to a top public school like the University of Tokyo often requires substantial private expenses—namely, expenses for after-school study programs and private tutoring services (Hirao 2007; Rohlen 1980). The highly competitive school environments and exam-based advancement systems in the two countries are argued to be conducive to the prevalence of private after-school education (also sometimes called *cram school* study or *shadow education*) (Stevenson and Baker 1992). Such education generally aims to enhance students' examination scores by helping them with the considerable memorization and repetitive practices that the exams require (Rohlen 1983; Russell 1997). Recent statistics indicate that about 60 percent of middle school students in Japan and more than 40 percent of their counterparts in Taiwan were enrolled in private after-school programs (Hirao 2007; Ministry of Education, Republic of China 1998, 2001). The percentages of high school students enrolled in such programs are likely to be higher in both countries.

Examination-oriented lessons are also available for recent graduates who fail the entrance exams to the schools of the next level they wish to attend. Most of those who intend to retake entrance exams the following year enroll themselves in private preparatory schools (known as another type of cram school) that provide full-time, examination-oriented training. In Japan, those who are in between schools and are studying for the next year's entrance exams are called *rōnin*, which originally referred to a samurai who does not belong to any master. Although a different term is used in Taiwan to describe those with the same status (i.e., *chongkaosheng*), for simplicity I refer to such individuals in both countries as *rōnin* hereafter. Passing the examinations of the most elite universities in Japan can sometimes take more than one year of *rōnin* study (Rohlen 1983). Hence, the cost of additional study in preparatory schools is frequently part of the private investment required for entering top-ranked Japanese universities. Similarly, the cost of *rōnin* study is part of Taiwan's private educational investment. Individuals who undergo *rōnin* study in Taiwan, however, are likely to be those who have failed to enter any university, rather than those who could not be admitted to top-ranked universities.[8]

To summarize, the school systems in both countries feature early tracking, strict age grading, an exam-based screening process, a hierarchical school system, and the prevalence of cram school study outside of regular schooling. Mary Brinton (1988, 1993) argues that these features are the factors that cause Japan's gender inequality in education opportunities. Because the tracking starts after middle school, and high schools are highly stratified, those who are not admitted to top-ranked high schools upon the completion of compulsory education generally have little chance of attending any university, not to mention a prestigious one. The feature of strict age grading, which discourages students from returning to school at a later age, also increases the importance of having an early success. The key to early success, according to Brinton, is parental investment. The exam-based, highly competitive screening process makes parental investment particularly crucial because those who can afford cram school tuition tend to perform better on examinations. Parents' willingness to pay for children's education also determines whether children can retake entrance exams after failing the first time. Brinton therefore contends that Japanese parents' preference for investing in their sons' schooling accounts for girls' lower educational attainment. Following this argument, parental investment and early success should also play crucial roles in shaping Taiwanese girls' educational opportunities. Yet, as the next sections show, parents' preference for educating sons over daughters has not been as detrimental to women's access to higher education in Taiwan as in Japan. The case of Taiwan therefore challenges the previous understanding of gender inequality in educational attainment in Japan.

TRENDS IN EDUCATIONAL OPPORTUNITIES

Before developing explanations for the differences in gender inequality in educational attainment between Japan and Taiwan, I use trends in educational opportunities to provide a detailed picture of what needs to be explained. I begin by giving a general idea about educational opportunities in Japan. Despite its policy of nine-year compulsory schooling, Japan's education expansion in the 1950s and 1960s made high school attendance nearly universal (Okano and Tsuchiya 1999).[9] By the 1970s, more than 95 percent of boys and girls had opportunities to continue their studies upon their completion of compulsory education. Among Japan's high school students, boys have been slightly more likely than girls to attend vocational, rather than academic, programs (Fujimura-Fanselow and Imanura 1991). For instance, 29 percent of male high school students and 25 percent of female high school students were enrolled in vocational schools in 2003 (MEXT, Japan 2004). Compared with high school education, tertiary education has been more difficult to obtain in Japan. From the mid 1970s to the mid 1990s, around 40 percent of Japanese boys with a high school education advanced to a university or junior college. The rate for their female counterparts was lower during most of the past half century. Japanese girls' tertiary education advancement rate nevertheless surpassed boys' in 1989 and remained slightly higher throughout the 1990s. In 2002, about 50 percent of girls and boys who had completed high school continued to study (MEXT, Japan various years).

Unlike in Japan, the advancement rates among middle school graduates in Taiwan have not been consistently high. The rates for both gender groups increased steadily from the early 1950s to the late 1960s—to more than 80 percent—and declined after 1971. This decline was a result of the 1968 extension of compulsory education to nine years, which led to sudden increases in middle school graduates starting in 1971. From the early 1970s to the mid 1980s, when all Taiwanese children had an opportunity to attend a middle school, only 60 to 70 percent of middle school students continued to study upon graduation. Despite increases in the advancement rates for both girls and boys since the mid 1980s, it was not until the mid 1990s that these rates exceeded 90 percent (Ministry of Education, Republic of China various years). Overall, Taiwanese individuals were less likely to pursue upper secondary education than their Japanese counterparts until the most recent decade.

The gap in educational opportunities between the two countries is even wider if the comparison is limited to the opportunities for attending academic high schools. The majority of Taiwanese students in upper secondary education were enrolled in vocational schools during past decades, whereas approximately three fourths of Japanese high school students were enrolled in academic schools. To illustrate, Figure 7.2 presents the estimated percentages of middle school students who advanced to general high schools, five-year junior colleges, and vocational high schools using enrollment statistics from the Taiwanese government.[10] Figure 7.2 shows a sharp decline in the estimated rates at which boys and girls advance to general, academic high schools since compulsory education was extended to middle school. From the early 1970s to the mid 1990s, only about 20 percent of Taiwanese students could attend academic high schools after middle school. Another 10 percent of middle school graduates attended five-year junior colleges. Most of the middle school graduates continued their studies in vocational high schools. This type of school has absorbed a particularly large proportion of female middle school graduates. By 1990, nearly 50 percent of Taiwanese girls advanced to vocational high schools upon their completion of compulsory schooling. Boys were slightly more likely than girls to attend academic high schools and five-year junior colleges. Thus, although female middle school graduates' average rate of educational advancement has been similar to their male counterparts' in Taiwan, they have been more likely to advance to schools of lower quality (namely, vocational high schools).

Attending an academic high school is the key to obtaining higher education in Taiwan, given that only a handful of vocational high school students continue to study.[11] Taiwan's rates of advancement among academic high

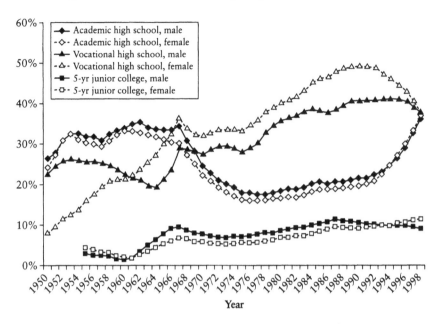

*Figure 7.2.*    Estimated advancement rates to various educational institutions among Taiwanese middle school graduates, 1950 to 1998.

s o u r c e :  Ministry of Education, Republic of China (Taiwan). *Educational statistics of the Republic of China*, various years.

*Note:* The advancement rates were calculated separately for boys and girls.

school graduates during the 1970s and 1980s were fairly stable—approximately 50 percent for girls and 40 percent for boys. These rates increased steadily after 1990 and reached 60 percent by 2001. The majority of general high school graduates who studied further headed to four-year universities,[12] but female graduates were more likely than their male counterparts to attend three-year junior colleges (Ministry of Education, Republic of China various years). Rather than attending three-year junior colleges, male high school students were more likely to become *rōnin* if they failed university entrance exams upon graduation. This gender difference, however, has diminished with the decline in the enrollment of three-year junior colleges.

Even though the gender gap in the opportunities of higher education has been narrowing in both countries, women and men are not always distributed evenly across types of tertiary institutions. Figure 7.3 presents trends in the shares of female students at various kinds of educational institutions. In Japan, the majority of junior college students have been female since 1955. Although those attending technical colleges have tended to be male, they have constituted only a small proportion of all those enrolled in higher educational institutions. In comparison with junior colleges, the percentage

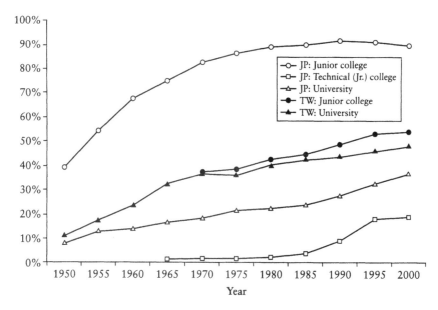

*Figure 7.3.*    Trends in the percentage of female students among students in tertiary institutions.

SOURCE: Ministry of Education, Republic of China. *Educational statistics of the Republic of China*, various years; Statistics Bureau, Management and Coordination Agency, Japan, *Historical statistics of Japan*, 1987; Statistics Bureau, Ministry of Internal Affairs and Communications (Statistics Bureau of the Management and Coordination Agency prior to 2001), Japan, *Japan statistical yearbook*, various years.

*Note:* JP, Japan; TW, Taiwan.

Except for 1950, the Taiwanese data are from the year following the one indicated in the figure. Hence, the percentages for 1955 in the figure are from 1956, those for 1960 from 1961, and so forth. I show the yearly data for Taiwan as in the same years as for Japan to simplify the presentation.

of female students in Japan's universities has been low. Even in 2000, after a substantial increase in women's university enrollment, the percentage was only 36 percent. Thus, consistent with previous research, Japanese girls who advance to tertiary education largely head to junior colleges (technical colleges not included), whereas their male counterparts are mostly enrolled in universities (Brinton and Lee 2001; Fujimura-Fanselow and Imamura 1991).

By contrast, among junior college students in Taiwan, there were more male than female students until the 1990s. The level of female representation among university students has been lower than that among junior college students. No more than one third of Taiwanese university students were female in the mid 1960s. The percentage of female students among the students enrolled in universities rose to 42 percent two decades later. The percentage further increased to 48 percent, nearly identical to the female share of the population age 18 to 21, by the end of the twentieth century. Despite the fact that it took several decades for Taiwanese women to obtain a share equal to men's at the university level, Taiwan's percentage of women among university students has been considerably greater than Japan's throughout the past half century. In fact, the female-to-male ratio among university students was more balanced in Taiwan in the mid 1960s than it is in Japan today. The degree of female dominance among junior college students has also been much higher in Japan than in Taiwan. Thus, Japan's level of gender segregation by type of tertiary institution has been greater than Taiwan's. Given the similarities between the two educational systems, Taiwan's higher level of gender equality in higher education is certainly surprising.

In addition to revealing the patterns of educational inequality in Japan and Taiwan, the trends just shown help illustrate the difference between these countries in the supply of highly qualified individuals—namely, those with a university education—in the labor market. Before the onset of Taiwan's higher education expansion in the late 1990s, only about 20 percent of middle school students attended academic high schools. Among these students, 40 percent might be able to pass university entrance exams upon high school graduation. These percentages mean that approximately 8 percent of each birth cohort would achieve a university education, given that virtually all university students come from academic high schools. Within this 8 percent, one third to two fifths were female. Thus, a Taiwanese employer with a strong preference for well-educated male workers had to select from a pool of about 5 percent of each birth cohort. In contrast, from 1975 to 1995, nearly all Japanese boys and girls were able to attend high school. During the same period, about 40 percent of the male high school students advanced to the tertiary educational level, and the vast majority of them went to universities, rather than junior colleges. Hence, near 40 percent of each birth cohort of males (equal to about 20 percent of each birth cohort) would attend a university in Japan.[13] Since about one in every five university students was female, we can estimate that the total percentage of a Japanese cohort receiving a university education was around 25 percent. This percentage was apparently higher than Taiwan's 8 percent. Perhaps more important, Japan's school advancement patterns enable a much greater supply of university-educated men than in Taiwan. Consequently, Japanese employers are far more able to indulge their preference for male workers than Taiwanese employers.

### The Opportunity to Attend Elite Universities

The discussion thus far has centered on women's and men's probabilities of attending universities in the two countries. Nevertheless, the "examination hell" that Japanese students experience has to do with the high level of competition to enter a small number of elite universities in that country, rather than attending university at all. Because the hierarchy of Japanese universities is clearly defined and well-known by the public, the ranking of an individual's university serves as a convenient indicator of the individual's "quality" compared with his or her peers. Not only does this perceived quality bring prestige and respect, it also affects individuals' long-term career prospects. Previous research shows that a disproportionately high proportion of Japan's elite in the public sector and the business world were educated at the University of Tokyo, the university commonly regarded as Japan's best university (Rohlen 1983). By contrast, in societies in which the ranking of universities is more debatable, such as the United States, the elite are not so concentrated in their educational backgrounds (Ishida 1993). Taiwan is similar to Japan in regard to the existence of a clear hierarchy among universities. For example, most Taiwanese would not hesitate to name National Taiwan University as the most preferred and most competitive university in that country. Graduates from this educational institution, as well as a few other prestigious universities, generally make up the majority of Taiwan's business and political elite. Similar to the case of Japan, an individual in Taiwan who attends a prestigious university is more than halfway to a good job and lifetime economic security.

The association between having attended an elite university and achieving better job prospects is not limited to men. The benefit of attending an elite university holds even for Japanese women, despite the fact that there is a sufficient supply of male university graduates in that country each year. Akira Wakisaka (2001) shows that female graduates from national universities, which are generally more highly ranked than private universities, are more likely to be assigned to managerial than clerical tracks in Japanese firms. In particular, women with degrees from the University of Tokyo are extremely unlikely to be placed in clerical tracks. Similarly, attending a top university is also associated with having a better first job and higher earnings for Taiwanese women (Yu and Chu 1998).[14]

The strong connection between university prestige and labor market positions makes it important to examine men's and women's chances to attend elite universities in the two countries. I use the University of Tokyo and National Taiwan University to exemplify women's relative opportunities for receiving an elite university education in Japan and Taiwan, respectively. The race to both universities is extremely competitive. During the past five decades, the University of Tokyo consistently admitted 0.2 to 0.3 percent of high school graduates each year. In comparison, being admitted to National Taiwan University has been slightly easier, primarily due to Taiwan's smaller population. Even so, only about 0.5 percent of the 18-year-old population

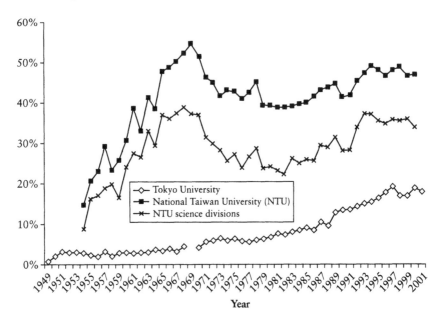

*Figure 7.4.*    Trends in the percentage of female students admitted to the University of Tokyo and National Taiwan University.

SOURCE: Komaba-50-Year-History Editorial Committee (2001). Aggregate statistics of National Taiwan University were obtained from Ming-Ching Luoh. See his study (2002) for details.

*Note:* The University of Tokyo did not admit any new students in 1969.

had an opportunity to attend National Taiwan University in the 1970s. This rate increased to approximately 0.6 percent in the 1980s and to near 0.9 percent today (Luoh 2002).

Figure 7.4 shows the percentage of female students among new entrants in the two universities across time. The differences between the two universities are striking. For the four decades after World War II, the percentage of female entrants at the University of Tokyo was less than 10 percent each year. It was not until 1994 that this percentage increased to more than 15 percent for the first time. In contrast, the percentage of female entrants to National Taiwan University reached 38 percent as early as 1961. This percentage decreased slightly from 1971 to 1990, but it was still more than 40 percent for each of these years. In the 1990s the percentage of female entrants increased again. By the mid 1990s, the gender ratio among National Taiwan University entrants was nearly identical to that among the 18-year-old population (Luoh 2002).

Japan and Taiwan have also differed in how the share of female students at top-ranked universities compares with the national average. The percentage of female students at the University of Tokyo has been consistently lower than that among all other Japanese universities. To illustrate, in 1975, 21 percent of Japanese university students were female, compared with only 6 percent of the entrants to the University of Tokyo. Similarly, Japanese women constituted 32 percent of all university students in 1995, but only 19 percent of the University of Tokyo entrants (Figures 7.3 and 7.4). Apparently, attending an elite university has been particularly difficult for Japanese women. Conversely, the gender ratio among entrants to National Taiwan University was more balanced than that among entrants to all other Taiwanese universities. Whereas the average share of female students across Taiwan's universities never surpassed 40 percent before 1986, the share of female entrants to National Taiwan University has rarely fallen to less than 40 percent since 1963 (Figures 7.3 and 7.4). Thus, despite their lower probability of receiving a university education than men, Taiwanese women's chances of attending elite universities were actually no worse than men's.

Were the differences in the gender ratio among students between the University of Tokyo and National Taiwan University attributable to the two universities' differing compositions of colleges and departments? Research shows that male and female students are highly segregated by field of study in higher education across the industrial world (Charles and Bradley 2002). Because male and female students tend to enter different fields, universities with an emphasis on customarily male fields, such as the natural sciences and engineering, may have a larger proportion of male students. Conversely, universities with greater strengths in conventionally female fields, such as the arts and humanities, may attract more female students. In both countries, the admission quota for each department in a university is set before the entrance exams. University applicants must decide whether they will major in natural sciences or social sciences and humanities, and take the entrance exams according to their choice.[15] Therefore, if a university allocates disproportionately higher quotas to natural sciences and engineering departments than to humanities departments, its student body is likely to be more male dominated, and vice versa.[16]

The University of Tokyo and National Taiwan University both have a wide range of colleges and departments. From 1949 to 2001, the average percentage of the University of Tokyo's new students who were in natural science-related fields (*rika*), including natural sciences, engineering, medicine, and agricultural sciences, was 52 percent, with a 42 percent minimum and a 55 percent maximum (Komaba-50-Year-History Editorial Committee 2001). Similarly, students in the sciences, engineering, and related fields outnumbered students in other fields (e.g., arts, humanities, social sciences, business) at National Taiwan University, constituting 57 percent of its new entrants, on average, from 1954 to 2000.[17] Not only was the difference in the ratio of science to nonscience students between the two universities small, but National Taiwan University actually had a slightly greater emphasis on the natural sciences and related fields, even though its proportions of female students were much higher over the years.

In addition, Figure 7.4 shows that even the percentage of female students in the four science-related colleges (i.e., natural sciences, engineering, agricultural sciences, and medicine) of National Taiwan University was higher than that at the University of Tokyo as whole. The fact that National Taiwan University's science-related colleges had smaller proportions of female students than the overall ones at the university indicates that Taiwanese women did concentrate in nonscience divisions. However, it was never as rare in Taiwan for a female student to attend the top university as in Japan. The University of Tokyo's relative focus on science compared with nonscience fields appears not to account for its extremely low level of female enrollment.

To sum up, despite their country's lower provision of university education, Taiwanese women have obtained a larger proportion of seats in universities than their Japanese counterparts throughout almost the entire second half of the past century. Furthermore, female students have had a particularly strong presence at Taiwan's elite universities, whereas Japanese women's presence at universities has decreased with the increase in university prestige. Explaining the puzzling differences in women's opportunities for higher education between the two countries is a major task for the reminder of this chapter.

## FAMILY AND GENDER INEQUALITY IN EDUCATION

As mentioned earlier, existing research often attributes Japan's gender inequality in educational attainment to parents' differential attitudes toward boys' and girls' schooling (Brinton 1993; Fujimura-Fanselow and Imamura 1991; Okano and Tsuchiya 1999; Ono 2004; Rohlen 1983). One major reason why parental attitudes are critical is that Japan's social norms discourage individuals from shifting back and forth between school and work. Since most Japanese individuals complete schooling before starting their first job, they must rely on their parents for the vast majority of their educational resources. Japanese parents are thought to prioritize sons' educational and occupational attainment over their daughters' because they expect their sons to provide financial support for them when they are old. Even unselfish parents tend to consider sons' education to be more worthy of their investment. The rationale of such parents is that women generally are rewarded less for their knowledge and skills as a result of gender discrimination in the labor market. Receiving less support from their parents, Japanese women are argued to have inferior educational opportunities compared with men's. In particular, because the cost of sending children to four-year universities, particularly prestigious ones, is substantially higher than that of sending them to junior colleges, parents are prone to sponsor sons to attend universities whereas they send their daughters to junior colleges at most.

Interestingly, Taiwan is also thought to exemplify the detrimental effects of patriarchal family norms on gender equality (Chu, Xie, and Yu 2007; Greenhalgh 1985; Hsiung 1996). Similar to Japan, the prevailing cultural practice is that sons, rather than daughters, are responsible for their parents' well-being when they are old (Lee et al. 1994; Lin et al. 2003). Previous research has shown that in the 1960s and '70s, Taiwanese parents frequently took advantage of the newly introduced employment opportunities for young women in export-oriented industries by sending their daughters to factory jobs at an early age (Kung 1994). With their daughters' earnings from factory work, Taiwanese parents were able to invest more in their sons' schooling, thus eventually enhancing their own welfare (Greenhalgh 1985). Other studies nevertheless contend that, rather than parents' selfish interests, the insufficiency of family budgets and parents' rational assessments of the gendered returns to education both account for the preference for educating sons over daughters in Taiwan. Hence, higher income parents are much less likely to remove their daughters from school for employment, even though Taiwanese parents generally devote more family resources to a child's education when the child is male (Parish and Willis 1993; Yu and Su 2006). Overall, regardless of why parents develop gendered strategies of educational investment, intrafamily gender inequality, manifested by differential educational opportunities for sons and daughters, has been well documented in Taiwan.

Earlier I showed that the overall rate of university attendance has been smaller in Taiwan than in Japan. It is arguable that parents' son preference is more detrimental to female educational attainment when the overall opportunities of university education are scarcer. When the competition is tighter, parents are more likely to feel the need to concentrate their resources on sons. Following this rationale, Taiwan's level of gender inequality in higher education should be greater than Japan's. The educational trends demonstrated in this chapter, however, indicate the opposite. One possible explanation for this counterintuitive finding is that Japanese parents have a much stronger preference for educating sons over daughters than Taiwanese parents. In a national poll conducted in 1993 by *Nippon Hōsō Kyōkai* (Japan Broadcasting Corporation), 70 percent of the respondents reported that, if they currently had a son in high school, they would like him to be educated at the university level, whereas only 9 percent reported junior college to be their preferred educational level. By contrast, 35 percent of the respondents reported the university level for a hypothetical daughter currently in high school, and 40 percent of them considered junior college as the optimal educational level for this daughter (The Japanese Public Opinion Database). Although the same opinion poll was not conducted in Taiwan, in 1991 the TSC survey asked respondents to report the minimum levels of schooling that they thought boys and girls generally should receive. Forty-one percent of the respondents chose some tertiary education for boys, whereas 25 percent did so for girls. Specifically, 26 percent of the respondents reported that boys must at least complete a university-level education, but only 13 percent considered that level to be the minimum required for girls. Interestingly, despite the different phrasings of the questions, respondents from both countries were exactly twice as likely to aspire for university education for boys as they were for girls (70% vs. 35% in Japan and 26% vs. 13% in Taiwan). This amazing similarity strongly suggests that parental educational aspirations and gendered investment strategies cannot account for the greater gender gap in university attendance, especially elite university attendance, in Japan than in Taiwan.

THE ROAD TO A UNIVERSITY EDUCATION

So far I have demonstrated the overall similarities in the educational systems and family norms in Japan and Taiwan. There are, however, a few seemingly small differences in educational policies, including those related to university entrance exams, between the two countries. Such differences, I argue, lead to Japan's greater obstacles against women in the process of university attainment. Here I examine the hurdles and challenges individuals must face and overcome to be eventually admitted to universities in the two countries. In doing so, I elucidate why Japanese women become increasingly disadvantaged along the road to a university education, whereas this is not the case for Taiwanese women.

### Challenges upon Middle School Graduation

As discussed earlier in this chapter, the competition for university entrance begins early in both countries. Passing the entrance exam to a general, academic high school constitutes the first necessary step. Hence, the story about who goes to a university has to start with who gets to the "right" high school. The selection of high school students is similar in the two countries. Public high schools of the same district rely on entrance examinations administered by their local boards of education to recruit students, whereas private schools may give their own entrance exams or hold exams jointly with other private schools.[18] One major discrepancy between the two countries, however, is that the probability of attending a general high school is much smaller in Taiwan. Unlike in Japan, the destinations of the majority of middle school graduates in Taiwan have been vocational educational institutions.

Taiwan's stronger emphasis on vocational education has important implications for women's and men's chances of university entry. To explain such implications, I must first discuss a few details about Taiwan's vocational educational system. Similar to universities, the student quota for each department or major is fixed in five-year junior colleges and vocational high schools. Students must select their majors before entering these schools and they are matched with the departments of their preference according to their entrance exam scores. Typically, the choices of major available at these educational levels are either business-related fields (e.g., accounting, finance, international trades) or applied sciences (e.g., electrical engineering, computer science). Male students generally concentrate in applied science programs across vocational schools. In 1970, for example, female students constituted only 16.8 percent of the five-year junior college students in applied science programs, and 6.5 percent of the vocational high school students in such programs. Although the female shares in applied science programs increased to 26.4 percent for five-year junior colleges and 14.3 percent for vocational high schools in 1985, these programs remained highly male dominated (Ministry of Education, Republic of China various years).

The large enrollment of male students in vocational school technical programs (prior to university expansion in the late 1990s) suggests that such education was considered appropriate for boys as far as Taiwanese parents were concerned. This type of technical training was particularly likely to be favored among parents who doubted their sons' ability to pass university entrance exams, given Taiwan's low rates of university entrance. Figure 7.5 indicates that from 1964 to 2000, Taiwan's five-year junior colleges and vocational high schools offered plentiful opportunities for boys' technical training. Five-year junior colleges often offered near 50 percent of the quota to those studying applied sciences, and the percentage of such students generally exceeded 50 percent in vocational high schools. By allocating more than half of the student quota to customarily male fields, five-year junior colleges and vocational high schools together attracted at least as many male as female graduates from middle schools. Had vocational training not been deemed helpful for boys' future careers, Taiwanese parents would probably have pushed their sons, but not daughters, to undergo *rōnin* study until the sons obtained admission to decent high schools. Such a scenario would have led to a much greater number of boys than girls competing for academic high school entrance. If so, admission to academic high schools, not to mention admission to universities, would have been much more difficult than it has been for Taiwanese women.

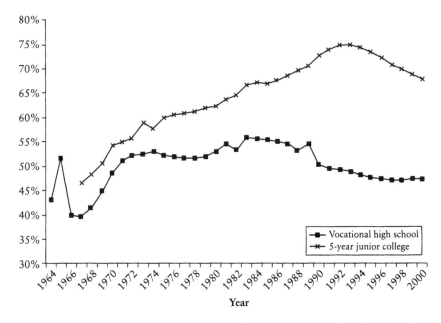

*Figure 7.5.* Percentage of students in applied science programs by educational level in Taiwan.

SOURCE: Ministry of Education, Republic of China. *Educational statistics of the Republic of China*, various years.

The hypothetical scenario just described can be found in Japan, but at the tertiary level. Unlike Taiwanese junior colleges, which have focused on technical or business training, the majority of Japan's junior colleges offer education in the liberal arts. As far as Japanese men's labor market prospects are concerned, the utility of two years of liberal arts study is low. Perceiving no "real" alternative for their sons upon failing university entrance exams, Japanese parents are likely to sponsor sons to become *rōnin* and take the exams the following year. Such parental support tends not to extend to daughters, because a junior college education in the liberal arts is viewed as a plausible option for women. As a result, male contestants are bound to outnumber female contestants in the race to a university, which contributes to an unbalanced gender ratio among Japanese university students.

Another major difference between Japan and Taiwan is at the high school level. This difference, paradoxically, has to do with Japan's colonial legacy in Taiwan. Nearly all Taiwan's top academic high schools were established under Japan's colonial rule. Following Japan's educational policy at that time, these schools were set to admit either boys or girls, but not both. The tradition of gender segregation remains in these schools today, whereas Japan shifted to coeducation during its postwar educational reform. Hence, almost all the highest ranked public high schools in Taiwan's major cities are single-sex schools. To illustrate, among the top 20 high schools with the most graduates admitted to National Taiwan University, only five of them recruit students of both sexes (Luoh 2002).[19] Because Taiwan's most selective public high schools are gender segregated, the ranking of the best high schools has to be gender specific, with the best school for girls differing from that for boys. These separate rankings lead to separate contests for boys and girls, despite the fact that they take the same entrance examination. Consistent with the logic of separate contests, each school district of Taiwan assigns separate admission quotas for boys and girls to all public schools in the district. Consequently, even among the lower ranked public high schools, which are often coeducational, the entrance scores required for admitting boys and girls differ. Thus, for public high school entrance, Taiwanese girls and boys actually compete with their own gender, rather than all those aspiring to attend such high schools.[20]

Although Taiwanese high schools' gendered admission policy originated from the colonial tradition of gender-segregated education, this policy has unintentionally raised women's educational opportunities, particularly the opportunities for receiving an elite education. To illustrate, I use the case of Taipei, the city that has produced the most elite university students (Luoh 2002). Taipei's public high schools generally admit more boys than girls (e.g., about 55:45 since 1990), similar to those in other districts (Broaded 1997). Despite this gendered policy, Taipei's six highest ranked high schools—of which three are for girls only, two are for boys only, and one is male dominant—together admit almost equivalent numbers of boys and girls. Thus, girls are guaranteed a similar number of seats as boys in the top six high schools in Taipei, which jointly generated half the students at National Taiwan University from 1982 to 2000 (Luoh 2002).

Had all Taiwan's top high schools been coeducational, girls would have attended prestigious high schools at lower rates. The evidence for this argument is that the required entrance score for the best girls' high school—Taipei First Girls' High School—has been consistently lower than that for the most prestigious high school for boys—Jianguo High School—despite the greater admission quota of the latter. In fact, from newspaper reports of the minimum entrance scores to Taipei's public high schools from 1980 to 1997, I find that a sufficient exam score for the best girls' high school was often not high enough to enter the second-best high school for boys.[21] This gender gap in exam performance, in part, resulted from the fact that Taiwanese parents tended to provide additional educational resources, such as private tutoring lessons, for boys (Yu and Su 2006). Gender segregation among the leading public high schools in Taipei, however, offsets girls' disadvantages by ensuring their equivalent number of seats to boys' in the district's top six high schools.

While most of Taiwan's top public high schools are gender segregated, almost all universities are coeducational in that country. Hence, there is no separate contest for university entrance by gender.[22] Interestingly, although students at Taipei's top two boys' high schools on average had higher entrance exam scores than those at the best girls' school, the latter had the highest percentage of students admitted to National Taiwan University in 1982 to 2000 in the country (Luoh 2002). The girls admitted to the best girls' high school appear to "catch up" with the boys in top schools during their high school years. To explain this change, it is noteworthy that Taiwan's elite high schools, regardless of whether they are boys' or girls' schools, compete intensively for higher advancement rates. In particular, a high school's advancement rate to prestigious universities, such as National Taiwan University, directly affects its ranking. This competition among elite high schools is conducive to the highly academic environments of elite girls' high schools, which reflect little of the societal expectation for girls to receive less education than boys. Such environments enable girls to realize their full potential by the time they take university entrance exams. In addition, because being at an elite high school signifies higher returns to parents' educational investment, once admitted to elite high schools, girls are likely to begin receiving greater educational resources from their parents. This increase in parental investment is also likely to contribute to their catching up with boys during their high school years. That Taiwanese girls in elite high schools eventually outperform their male counterparts reveals the importance of having a gender-specific admission policy at the high school level. Such girls would not be given equivalent opportunities for higher education as similarly talented boys had there not been nearly equal quotas for girls and boys in the top-ranked high schools.

I should note that Japan also has some single-sex high schools. Fujimura-Fanselow and Imamura (1991) contend that gender segregation among a handful of private high schools in Japan constitutes an impairment of gender equality in educational opportunities because the best private high schools are exclusively male. As private Japanese high schools increasingly outrank public high schools in the number of students admitted to elite universities (Kariya and Rosenbaum 1999), the exclusion of girls among some elite private high schools further exacerbates gender inequality in Japan's higher education. Gender segregation among Taiwan's schools has the opposite effect on women's educational opportunities because it is particularly common among top-ranked *public* high schools. As discussed earlier, this segregation compels local governments to separate student quotas of public high schools by gender. Moreover, in part as a result of the legacy of Japan's colonial rule, for every elite public high school for Taiwanese boys there generally is an equivalent girls' high school. The admission policy formulated under these conditions essentially functions as affirmative action for Taiwanese girls. The same policy, however, cannot be observed for Japan's private sector (or Taiwan's). There is generally no incentive for the private sector to even nominally ensure some level of gender equality. Private schools thus would not offer girls equal (but separate) educational opportunities simply because the top schools are exclusively male.

### The Design of University Entrance Examinations

Part of the reason why male students have dominated Japanese universities has to do with the gender composition of applicants to four-year universities. Male applicants have outnumbered female ones by a large margin. Using aggregate statistics from Japan's School Basic Survey (MEXT, Japan various years), I find a .99 correlation between the percentage of female students within national universities and the percentage of female applicants to such universities from 1969 to 2005. That is to say, the change in the gender ratio among students of Japan's national universities almost perfectly reflects that among applicants for these universities. To the extent that sending a university application signifies a person's educational aspiration, this strong correlation suggests that the low proportion of women in Japan's four-year universities is largely a result of their low aspirations to attend such educational institutions.

The discussion thus far sheds some light on the reasons for the relatively few female applicants to Japan's four-year universities. In both Japan and Taiwan, only students in highly ranked academic high schools are likely to have a reasonable chance of entering a university, especially an elite university.[23] To illustrate this relation, nearly 50 percent of National Taiwan University students came from four high schools—two girls' and two boys' high schools in Taipei—during 1982 to 2000 (Luoh 2002). The association between elite high school attendance and admission to prestigious universities is similarly strong in Japan (Kariya and Rosenbaum 1999). However, whereas Taiwan's high school system ensures that almost half the "real contenders"—that is, students of highly ranked high schools—are female, highly ranked Japanese high schools generally consist of much larger proportions of male students (Fujimura-Fanselow and Imamura 1991). Thus, Japan's gender composition of elite high school students accounts in part for its extremely unbalanced gender ratio among university applicants.

The story of why relatively few female students in Japan aspire for a university education, however, does not end with the gender imbalance of its top-ranked high school students. The specific design of Japan's university entrance exams also helps dampen women's educational ambitions. Perhaps the best way to explain the effect of the design of Japan's university entrance exams is to contrast it with Taiwan's. As discussed previously, both countries rely heavily on standardized tests for university admission. Nonetheless, there are key differences in the designs of their entrance exam systems. I argue that these seemingly small differences have important implications for women's access to universities, especially elite universities.

Japan's university entrance exam system features separate exam policies for the public and private sectors. Private universities hold their own entrance exams individually and select students based on their performance on the university-specific entrance exam. In addition to the exam contents and formats, private universities are also free to choose their own time for entrance exams, as long as it is within the exam season (February and March). The exam system for public universities is more regulated. I pay special attention to Japan's national universities' exam policies because such universities are generally those that most Japanese students aspire to attend. Until 1979, Japan's public university admission system relied on joint entrance exams. Under the joint system, Japan's public universities were officially divided into first- and second-tier groups. Each year, the first-tier universities would offer a uniform entrance exam together, and the second-tier universities would offer their exam jointly at a different time. This joint entrance exam system essentially allowed students to apply for all participating universities simultaneously. Thus, anyone whose exam score was in a percentile above the overall admission percentile would be able to attend a public university.

In 1979, Japan's public universities shifted to a two-stage entrance exam system, in which an applicant takes a nationally administered uniform achievement test and then an exam administered by the university to which the applicant aspires to enter. The joint first-stage achievement test is used merely as a screening device to qualify applicants for the second stage, a university-specific entrance exam. The focus of the new system is university-specific entrance exams. Applicants must pass the specific exams administered by the respective universities to which they wish to be admitted. Top-ranked private universities may also use the first-stage achievement test scores to screen applicants for their own entrance exams, but they do not have to adopt the two-stage exam system as public universities do.

One major impact of Japan's shift to a two-stage entrance exam system is a sharp reduction of university choices for applicants because public universities are required to hold the second-stage exams on the same dates. Specifically, national universities are expected to offer two opportunities for taking second-stage exams each year. As these exams are held on the same dates, university applicants are virtually given only two choices of national universities during the entire exam season.[24] Furthermore, the two opportunities for second-stage exams are not equal because universities generally recruit more than 70 percent of their students from those taking the first university-specific exam. Those taking the second university-specific exam have to compete for the remaining quota. Given these policies, students have to plan carefully for which national university's exam to take and in what order. Overall, the reform of the public university exam system in 1979 greatly enhanced the importance of university applicants' strategic planning for which exams to take.

With only two choices of national universities each year, students can easily miscalculate their chances and end up with no admission. This scenario is particularly likely among those who aim for the most prestigious universities, which are extremely competitive. Upon failing both exams to elite universities, students face few choices other than becoming *rōnin* and taking the entrance exams again the following year. Had they been given opportunities to attend less prestigious and yet highly regarded public universities, some students may have been willing to forgo the hardship of *rōnin* study. In this sense, the change in the exam system in 1979 not only increased the number of *rōnin*, but it also lowered students' chances of gaining admission to a national university.

The importance of individuals' educational aspirations and their family's expectations for them, independent of their abilities, also rose with Japan's adoption of a two-stage exam system. By allowing only two chances to take university-specific exams, Japan's national universities' admission policy compels applicants to consider seriously (1) how important it is for them to enter a highly prestigious university and (2) how undesirable their situation will be if they fail. Japanese men and women are likely to have different answers to these questions. Not only are the economic returns to elite education considered smaller for women than men, but women are also less likely to be supported by their families for undertaking *rōnin* study if they fail university entrance exams (Brinton 1993; Brinton and Lee 2001). As a result, when given limited choices for the universities where they can take entrance exams, Japanese women are more likely than men to take the conservative route and try less competitive universities. Women with the ability to attend the highest ranked universities are therefore likely to choose to take second-tier universities' entrance exams. This tendency in turn explains why the number of female students in Japan's elite universities has been extremely small.

To illustrate the effect of the exam system on women's educational opportunities, Figure 7.6 shows the percentage of women among the students admitted to national and private universities from 1973 to 1982 in Japan. Private universities generally had smaller proportions of women than national universities in Japan, especially before the national universities shifted away from the joint exam system in 1979. This difference suggests that a system in which each university administers its own entrance exam, such as

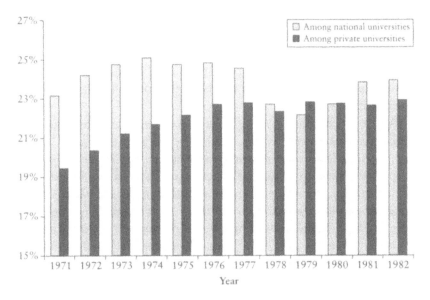

*Figure 7.6.* Percentage of female students in four-year universities by university ownership.

SOURCE: MEXT, Japan, *School Basic Survey*, various years.

one used by Japan's private universities, is conducive to a higher level of gender inequality. Of course, private universities' higher tuition might also contribute to the lower percentage of female students compared with national universities. The tuition difference, however, cannot account for the sudden decline in the percentage of female students among national university students since 1978. This decline appears to have resulted from the shift to the two-stage system in 1979. Why did the female percentage begin to decline the year *before* the new system was implemented? Aggregate statistics published by the Japanese government indicate that the number of female applicants for national universities was unusually small in 1978.[25] Perhaps a particularly large number of women veered away from university exams that year because the consequences of failing them seemed worse; taking the exams again in the next year required adaptation to a completely unknown exam system. Not only were the female shares among national university students lower in 1979 to 1980 than previous years, they also were akin to those among private university students. That is to say, when public universities shifted from a joint to a separate entrance exam system, they became more similar to private universities in their students' gender composition. The removal of a joint exam system was apparently a setback to the steady growth of the female share of national university students in previous years.

For Japanese students who are willing and have the financial resources to attend private universities, their exam options are certainly not as limited as those aiming at only national universities. In theory, students can apply for nearly all private universities at once. In reality, however, individuals still need to choose strategically which private universities' entrance exams they will take to best utilize their energy and resources (e.g., for application fees), as well as to maximize their chances of success. Besides, private universities' entrance exam dates may still overlap. That is to say, even those aiming at private universities face trade-offs because it is possible to make the wrong decision, which will result in a less than optimal outcome. Therefore, the mismatching of universities to applicants is inevitable even among those aspiring for private universities. For women, miscalculation and mismatching mean they might be admitted to a private university that is only slightly more prestigious but much more expensive (with two extra years of tuition) than a junior college. Between a mediocre private university and a junior college, many Japanese parents are likely to prefer to send their daughters to the latter. In this sense, even the exam system for private universities in Japan constitutes an impediment for women's university attainment.

Taiwan's university entrance exam system is similar to the system adopted by Japan's public universities prior to 1979, but its application is more extensive. The Ministry of Education in Taiwan adopted a joint entrance exam policy for university admission in 1954. Unlike for high school entrance, for which several exams are used for schools of different districts, a uniform national entrance exam is held for all universities across Taiwan, regardless of whether the university is public or private. This national joint exam is held on the same dates each year to determine admission for all individuals who aspire to enter a university the coming fall. Applicants for science-related departments take tests on somewhat different subjects (e.g., physics, chemistry, biology) from those taken by applicants for liberal arts or social science fields (e.g., history, geography). Nevertheless, all departments within the broadly defined field (e.g., natural science, nonnatural science) across universities rely on the same entrance exam for admissions. Applicants with higher examination scores are given higher priority to pick their most preferred among the departments with admission quotas that have not been met. Under this matching system, individual departments have little autonomy in selecting students, other than encouraging applicants to rank the department higher in their preferences (e.g., by providing financial incentives). Those less preferred by students naturally require a lower minimum score for entrance. The minimum entrance exam scores required for admission generally make up the rankings among all departments in the broad field across universities. Over the years, the rankings of Taiwan's departments have varied fairly little, suggesting a high level of homogeneity among university applicants' preferences for departments.

Within the general design just described, Taiwan's university entrance exam policies have undergone a few revisions. For example, since 2002 individual departments have gained some autonomy in selecting students by choosing which subject tests they will take into account for admission. As a result, students today can choose to take just the subject tests required by the departments they wish to attend. Despite this, the matching of applicants to departments is still, and has always been, based on the applicants' scores of the tests held jointly by all universities. That is to say, no modifications of Taiwan's university admission policies have altered the fact that students essentially have only one university entrance exam to take each year.

Because there is merely one uniform exam, and thus one application fee, for all universities in Taiwan, nearly all individuals upon high school graduation could be persuaded to "give it a try." In fact, most academic high schools automatically register all their seniors for the university entrance exam. Under the joint exam system, as long as an individual's exam score reaches the percentile to be admitted to any university, he or she will be matched with a university program. Even though Taiwanese parents may prefer to educate their sons over their daughters, they are unlikely to deny their daughters' university entrance if admission is granted. This process of matching students to university programs therefore helps reduce the influences of gender-specific educational aspirations and the family's differential support for boys and girls.

In addition, under the single-exam system, Taiwanese applicants are more likely than their Japanese counterparts to be convinced that they have obtained admission to the best possible universities. For this reason, they are also more likely to accept the outcome of the contest. This difference is evidenced by the fact that the proportion of *rōnin* among each year's applicants is smaller in Taiwan than in Japan. To illustrate, in 2003, 16 percent of the university applicants in Taiwan had attended private preparatory schools for *rōnin* study, though as many as 23 percent of the applicants were not recent high school graduates (College Entrance Examination Center 2003, 2008). By contrast, about 30 percent of Japan's university applicants in the same year had taken the entrance exams in previous years (MEXT, Japan 2004). Because those undertaking *rōnin* study are predominately male in both societies, the more such individuals are among university applicants the less balanced the gender composition of such applicants. That Japan's exam system encourages *rōnin* study more frequently thus contributes to its smaller proportion of female university applicants than in Taiwan.

Not only is Japan's exam system conducive to a larger number of *rōnin* students, but those undertaking *rōnin* study tend to do so for different reasons in Japan than in Taiwan. Because Taiwan's university applicants are likely to consider the admission they receive as the best possible one, only those who fail to receive any university admission are likely to undertake *rōnin* study. In contrast, many of Japan's *rōnin* students could have been admitted to some university, but failed because they used the wrong exam strategies. Hence, the average academic ability of Japanese *rōnin* students should be higher than Taiwanese ones. That is to say, Japan's *rōnin* students are more likely than their Taiwanese counterparts to be a threat to the most competitive contenders in the race—that is, recent graduates from top-ranked high schools. This difference explains why those with *rōnin* experience seem to constitute a much smaller proportion of Taiwan's elite university students than Japan's. According to Thomas Rohlen (1983), 35 percent of students admitted to Tokyo University in 1980 had taken the entrance exam for the second time and 10 percent for the third time or more. Although I have no comparable data for Taiwan, Ming-Ching Luoh's (2002) study suggests that the majority of the students admitted to National Taiwan University are recent high school graduates.[26] Furthermore, the College Entrance Examination Center in Taiwan (2001) reported that the percentage admitted to four-year universities among recent high school (and vocational high school) graduates was 63 percent in 2001, but it was only 47 percent among those who had graduated in previous years (i.e., *rōnin*). Given their generally worse exam performance, *rōnin* students are unlikely to compete well in the race to Taiwan's elite universities.

The different extents to which *rōnin* experience is associated with elite university entry between Japan and Taiwan have important implications for women. As far as *rōnin* study is not essential to individuals' chances of entering highly ranked universities, parental preference for sponsoring sons' *rōnin* study over daughters' *rōnin* study would not harm women's opportunities of elite university education substantially. Therefore, despite high levels of intrafamily gender inequality in both societies, Taiwanese women's opportunities for university education, particularly elite university education, are more equal to men's compared with their Japanese counterparts.

SUMMARY AND CONCLUSION

The analysis and discussion presented in this chapter point to the need to explore more than broad East–West differences in educational and family systems. Subtle differences in educational systems can have important implications for gender inequality across societies. Japan's and Taiwan's educational systems both emphasize early success, which generally makes family support critical. Both sets of family norms prescribe a preference for investing in sons' education over daughters'. Nevertheless, while Japan's system does nothing to compensate for the social and family norms that hamper girls' educational aspirations, several of Taiwan's institutional arrangements and selection mechanisms at various educational levels help increase women's chances of attending four-year universities, especially prestigious ones. To be specific, first, Japan's colonial legacy of gender-segregated education at the upper secondary educational level contributes to Taiwanese girls having relatively equal access to elite high schools as boys. This access ensures girls' competitiveness in the long-distance race for university entry. Second, the Taiwanese state's effort to prepare technicians for economic development historically has channeled a considerable number of male students into the vocational track at the upper secondary level, resulting in relatively good odds of university entry for girls remaining in the academic track. Third, Taiwan's university entrance exam system makes applicants' own educational ambitions and strategic planning, as well as their family's sponsorship, much less important in determining university entry than it is in Japan. Related to the design of the university entrance exam system, *rōnin* study is more popular in Japan than in Taiwan because mismatches are more likely under Japan's exam system. The different designs of the exam systems also contribute to the fact that *rōnin* experience is more critically associated with elite university entry in Japan than in Taiwan. Thus, Japanese children's chances of attending elite universities are closely tied to whether their parents are willing to sponsor their *rōnin* study, and whether they are willing to undergo the hardship of *rōnin* study, whereas Taiwanese children's are less so. In other words, because of the importance of *rōnin* study in Japan, parents' son preference, as well as girls' generally lower educational aspirations, translates more easily into low female presence at elite universities than in Taiwan.

Overall, the institutional differences just discussed between Japan and Taiwan allow gender inequality at the family and society levels to manifest less in the process of educational attainment in Taiwan. One may still wonder: Could the differences in labor market practices between these two countries also affect women's relative opportunities for higher education? To elaborate, because of Japanese employers' preference for recruiting recent school graduates, managers' only way to distinguish job candidates has been based on their educational credentials. This reliance on educational credentials, along with a shortage of employer change opportunities, is thought to make elite university attendance extremely important for Japanese men (Rohlen 1983). Hence, it is arguable that university prestige is more closely associated with lifetime job prospects for men in Japan than in Taiwan. This difference could explain why Japanese men are more likely than Taiwanese men to undertake *rōnin* study even when they are able to attend some university, resulting in Japanese women's lower chances of being admitted to elite universities. In this sense, Japan's particular employment practices can be thought to have accounted for women's relatively small presence at elite universities during the past several decades.

In addition, one may suspect that rather than the design of the educational system, Taiwanese women's comparatively great economic opportunities have encouraged girls to have high aspirations for educational achievement. Such aspirations can be argued to cause Taiwan's relatively high level of gender equality in tertiary education. In other words, Taiwan's relatively large female share among elite university students can be thought to have resulted from women's improving employment opportunities during the past several decades.

I certainly do not deny that the differing labor market conditions may have somewhat contributed to the smaller gender gap in higher education in Taiwan than in Japan. After all, much of this book is about precisely how national labor market institutions shape gender stratification. I nevertheless call attention to the specific arrangements of educational institutions and entrance exam systems, since their effects on women's educational opportunities have been generally overlooked in previous research. The evidence presented in this chapter appears to support the view that these structural arrangements account for a substantial part of the discrepancy in women's relative opportunities to receive a four-year university education, especially an elite university education, between the two countries. More specifically, first, I have shown that Japanese national universities' shift from a uniform exam system to a university-specific exam system led to a decline in women's presence at such universities. This association corroborates the importance of university entrance exam policies. Second, Taiwanese women had relatively equal access to National Taiwan University as early as the 1960s, when the majority of working women held farm or factory jobs in that country. That is to say, women achieved relatively equal access to elite universities even before they had opportunities to utilize such education in Taiwan's labor market. Thus, women's economic roles alone cannot fully explain Taiwanese women's relatively greater chance of attending elite universities. Rather, Taiwan's educational system, including its gender-segregated elite high schools and entrance exam policies, has played a crucial part in shaping gender equality in higher education.

## CHAPTER EIGHT

# Conclusion

I began this book with a puzzle concerning the transformation of women's working lives. During the second half of the twentieth century, Japan and Taiwan experienced markedly different levels of improvement in women's employment opportunities. As previous chapters have shown, Taiwanese women who started their employment careers soon after World War II were not much different from their Japanese counterparts. They participated in the labor force for a short period of time before marriage, with the expectation of leaving their jobs for childbearing and child rearing. Many of them held jobs requiring relatively few skills in factories or farms. Although some of these women did return to the labor market after their children grew up, their career processes were by no means similar to men's. Forty years later, the situation has changed considerably. Despite having less education, somewhat more conservative gender attitudes, and arguably less legal support for their rights than Japanese women, Taiwanese women are observed to have higher earnings and occupational status relative to men. So what happened?

The answer to this question is rather complex. I have argued that because of the particular economic structures in which they were embedded, business organizations responded differently to market shifts that generated a great demand for labor in Japan and Taiwan. The organizational reactions to these shifts played a key role in shaping the workplace dynamics that affect how women assess the feasibility of combining their job and family responsibilities. At the microlevel, it is women's perceptions of the compatibility between work and family that directly impact their employment trajectories over their life course. These individual trajectories, taken together, account for the divergence in gender stratification between Japan and Taiwan.

To be specific, Japan's dualist economic structure, with large enterprises dominating the market, was conducive to the genesis of the permanent employment system as its economy faced a rapidly increasing demand for labor during the early twentieth century. In the decades after World War II, by favoring large enterprises and capital-intensive industries, Japan's industrial strategies further institutionalized the permanent employment system. Such strategies also led to small increases in labor demand. With a labor surplus, Japanese employers could compensate for the inflexibility of the permanent employment system by normalizing excessive job demands for primary workers, while compelling timely exits of secondary, often female, workers. Consequently, women who attempt to keep their jobs beyond marriage must deal with either hostile workplaces or harsh working conditions. Because their job exits enable firms to save more in labor costs under that employment system, Japanese women holding white-collar jobs and working in large firms have been particularly likely to be pressured out of the labor force upon marriage or childbirth. As single women have increasingly entered white-collar occupations and taken jobs in large firms, the overall rate of postmarital job exits has remained high in Japan. Thus, despite increases in Japanese women's education and career aspirations (Ojima 2001; Schoppa 2006), the changes in their employment continuity and long-term occupational attainment have stalled.

By contrast, in part as a result of the state's political concerns, firms in Taiwan followed somewhat different industrial strategies. The emphasis on exports from light industries, in particular, led to frequent labor shortages and the dominance of small- to medium-size business establishments in the economy. Such organizational structures restricted employers' solutions to labor shortages. Specifically, a lifetime employment system like Japan's requires a large investment in training workers, as well as hierarchical wage and promotion structures within organizations. In the small-firm-based Taiwanese economy, however, few employers could afford much in training costs, and even fewer could promise workers upward mobility over the long run. Therefore, implementing a lifetime employment system was far from feasible in Taiwan. Instead, Taiwanese employers' response to the rising labor demand was to expand their labor pool by incorporating married women into the workplace. This attempt, along with the often informal work climates of small firms, contributed to the development of workplace practices that generally facilitate women's ability to combine work and family.

In Taiwanese workplaces where highly qualified labor is preferred, the incentive to integrate married women has been even greater, because there has been a shortage of highly qualified male labor. That women with higher income potential have been more likely to work continuously over their life course essentially accounts for Taiwan's shrinking gender gaps in employment trajectories and economic status. As economic development and educational expansion improve single women's occupational attainment, the overall probability that Taiwanese women will have continuous employment careers—like men's—also increases. Given this, explaining Taiwan's short-age of highly educated men is critical to this study. As demonstrated in Chapter 7, this shortage results from Taiwan's restricted access to receiving a university education, as well as from the high level of gender equality among university students, especially those in elite universities. Both features can be linked to the state's endeavor to prepare more midlevel technicians than highly educated citizens for the developing economy, which had been domi-nated by low-skilled industries through the early 1990s. Specifically, until re-cently, the Taiwanese system channeled most male students into vocational schools, thereby reducing the competition for university admission faced by girls remaining in the academic track. Moreover, despite a widespread pref-erence for educating sons over daughters among Taiwanese parents, girls are gaining ground at the high school level as a result of the affirmative action-like admission policy designed to preserve gender segregation among elite public high schools—a legacy of Japan's colonial education. The use of a single, uniform exam for university entrance across the nation also helps minimize the impacts of parental gender preferences and students' own edu-cational aspirations, which are often shaped by the society's predominant gender ideology. Taiwan's exam system thus helps facilitate a high level of gender equality in the enrollment of elite universities.

Although Japan's educational system shares many features with Tai-wan's, it does not have similar admission policies that ensure girls' seats in elite high schools. More important, unlike in Taiwan, the system in Ja-pan allows parental preferences for investing in sons' schooling to be easily translated into gender inequality in education. To begin, Japan's schooling system provides far fewer opportunities for nonuniversity technical train-ing, making a university education nearly the only "appropriate" pursuit for boys. This notion, along with the great importance for Japanese men to obtain good first jobs for which high educational credentials are necessary, leads boys with any possibility of succeeding to put themselves through "ex-amination hell," competing intensely for limited spots at universities (par-ticularly elite universities).

The strong expectations for men, but not women, to attend universities, however, are not the only reason for Japanese women's inferior educational attainment. By allowing students to take entrance exams at only two national universities each year, Japan's two-stage entrance exam system amplifies the importance of family sponsorship and strategic planning. Those unlikely to be sponsored by their families for an additional year of exam preparation—namely, women—can hardly afford any risk when deciding to which schools to apply. For this reason, Japan's top-ranked public universities have always been extremely male dominant. Furthermore, for Japanese students, whether they will be admitted to a highly regarded university depends not only on their academic ability but also on their exam strategies. Given this, they are quite likely to find the outcomes of their university applications unjust and are willing to try again the following year. This sentiment, together with a belief in the enormous impact of attending a highly prestigious university on men's careers, contributes to the exceptional popularity of *rōnin* study in Japan.[1] This popularity makes it difficult for those without *rōnin* experience to be competitive. Rarely receiving family support for *rōnin* study, women are bound to be seriously disadvantaged in this system.

Because of the educational system and labor market conditions just summarized, Taiwanese women with more education are lured to stay in the labor force by not only better paying jobs, but also by a greater leverage for negotiating family-friendlier job conditions. Conversely, Japanese women with more education and higher income potential are less likely to combine employment and motherhood, since their qualifications only increase management's incentive to pressure them to quit. As noted earlier, these different patterns of labor force exits among women are key to understanding the differing paces of change in gender inequality between Japan and Taiwan. Equally noteworthy is that these exit patterns also account for changes in family dynamics, leading to further divergence in women's employment behaviors between the two countries. To be specific, the greater tendency for Taiwanese women with better paying jobs to remain in the labor force after marriage resulted in greater family consumption and higher living standards, as middle- and upper middle-class families became wealthier by having dual earners. This change virtually eroded the possibility for Taiwanese households to maintain a middle-class standard of living with only the husband's wage. Consequently, among the current generation of Taiwanese women, even those who wish not to spend their married lives in the workplace must do so for their family's sake. In contrast, with well-educated Japanese women being more frequently pushed out of the labor force for motherhood, the social expectations of mothers' involvement in child development increased over time. Mothers—not parents in general—became regarded as not only the best caregivers, but also the most critical educators of their children. This elevated emphasis on mothers' importance increased the conflict between women's family and work roles, making combining employment and motherhood less feasible for Japan's current generation of women.

In this book I pay great attention to women's decisions to leave the labor force upon marriage and childbirth because these decisions essentially determine the extent of the similarity between men's and women's employment careers. When more women work continuously in the economy, their employment careers are likely to converge with men's in terms of not only their trajectories, but also the economic returns to their labor. The comparison of Japan and Taiwan reveals that the less similar women's and men's employment trajectories, the more severe the penalties for women who work discontinuously. A greater gender disparity in continuous employment strengthens employers' reluctance to accept married women as suitable workers, which in turn reduces women's likelihood of returning to jobs comparable with their premarital ones after interruptions. As I have shown in Chapters 2 and 6, the downward mobility Japanese women generally suffer after work interruptions—by taking lower status, worse paid, and often contingent jobs—largely explains the high level of economic inequality between men and women in that country. Japan's lifetime employment system also exacerbated the situation for women by preferentially rewarding those working continuously within the same firm, not to mention the incentive it created to keep female reentrants in jobs exempt from the extensive benefits entitled to permanent employees. In comparison, as the rate of continuous employment increased among Taiwanese women, employers began to view married women as part of the usual labor force, just like men and single women are. This change makes Taiwan's labor market more forgiving toward married women who attempt to resume employment after taking time off.

Thus, of the two countries, the one that impairs women's continuous employment more also penalizes them more for working discontinuously. Seemingly paradoxical, this combination is hardly coincidental, however. Precisely because women's work and family roles are made incompatible, women who give any signal of favoring their family roles are deemed incapable of fulfilling worker obligations. Women therefore pay a higher price for interrupting their careers during childbearing years in labor markets where combining job and family responsibilities are more difficult. It is through paying a higher cost for every critical decision they make over their lives that Japanese women suffer from a wider gender economic gap than Taiwanese women.

FURTHER DEVELOPMENT IN THE NEW CENTURY

The empirical evidence reported for Japan and Taiwan in previous chapters is largely based on survey data collected through the mid 1990s. Scholars and observers of East Asia, however, have called attention to social and economic changes in the region, especially in Japan, since the 1990s (e.g., Ahmadjian and Robbins 2005; Bongaarts 2001; Mason 2001a, b; Raymo and Iwasawa 2005; Rindfuss, Choe, Bumpass, and Tsuya 2004). Among the changes often noted are rapid declines in marriage and birth rates in recent years, as well as major restructuring in response to macroeconomic shifts of the 1990s. These changes have the potential to reshape women's employment opportunities by altering either their family processes or long-term career prospects. In the case of Japan, the state has also responded to recent demographic and economic challenges by implementing new policies, of which a few are directly associated with women's economic opportunities. Given all this, one naturally wonders the extent to which the employment trajectories I have documented for Japanese and Taiwanese women have remained since the mid 1990s. Also in question is whether we can expect a further divergence or a future convergence in women's working lives between the two countries. With recent survey data I address these questions in the following section.

### New Crises; Emerging Opportunities?

For Japan, the decade since the mid 1990s has featured major crises. On the one hand, the economic recession that originated with the burst of the "bubble" in 1989 continued. With its real growth averaging just 1.3 percent per year between 1990 and 2005, Japan underwent the longest and most severe economic stagnation since World War II. This decade and a half of recession exerted enormous pressure on the permanent employment system, the existence of which has long failed to be justified by the market rationale. Although researchers and commentators still debate about the extent to which the Japanese employment system has actually transformed, it is clear that workers' expectations of lifetime employment and seniority-based promotions had been severely dampened by the start of the new century (Ahmadjian and Robbins 2005; Kato 2001; Kelly and White 2006; Lincoln and Nakata 1997; Schoppa 2006; Thelen and Kume 1999).

On the other hand, the demographic crisis Japan has been facing, with its population aging rapidly, has become more conspicuous since the 1990s, due to a persistent decline in the birthrate. As Japan's fertility continues to be near the lowest among industrialized countries, politicians and observers alike cast serious doubts that its population structure can sustain further economic development, much less ensure the elderly's future welfare. Because the trend toward less and later marriage has been a key contributor to this fertility decline, the popular discourse generally considers the demographic crisis as resulting from women opting out of marriage. Therefore, one prevalent view regarding the remedy for the crisis is that there should be more support for child rearing, and that the women's conflict between work and family should be reduced. Based on this view, revisions of the EEOA were implemented in 1999, making it mandatory—rather than recommended, as in the old version—for employers to treat women and men equally in recruitment, assignment, and promotion (Yamakawa 2001). In addition, the Basic Law for a Gender-Equal Society, which aims to enable men's and women's participation in both family activities and workplaces as equal partners, was enacted in 1999. To facilitate the agenda set in this law, the Japanese government also established the Gender Equality Bureau under the Cabinet Office in 2001 (Melkas and Anker 2003; Osawa 2005).

It is not difficult to see the potential impact of the changes just described on women's employment. Because Japan's lifetime employment system provided an incentive for employers to discourage women's continuous work, the dismantlement of this system can be argued to benefit female workers. Similarly, the enactment of laws that facilitate gender equality in the workplace and enhance childcare support for families might increase the compatibility between employment and motherhood. If combining job and family responsibilities becomes easier, or the workplace becomes less hostile, Japanese women with higher status and better paying jobs should become more likely to remain in the labor market after marriage and childbirth. That is to say, we would see changes in Japanese women's job exit dynamics since the mid 1990s. To examine this possibility, I perform a series of multinomial regression analyses of how marriage is associated with women's current type of employment (including nonemployment), using the 2003 data from the Japan General Social Survey (JGSS).[2] Because the JGSS data do not include full information about respondents' work histories, it is not possible to tell exactly which groups of working women are more frequently leaving the labor force upon marriage. Nevertheless, a comparison of labor market positions between single and married women allows me to estimate which types of positions are more compatible with married women's family lives.

Figure 8.1 presents partial results from the series of multinomial regression analyses, with the black bars representing the effects of marriage on Japanese women's odds of having a given type of job rather than another (e.g., office vs. factory jobs; full-time vs. part-time jobs). In addition to marital status, the regression models also include years of schooling, age, presence of a preschool child, and residence in urban areas as independent variables.[3] Starting with the first black bar on the left in Figure 8.1, married Japanese women are about half as likely as single ones to be in office rather than factory jobs. At the same time, they are far more likely to be employed by small- or medium-size firms, rather than large-scale ones, compared with those who have never married. Furthermore, married women are about three times as likely as single women to be in part-time or temporary jobs rather than full-time regular jobs.[4] These results are highly consistent with the dynamics I have shown in previous chapters with data through the mid 1990s. The significant negative associations between marriage and office jobs, as well as marriage and large-firm employment, suggest that single women holding white-collar occupations or working in large-scale enterprises are still more likely to leave their jobs upon marriage or pregnancy than those with other work. At the same time, the particularly strong tendency for married women to hold part-time or temporary jobs is consistent with the results

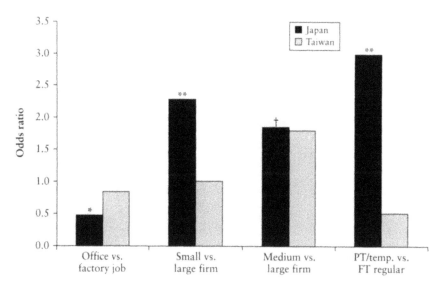

*Figure 8.1.*    Likelihood of labor market positions of married versus single women, Japan and Taiwan.

SOURCE: Japan, 2003 JGSS; Taiwan, 2002 TSC, part I.

*Note:* "Single women" refers to women who have never been married. PT, part-time work; FT, full-time employment. Each bar indicates the ratio of married women's odds of holding a specified type of job, rather than the other, to the odds of the same job situation for single women. The odds ratios are based on the multinomial regression results shown in Appendix B, Tables B.8 through B.10. An odds ratio equal to one indicates there is no difference between married and single women in the likelihood of being in one labor market position rather than the other.

†$p < .10$, *$p < .05$, **$p < .01$.

presented in Chapter 6, which indicate that many of them are pushed into such jobs when they resume employment after their children grow up.

Because the JGSS sample includes many older respondents who are likely to have been through marriage and childbirth before the 1990s, an analysis based on the full sample may not be the best way to identify changes among recent cohorts of women.[5] For this reason, from the sample I selected women who had ever been married and had preschool children to represent those who experienced marriage and childbirth relatively recently. For simplicity, I refer to such women as *recent mothers* hereafter. I compare their current occupations with those of single women. Assuming that women's broad occupational categories hardly change from before marriage to the time they have young children, the differences in occupational distributions between single women and recent mothers would have to be related to those exiting the labor force around the time of marriage and childbirth. Thus, a comparison of these two groups tells us which types of occupations tend to

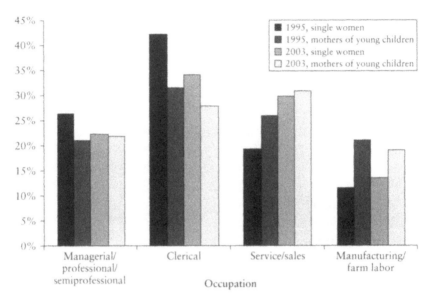

*Figure 8.2.* Comparisons of Japanese women's occupational distributions.

SOURCE: 1995 SSM, parts A and B, and 2003 JGSS.

*Note:* The JGSS sample is weighted.

be associated with more postmarital exits. To reveal whether there has been any change over time, I also compare the occupational distributions of the same two groups of women in the sample of the 1995 SSM.[6]

Figure 8.2 shows the occupational distributions among single women and recent mothers in both 1995 and 2003 for Japan.[7] During both years, the proportion holding manufacturing jobs among recent mothers was higher than that among single women. Conversely, the proportion of single women in clerical occupations was higher than that of recent mothers. These findings once again suggest that women with manufacturing jobs are more likely than those with clerical jobs to continue working upon marriage and childbirth.

But have Japanese women's job exit dynamics changed in any way between 1995 and 2003? Looking at the differences between single women and recent mothers in their percentages in upper white-collar (i.e., managerial, professional, and semiprofessional) and clerical occupations, one may argue that the drop in the proportion of women holding white-collar jobs with childbirth decreased from 1995 to 2003. Likewise, Figure 8.2 suggests a smaller increase in the proportion of women in manufacturing occupations after childbearing in 2003 compared with 1995. All this seems to imply that the probability that women with white-collar jobs will remain in the labor force upon childbearing has increased slightly in recent years, even though they still exit their jobs at a higher rate than their blue-collar counterparts.

When shifting attention to the change in single women's occupations from 1995 to 2003, I nevertheless derive the conclusion that the view just described may be overly optimistic. Single women's jobs have become worse in Japan, judging from their occupational status. Compared with 1995, smaller proportions of them were in upper white-collar and clerical occupations in 2003. At the same time, larger proportions of single women held manufacturing, service, and sales jobs, which are likely to be paid by piece rates and are exempt from firms' promotion or benefit schemes. That is to say, as a result of Japan's economic stagnation since the 1990s, even single women now face difficulties obtaining jobs that promise stability and wage increases (at least until they enter motherhood). For this reason, those who are able to find such jobs appear to be more likely to hold onto them than before. Despite this, the deterioration of single women's occupations has, on the whole, depressed women's employment opportunities. When comparing recent mothers' occupational distributions in 1995 and 2003, it is clear that there is virtually no improvement in married women's occupational attainment. The number of married women in Japan's white-collar workplaces is still small, making it difficult for employers to recognize them as suitable candidates for the more promising, long-term jobs.

Other recent statistics also corroborate that for Japan, the decade since the mid 1990s in many ways was a continuation of the previous ones, as far as married women's employment is concerned. Based on a national survey conducted among women in their thirties and forties in 2006, Japan's Gender Equality Bureau (2007) reported that about three fifths of the mothers in the sample interrupted their employment careers. Even among married women without children, almost half left the labor force around the time of marriage. These statistics appear to be quite similar to what I have shown with the SSM data from 1995 (e.g., see Figure 2.2), if not indicating an even stronger propensity for work interruptions among women.

In contrast, despite suffering occasionally from regional and global economic recessions, the Taiwanese economy, on average, grew 4.4 percent annually from 1996 to 2005. This relative stability, however, does not necessarily indicate a lack of other changes that may have reshaped women's economic opportunities. First, in response to the economy's maturing, the state shifted its strategy to promoting more skill- and capital-intensive industries (rather than labor-intensive ones) in the 1990s (Hsu and Chiang 2001). The growing dominance of high-technology-based enterprises in Taiwan's economy, along with the massive movement of factories to China by labor-intensive industries, has slowed down the increase in aggregate labor demand. The second major transformation since the 1990s was Taiwan's continuation of democratization. This political process has subjected the government to unprecedented pressure to address various social demands, including one for expanding opportunities for higher education. This demand, in conjunction with the government's plans for economic upgrading, led to a rapid increase in four-year universities and colleges. From 1995 to 2000, for example, not only did the number of four-year universities and colleges more than double, but the number of students enrolled in such institutions also rose by 80 percent. In 1999, Taiwan's number of university students surpassed that enrolled in junior colleges for the first time since 1969 (Wang 2003).

Looking back at what helped Taiwanese women economically, one might expect the changes just described to be detrimental to them. To begin, the barely growing labor demand Taiwan has experienced in recent years may reduce employers' incentive to hire and retain married women. To make matters worse, the recent expansion of university enrollment has greatly enhanced the supply of highly educated men. Without a shortage of male labor, managers may be less willing to accommodate women's family responsibilities. In addition, working conditions in Taiwan might be expected to become harsher and less compatible with women's family lives as its economy transforms. With the rise of larger and more promising enterprises (mostly in the high-technology sector), there is now more differentiation in the quality of jobs in the Taiwanese labor market. The competition for the "good jobs" allows managers that offer such jobs to demand longer working hours from workers. Corroborating this argument, Taiwan's mass media frequently report the extremely long hours that employees in prestigious and well-paying large enterprises have to spend at work. It is therefore possible that Taiwanese women are becoming more likely to find their job conditions incompatible with their family responsibilities. Plus, the demand for Taiwanese women's time at home may be increasing as their husbands work more hours. If so, we might observe a reversal of Taiwan's persistent increase in women's continuous employment.

Does the empirical evidence support these speculations, though? I performed the same multinomial regression analyses of women's current labor market positions, as those reported earlier for Japan, using data from the TSC conducted in late 2002. I present partial results from these models (i.e., the gray bars) alongside those for Japan in Figure 8.1, and show the full regression coefficients in Appendix B, Tables B.8 through B.10.[8] According Figure 8.1, married Taiwanese women are not significantly different from single ones in their associations with certain occupations, firm size, or types of employment. That is to say, unlike women in Japan, Taiwanese women appear no more likely to exit from office jobs than factory jobs, or from jobs in larger firms, upon marriage. They also seem to be less likely to hold part-time or temporary jobs than single women, even though the effect is not statistically significant.

To interpret the results just described, it is important to keep in mind that job prospects generally improve for every new cohort of Taiwanese women. If no woman ever left her job, single women, who are usually from a newer cohort, would be more likely than married ones to be in white-collar than blue-collar occupations, as well as larger and more established firms. The lack of differences in occupation and firm size between single and married women, as shown in Figure 8.1, thus suggests that among the married ones, those with worse jobs might have been "weeded out" upon marriage or childbirth. To provide further evidence, Figure 8.3 shows, by their first occupation, the percentage of working-age, ever-married women currently in the labor force, based on the TSC data from late 2002.[9] Almost 90 percent of those who started their careers in professional or managerial occupations held current jobs, despite having married. The percentage is lower for those who started with semiprofessional occupations, followed by clerical, service and sales, and manufacturing occupations, in that order. Although we do not know for sure, the married women in the labor force were highly likely to have worked continuously since before they married.

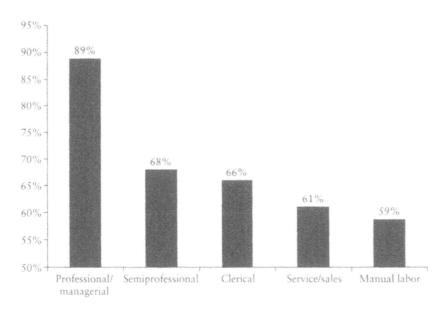

*Figure 8.3.*    Percentage of ever-married, working-age Taiwanese women in the labor force by their first occupation.

SOURCE: 2002 TSC, part I.

*Note:* The percentages are calculated among female respondents who were no older than 55 years of age and had been married by the survey time. The sample is weighted.

Thus, the pattern shown in Figure 8.3 suggests that Taiwanese women in higher status occupations are more likely to continue their jobs after marriage (and probably childbirth), just like those from previous generations. This pattern remains when I look at only those who entered marriage and motherhood relatively recently.[10]

Using the information on the time respondents spent searching for their first jobs since school completion in the 2002 TSC, I further investigate whether the recent increase in the supply of university-educated men has affected women's employment opportunities. Interestingly, it took male university graduates significantly longer (by three months) to locate their first jobs than their female counterparts. Also, not only did younger women tend to spend less time looking for their first jobs, but university-educated women younger than age 30, whose first job search would have occurred after the educational expansion of the 1990s, found their first jobs particularly promptly. Almost two thirds of them did so within a month. To the extent that the time expended in the job search process indicates the difficulties a particular demographic group faces in the labor market, there is no evidence that women, particularly highly educated women, have become less desirable as workers since the mid 1990s.

The results revealed by the data from late 2002, therefore, suggest that the period since the mid 1990s is merely a continuation of the previous decades for women's employment in Taiwan, just like it is in Japan. Taiwanese women's employment decisions still largely depend on their own income potential: Those who are able to obtain better paying and more promising jobs generally are more likely to stay in the labor market after marriage and childbirth. So long as single women continue to obtain relatively promising jobs (as they seem to be doing), the overall likelihood for women to interrupt their employment careers should continue decreasing in Taiwan.

### Explaining the Continuation After the Mid 1990s

The empirical evidence suggests that despite all their social and economic transformations, Japan and Taiwan have continued to diverge in women's employment trajectories since the mid 1990s. This naturally raises the question of why there has not been more change in either country. How can we explain the lack of effect of the dismantlement of Japan's permanent employment system on women's job opportunities, given that this system played such an important role in obstructing these opportunities? Also, doesn't the persistent increase in Taiwanese women's continuous employment challenge the importance of the shortage of comparably qualified male labor for women's job opportunities?

One clear lesson we have learned from comparing the historical trajectories of Japan and Taiwan is that workplaces tend to respond to workers' family roles when the lack of female labor poses a threat to the profits of enterprises and their owners. Such a threat is almost the only reason why women's working conditions improve in societies where there is little cultural or legal support for gender equality, as in the cases of Japan and Taiwan. Given this, it is understandable why Japan's economic restructuring of the 1990s has failed to affect women's employment patterns. The economic stagnation from 1990 to 2005 severely decreased the growth of jobs in Japan. Furthermore, few new jobs created during this period were regular full-time ones, as contingent employment contracts helped management reduce labor costs and maintain personnel flexibility, particularly in a time of recession. Figure 8.4 shows changes in the numbers of male and female employees in full-time regular (standard) or part-time temporary (nonstandard) positions from 1996 to 2007 in Japan. Women evidently experienced negative job growth during these years, regardless of whether they were willing to accept temporary, irregular positions. Even after 2005, when the Japanese economy was on its way to recovery, women gained hardly any standard job opportunities. Japanese men also suffered substantially from 1996 to 2006, as the

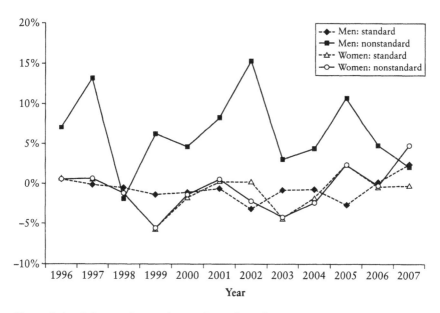

*Figure 8.4.*   Job growth rates by gender and employment status in Japan, 1996 to 2007.

S O U R C E : Statistics Bureau, Ministry of Internal Affairs and Communications, Japan, Labour Force Survey, various years (www.stat.go.jp/data/roudou/2.htm).

*Note:* The job growth rate is calculated as the percent increase or decrease in the number of employees of a given category from the previous year, using numbers reported for February of each year. Self-employed jobs are excluded from the calculation.

number of them holding standard jobs decreased steadily. During this time, nonstandard jobs appear to have been the only new jobs available for men. Taken together, these trends indicate that at no point since the mid 1990s did Japanese employers actually "need" to utilize women in the workplace. In this sense, the force that drives women's workplaces to change has been absent.

In addition, women's working conditions in postpermanent employment Japan are not entirely different from before. The dichotomous definitions of work—permanent versus temporary—originally associated with the permanent employment system linger and perhaps strengthen with the increase of contingent employment contracts. Since the 1990s, the number of agencies in Japan that dispatch workers to firms requesting short-term personnel support has increased rapidly. This increase partly results from the revisions of the Worker Dispatch Law enacted in 1999 and 2004, which allow managers to use temporary, dispatched workers for a wider range of jobs and for as long as three consecutive years. As described in Chapter 6, temporary employees are generally exempt from union protection, promotions, wage increases, and fringe benefits, not to mention job stability. By raising social consciousness about the differences between regular and irregular jobs, the growing prevalence of contingent employment arrangements helps preserve a dichotomous view about work in the absence of the promise of lifetime employment. Fearing the alternative, regular Japanese employees continue to devote enormous time and energy to work, at the expense of their family time, so that they are seen as worthy of such "good jobs."[11] Consequently, the working conditions for women who are fortunate enough to find regular full-time jobs remain highly incompatible with their family roles. As for women who begin their careers with temporary jobs, a group whose number is on the rise during the past decade (Genda and Kurosawa 2001; Kelly and White 2006), working continuously may not even be an option. Besides, as I discussed in Chapter 6, the very nature of nonstandard employment in Japan makes it hardly worthwhile for women to remain in jobs of this type after childbirth.

If the Japanese economy failed to instigate changes in women's working conditions, what about the laws the state has promulgated since the late 1990s? The primary reason for the small effect of Japan's laws aiming at enhancing gender equality is that they are relatively weak on enforcement, especially when such enforcement may conflict with the interests of enterprises. One issue to keep in mind is that the Japanese government has been facing economic and demographic crises simultaneously, with the economic problems being more pressing. It would be against the state's interest to promote gender equality at the expense of business profits. Thus, even the revised EEOA only halfheartedly deals with discriminatory treatment against women within firms, since such treatment helps keep labor costs low. For the same reason, employers who fail to comply with this law are subject to almost no sanctions other than having their names publicized (Gelb 2000).

Likewise, the implementation of the Basic Law for a Gender-Equal Society is mostly limited to areas that do not impact business operations. For example, as I observed during my field trips to Tokyo and Kansai metropolitan areas in late 2002, much of government funding went to new facilities that offer counseling, social activities, and other support for mothers who are full-time caregivers. Older government agencies, such as public job search offices, also added temporary childcare facilities for the convenience of mothers seeking ways to reenter the labor force. Women who are contemplating the decision to leave the labor force upon pregnancy, however, are unlikely to appreciate the enforcement of the law because it barely reaches the workplace. In a meeting with government officials in charge of gender equality issues, I asked what they have done regarding the difficulties women face in the workplace. With a tone of embarrassment, one official answered: "Not much. We look for companies that provide family-friendly work environments and publicize their names. We recommend that other companies learn from such examples. That's about it."

As I have shown in this book, what compels women to exit their jobs upon marriage or pregnancy is often their perception of the incompatibility between work and family based on their actual workplace dynamics or job conditions. Relying on legal actions per se to transform workplaces is never easy, because workplace dynamics that create conflict with women's family obligations are often too subtle for a law to remedy. In the case of Japan, the likelihood that laws will shake up the workplace seems particularly slim because the relevant laws were formulated and implemented in a way that was not meant to reshape women's working conditions. It is therefore not surprising that Japanese women's employment trajectories are virtually unchanged, despite legal improvements since the late 1990s.

In the previous discussion, I emphasized the importance of market conditions that favor (or disfavor) the use of female labor for understanding women's postmarital employment. Does this same rationale explain the continuation of the increase in women's postmarital employment in Taiwan? The short answer is yes, at least in part. That is to say, the persistent increase in Taiwanese women's labor force participation after marriage has to do with the absence of dramatic changes in the labor demand for women since the mid 1990s. It is certainly true that Taiwan's transition to a more skill- and service-oriented economy has led to fewer new jobs being generated each year. Nevertheless, the period since the mid 1990s is featured by slower growth of not only labor demand, but also labor supply. The changing labor supply to some extent offsets the impact of Taiwan's economic transformation on women. The first factor contributing to the lessening growth of the labor supply is the rapid expansion of higher education. Newly established colleges and graduate schools have absorbed a substantial proportion of the youth who would otherwise be in the labor market. Second, declining drastically since the 1950s, Taiwan's fertility has fallen below the replacement level since 1985 (DGBAS 2007:27). As a result of this trend, Taiwan has become the country with the second-lowest level of population growth across East and Southeast Asia, next only to Japan (Feeney and Mason 2001). The attenuation of population growth has ensured a small increase in labor supply during recent years.

In addition to the limited influence of Taiwan's changing labor demand, the increase of high-technology-based, capital-intensive firms during the past decade also has relatively small effects on its labor force as a whole. Such firms, despite their increasing visibility, actually employ a very small proportion of Taiwan's labor force. In 2006, for example, only 5.4 percent of workers were hired by companies with more than 500 employees, a category that includes most of Taiwan's high-technology firms. That percentage was 3.7 a decade ago (DGBAS 2006). Although the growth rate of enterprises of this scale is substantial, relatively few Taiwanese workers are affected by their employment practices, regardless of how family irresponsive these practices may be. Meanwhile, the Taiwanese economy continues to be dominated by small firms. As of 2001, the average number of employees among Taiwanese enterprises was only seven (DGBAS 2001a). Thus, Taiwanese workplace atmospheres remain relatively informal and to the workers' advantage, in the sense that they can negotiate some scheduling flexibility, as well as other family-responsive working conditions.

Aside from the absence of major structural changes in the labor market, a few social transformations that were set in motion during the previous decades have played important roles in persistently pushing for women's continuous employment since the mid 1990s. First, as demonstrated earlier in this book, the convergence in men's and women's employment trajectories over time has raised not only employers' acceptance of married women as effective workers, but also overall social support for women's, particularly mothers', employment in Taiwan. Once married women's employment increases to the extent that it is taken for granted, the reversal of this trend would require extreme exogenous shocks that lead women to ignore their own income potential and employers to overlook the benefit of having an additional source of labor supply (e.g., lower wages to workers).

Second, one major consequence of Taiwanese women's changing employment behaviors is the increase in the average family living standard. As shown in Chapter 5, having a working wife has become the key to maintaining a middle-class lifestyle for Taiwanese families. This is conducive to the emergence of social norms in which married women's participation in the labor force is not only their right, but also their obligation to the family. Statistical results from the ISSP in 2002 confirm this sense of obligation in Taiwan. Among the respondents, 87.7 percent of women and 72.2 percent of men reported to agree that both husband and wife *should* contribute to household income. Therefore, with the exception of those marrying the very wealthy, women of recent generations are strongly expected to participate in the labor force despite childbearing and child rearing. Those who do not comply with this expectation are considered not only wasteful of their human capital, but also selfish in the sense that they are unwilling to work for their family's well-being.

To summarize, while the transformation in Taiwanese women's economic lives gains momentum through the associated alterations in social dynamics, the institutional arrangements that deterred Japan's change evolve in a way that offers no challenge to the status quo. If the past informs the future, then Taiwan's chance of closing the gender economic gap will continue to exceed Japan's. That being said, Western media and observers have been speculating for some time that Japan's shrinking work-age population may serve as one extreme force that will shatter its current system of gender stratification.[12] Although the everlasting economic stagnation has masked the problem of a decreasing labor supply, Japanese management is thought to have to accommodate women in the workplace, because the extremely low birthrate will eventually cause a labor shortage. This speculation is certainly in line with the argument I have presented. Nevertheless, I would be cautious in predicting how soon that day will come. For several decades, Japanese management has been able to handle the declining fertility rate by taking advantage of the increase in married women reentering the labor market, while offering no real career opportunities to women. As long as Japan's dualist work structure remains, firms are likely to continue to rely on this same strategy, especially since it benefits them to keep women in secondary jobs that pay less. Only when the labor shortage becomes so severe that Japanese women gain sufficient bargaining power to overthrow institutional barriers are we likely to see Japan and Taiwan begin to converge in women's career trajectories. Given how resilient Japan's labor market arrangements have been, I am afraid that it may still take quite a while for this convergence to occur.

IMPLICATIONS FOR UNDERSTANDING
GENDER AND SOCIAL CHANGE

As stated at the beginning of this book, one broader question that motivates comparative studies of gender inequality is why industrial societies differ so widely in the pace at which they improve women's employment opportunities.

In an attempt to shed light on this question, I close the book by discussing what this comparative study has contributed to our understanding in general. To start, the story I have unveiled has particularly important implications for change in women's economic status in industrializing countries, where political and cultural support for gender equality is generally insufficient. I have demonstrated that women's opportunities in the labor market are directly or indirectly shaped by various macrosocial conditions, including the regime's political and industrial strategies, the preexisting structure of business networks, and institutionalized employment practices. Beyond the experiences of Japan and Taiwan, I argue that how likely the gender economic gap may narrow in countries lacking political and cultural pushes for it depends greatly on whether the macrostructural context is conducive to incorporating married women's labor at a critical juncture, when new and better jobs are generated during the course of economic development. An understanding of how women's employment opportunities evolve thus requires greater attention to the interactions of the market, the state, and the economy's structural arrangements.

By comparing two societies that share many values resulting from historical intermixing, this study also provides a valuable lesson regarding the importance of institutional contexts. The extent to which cultural norms and preferences affect women's economic opportunities ultimately depends on whether the institutional arrangements in schools and labor markets tend to amplify or lessen the influences of these norms and preferences. For example, adopting a uniform achievement test for university entrance across the nation largely reduces the roles of family norms and parental preferences in Taiwanese women's educational attainment. Such an exam policy essentially enables the improvement of women's economic conditions despite a strong cultural preference for educating sons over daughters. Similarly, by adding material incentives, the institutionalized practices about recruitment, payment, and promotions encourage Japanese employers to act upon their cultural belief that men are more suitable workers. Therefore, rather than social norms and values per se, a theory of comparative gender inequality needs to focus on the institutional processes that shape the manifestation of cultural beliefs and hence women's socioeconomic attainment.

An additional insight this book offers for gender stratification research is that the development of women's economic roles is highly path dependent. Not only does the onset of change (or the lack thereof) often depend on exogenous forces that may result from historical incidents (e.g., the Taiwanese regime's preference for sponsoring small enterprises), but the path of change (or nonchange) is also paved by other social transformations that reinforce the initial development. That is to say, once change in women's employment behaviors takes place, alterations in other aspects of the society are also set in motion. Such subsequent alterations tend to further the movement. To illustrate, my analysis has demonstrated how the transformation of Taiwanese women's work trajectories is linked to changes in the society's income distribution, expected living standards, and popular support for female employment. These changes essentially redefined women's gender roles by having them take on the roles of coprimary earners in the family. This redefinition then accelerated the transformation of women's employment careers.

Because change in women's economic behaviors has important consequences for social norms and family budgets, the reversal of this change, with women increasingly giving up their income opportunities to become full-time homemakers, is highly difficult. Taiwan is not the only case that suggests so. A parallel example can be found in China, a formerly socialist country where women were obligated to be employed until retirement. Although scholars and critics generally suspect that China's economic reform may sweep away the socialist sponsorship for gender equality and hence increase women's economic disadvantages, recent research shows only a small decline in its female labor force participation (Tang and Parish 2000). Perhaps in part a result of women's persistent presence in the workplace, the gender wage gap has also been found to be relatively constant despite China's rather dramatic transition to a market economy (Shu and Bian 2003). The fact that Chinese women continue to work frequently and continuously corroborates the conclusion I derive from the Taiwan case: There is no easy reversal of the increase in women's employment over their life course. This understanding should help inform researchers interested in gender and social change in societies with comparatively high female employment rates, such as certain industrialized countries and formerly socialist countries that are in transition to becoming market economies.

As mentioned earlier, the argument about path dependence is not limited to cases in which change in women's economic roles can be observed. The force stalling change is just as resilient as that pushing for it. A social institution that resists alterations of women's economic roles can be reinforced by the actions of related agencies whose options are constrained by the institutional setup. Even in a time of instability, existing institutional arrangements can shape the directions of their own transformations—usually in a way that allows their beneficiaries to maintain the status quo. Japan's permanent employment system exemplifies such institutions. Because the highly gendered employment system left women few options but to exit their office jobs when rearing young children, they had to come to terms with their depressed careers by embracing the roles of "educational mothers." The growing prevalence of educational mothers, in turn, raised the standards of child rearing in Japanese society. The changing norms regarding motherhood then reinforced the need for a gender-segregated employment system that differentiates both job responsibilities and rewards based on gender. Even when the permanent employment system faced severe challenges after the 1990s, the system could preserve its essence during the transformation, with firms' core employees provided with relatively high job security while the rest had extremely unstable job conditions. The lingering dualist work structure means that it remains rare for women to have the type of jobs they most wish for: full-time regular jobs *without* overtime work (see Gender Equality Bureau, Japan [2007] for the most desirable job traits for women). That is to say, women still must choose either family or career; they cannot have both. In this sense, the transformation of the permanent employment system only reinforces existing workplace norms, thus continuing to repress change in women's employment careers.

Because economic inequality between men and women is a dynamic process shaped by antecedent conditions in society, to gain a comprehensive understanding of worldwide variations in this regard researchers need to extend beyond cross-sectional comparisons and focus more on the differing trajectories of gender stratification between countries. Previous research that compares women's employment often relies on typologies that are developed based on information at a given time point (Chang 2000; Stier et al. 2001; Van der Lippe and Van Dijk 2002). Such typologies generally overlook the nature of interdependence among factors affecting women's work in the society, such as cultural norms and institutionalized workplace practices. Cross-sectional studies with a typology-based framework therefore can face great difficulty identifying the precise and initial cause for some countries to develop different levels of gender inequality. Thus, beyond the specific cases of Japan and Taiwan, this study informs future research on comparative gender stratification by demonstrating the benefit of incorporating changes over time into the explanatory framework.

Another general lesson from this research is that the likelihood of closing the gender gap in economic status is largely shaped by the workplace atmospheres and working conditions women face. For this reason, policymakers aiming to improve women's overall economic chances must ensure that any policy implemented by the state can actually penetrate workplaces and have real influences on individual women. Of course, this is easier said than done. It is nevertheless possible for the law to enforce changes, even minute ones, in the workplace by granting women their right to reasonable working conditions. One example appeared in a June 10, 2007, *New York Times* report, which cited a lawsuit won by a South Korean woman against her male supervisor for pressuring her to drink alcohol during after-work gatherings, which the boss routinely organized to have the subordinates bond. According to the report, this ruling helped shake Korea's male-centered corporate culture, in which bonding through heavy drinking after normal business hours was considered necessary. In the same fashion, a court could rule it illegal to compel workers, both female and male, to attend after-work company outings that cut into their family time. Any small step made through such rulings may transform workplaces a little, thus making combining work and family easier for women (as well as for men).

On a final note, in this book I have demonstrated how change in women's employment trajectories helps bridge the gender gap in the workplace. It is, however, worth highlighting that the transformation in women's economic lives in Taiwan has not been accompanied by alterations of the unequal distributions of family responsibilities between men and women. Even though Taiwanese women are likely to find it easier to combine employment and motherhood than their Japanese counterparts, they do not seem to be able to negotiate more equal sharing of family responsibilities with their rising wages. As prior research shows, Taiwanese men's participation in domestic work barely increases with their wives' increasing contributions to household income (Tang and Parish 2000). During my fieldwork in Taipei, I also heard a few working mothers complain that they were always the ones who needed to deal with unexpected situations related to their children during working hours. Their full-time jobs appear not to enable them to transfer part of the child-rearing responsibility to the father, not to mention the responsibility for housework.

The lack of concurrent changes in women's working and family lives can perhaps explain why Taiwan is experiencing a dramatic increase in the number of women who delay marriage and childbearing, just like Japan. As stated earlier in this chapter, women's postponement of marriage in Japan is often thought to result from the fact that they are forced to choose either career or family. Since Taiwanese women historically have been relatively able to combine motherhood and employment, this reasoning does not seem to apply to that country. Instead, the experience of Taiwan suggests that simply making it feasible for married women to keep their jobs may still be insufficient to encourage women to step into marriage. Given that women are opting out of marriage in both countries, perhaps the root of this behavioral pattern has to do with what marriage represents to today's women—namely, an unfair institution that brings more restrictions than benefits. Regardless of whether their grievance is about lost career opportunities or an unequal division of labor at home, women in both countries are likely to continue avoiding marriage as long as it leads to unfair disadvantages either at home or in the workplace. The key question is: Will this relatively silent protest force social change in the directions women wish for? So far it does not seem to have helped Japanese women gain more equal treatment in the workplace, despite the great public attention it attracts. I am more optimistic about the possibility of change in Taiwan because the targets of the protest—men who are reluctant to share family responsibilities equally—will indeed suffer from it. Despite this, it not clear how long it may take for this opt-out protest to be effective. In this sense, the transformation of women's economic lives constitutes only the beginning of a series of changes that would be required to achieve gender equality in both societies. Even in Taiwan, the society where we observe greater progress in closing the gender gap in employment opportunities, the story regarding the trajectory to gender equality is still far from finished.

Most of the analyses reported in this book are based on data from two nationally representative surveys: part A of Japan's 1995 Social Stratification
and Social Mobility Survey (SSM) and the second part of the 1996 Taiwan
Social Change Survey (TSC). The SSM has collected detailed work and life
history information through face-to-face interviews from a representative
sample of Japanese men age 20 to 69 every decade since 1955. The survey
also has included a female sample with the same age range since 1985. Each
wave of the SSM is generally conducted by a research committee consisting
of several social inequality scholars. Although different waves of the SSM
share a considerable number of questions, their samples are independent.
The survey's primary sampling frame is a list of eligible voters in Japan.
Because of its extensive job history data, the SSM is the primary source for
labor market research on Japan, particularly when career trajectories are
concerned (Cheng and Kalleberg 1996, 1997; Ishida 1993; Sakamoto and
Powers 1995; Yu 2005, 2006).

The 1995 wave of the SSM used three questionnaires, and all were administered to both women and men. Nevertheless, only questionnaire A of
the 1995 SSM asked respondents to report detailed information about each
job they had experienced up until the time of the survey. This questionnaire
also asked about the years when respondents completed schooling, became
married, and had their first and last children, and asked them to list their
current income. Because of this book's emphasis on life course trajectories
and work histories, I relied on this part of the 1995 SSM data for most of
the analyses on Japan. In Chapter 8, however, data from both questionnaires
A and B of the 1995 SSM were used for the descriptive analysis regarding
the characteristics of respondents' current jobs. The primary reason for including data from both questionnaires was to ensure a sufficient number of
cases, since that analysis is based on certain subgroups of the sample (e.g.,
women with preschool children at the time of the survey). Lacking comparable information on respondents' current or previous jobs, questionnaire C

of the 1995 SSM was excluded from the analyses reported in Chapter 8 and elsewhere. Thus, except for a small part of Chapter 8, data from questionnaire A of the 1995 wave of the SSM were the only SSM data used in this book. For simplicity, hereafter the SSM refers to this specific part of the SSM conducted in 1995.

With respect to the analyses on Taiwan, the primary source of data is the 1996 wave of the TSC. Conducted by the Institute of Sociology, Academia Sinica in Taiwan, the TSC is a yearly study that serves similar purposes as the General Social Survey project in the United States (conducted by the National Opinion Research Center, University of Chicago). Since 1985, two or three surveys targeting different themes have been administered to Taiwanese adults each year. The second questionnaire of the 1996 TSC was among the few surveys in Taiwan that asked respondents about their entire life and work histories. The questions included in this questionnaire were highly comparable with those in the SSM, and were more detailed. For example, while the 1995 SSM asked about the ages of respondents' oldest and youngest children, the 1996 TSC recorded the year in which each of the respondents' children was born. Similarly, the 1995 SSM asked when respondents' most recent marriage occurred, whereas the 1996 TSC collected information about the respondents' entire marital histories.

Although both surveys include self-reported, retrospective records of respondents' life events by year, their samples are slightly different. Namely, the Taiwanese sample contains men and women age 25 to 60. To make these two data sets comparable, I selected only respondents 25 to 60 years of age from the SSM survey data. This selection results in 904 men and 1,080 women in the Japanese sample, and 1,452 men and 1,379 women in the Taiwanese sample. All the analyses presented in the book are based on these samples or subgroups selected from these samples. Reflecting their demographic compositions, the Japanese sample is, on average, older than the Taiwanese sample (also see Appendix B, Table B.1). In addition, women and men in the Japanese sample have higher educational levels than their counterparts in the Taiwanese sample. The percentage of respondents in the labor force is also slightly higher in Japan than in Taiwan. All these differences are consistent with the differences observed between the two populations.

Because I am specifically interested in understanding women's employment behavior after marriage, for the analyses appearing in Chapters 4 through 6 I generally selected from the samples women who had ever been married. Due to the difference in age distributions, the Japanese sample contains 7.4 percent single women, whereas the Taiwanese sample contains 9.1 percent. The difference is rather small and should not introduce serious bias into the comparison (see Yu [2005] for a more detailed comparison of women's marital status in the two samples). Among Japanese women who had ever married, 3.3 percent were divorced and 3.8 percent were widowed at the time of the survey. By contrast, the ever-married sample for Taiwan consists of 4.1 percent of women who were divorced or separated and 6.2 percent of women who were widowed. Overall, these two samples of ever-married women are similar in their levels of marital stability. Given that the proportions of women who were divorced or widowed are small in the two samples, for simplicity I sometimes refer to the ever-married women in the samples as married women in this book.

Because the SSM did not ask whether respondents had any prior marriages, I had to assume that their current or most recent marriage was also their first marriage in any analysis concerning the first marriage. Since Japan had low divorce and remarriage rates until the most recent decade (Raymo, Iwasawa, and Bumpass 2004; Rindfuss et al. 2004), this assumption should be accurate for the vast majority of the respondents. Thus, I expect the impact of any bias caused by this assumption to be small.

A large part of the analyses reported in Chapters 4 through 6 uses an event history approach. Because a major focus of this book is how changes in economic status and family conditions shape women's decisions regarding employment, an event history approach that is sensitive to changes in individual experiences throughout time is the most appropriate for the analyses of women's labor force exits and reentry. To fit the discrete time event history models presented in the book, I transformed the SSM and TSC samples into person-year observations with time-varying job and family characteristics, based on respondents' reports of their life events and work experiences. Rather than the individual, the unit of analysis for event history models is the person-duration of exposure to the outcome of interest. Thus, respondents have as many observations as the number of years they were at risk of the specified outcome in the analytical sample (Yamaguchi 1991). The results of the models using such data are presented in Appendix B, Tables B.3 through B.6.

A few other data sets were used for the descriptive analyses presented in this book. They are from other waves of the TSC, as well as various waves of the International Social Survey Programme (ISSP) and the Knowledge, Attitude, and Practice of Contraception (KAP) Survey. The ISSP collects information annually on topics relevant to social science research from nationally representative samples of men and women across several participating countries. The ISSP data used in the book are drawn from the 1994 and 2002 waves, which focused on family and changing gender roles. The KAP contains eight waves of survey data on Taiwanese women of childbearing age, conducted collaboratively by the Department of Health, Bureau of Health Promotion in Taiwan, and the Population Studies Center at the University of Michigan from 1965 to 1998. Because one aim of the KAP was to understand women's attitudes toward their family roles, the KAP data from various years enabled me to portray changes in gender attitudes among Taiwanese women throughout time.

In the concluding chapter, I used two additional data sets from Japan and Taiwan to estimate changes since the mid 1990s (e.g., for the analyses presented in Appendix B, Tables B.8–B.10). The data for Japan are drawn from a recent wave of the Japanese General Social Surveys (JGSS) project, which is the Japanese version of the General Social Survey in the United States. Conducted by the Osaka University of Commerce and the University of Tokyo, the JGSS has collected information concerning Japanese adults' attitudes and behaviors almost annually since 2000. The specific data used for the analysis reported for Japan in Chapter 8 were collected in late 2003, consisting of a sample of 3,663 men and women age 20 to 89. Concerned primarily with Japanese citizens' attitudes toward social issues, the 2003 JGSS includes few questions about respondents' work and life histories, though it provides detailed information about respondents' current jobs.

The analysis for Taiwan reported in Chapter 8 is based on the first survey of the TSC conducted in late 2002, which focused on social strati-fication. This part of the 2002 TSC contains a nationally representative sample of men and women age 20 years and older. A total of 1,992 men and women were included in this sample. Although the age range of the 2002 TSC in theory is wider than that of the JGSS, only three respondents in the Taiwanese sample were older than age 89 at the time of the survey. The 2003 JGSS sample nevertheless has a higher average age than that of the 2002 TSC sample, which is consistent with the population characteristics in Japan and Taiwan. Part I of the 2002 TSC asked a series of questions about respondents' first and current jobs, as well as asked questions regarding the characteristics of their family of origin. Similar to the 2003 JGSS, this survey does not include information about respondents' complete work and life histories. I therefore had to rely on cross-sectional information to estimate the job exit patterns among women.

TABLE B.I

*Descriptive statistics of the SSM and TSC samples by gender.*

| | JAPAN | | TAIWAN | |
|---|---|---|---|---|
| | *Men* | *Women* | *Men* | *Women* |
| Age group, y | | | | |
| 25–34 | 20.1 | 20.9 | 29.8 | 31.3 |
| 35–44 | 28.3 | 30.3 | 37.9 | 38.6 |
| 45–54 | 34.3 | 34.0 | 23.7 | 20.5 |
| 55–60 | 17.3 | 14.8 | 8.7 | 9.6 |
| Marital status | | | | |
| Never married | 15.7 | 7.4 | 16.0 | 9.2 |
| Married | 81.6 | 86.5 | 80.2 | 81.1 |
| Divorced/separated/widowed | 2.7 | 6.0 | 3.8 | 9.7 |
| With children | 77.9 | 85.7 | 79.4 | 88.0 |
| Living with extended kin (e.g., parents-in-law)* | 29.9 | 30.4 | 42.3 | 33.4 |
| In the labor force | 96.9 | 66.3 | 90.4 | 60.7 |
| Highest educational level | | | | |
| University and above | 26.9 | 8.2 | 12.6 | 7.4 |
| Junior college | 1.8 | 12.5 | 13.7 | 10.1 |
| High school | 49.9 | 57.6 | 26.3 | 26.4 |
| Middle school | 21.1 | 21.6 | 19.7 | 16.2 |
| Primary school and below | 0.3 | 0.1 | 27.7 | 39.9 |
| Living in urban areas | 76.0 | 72.7 | 49.7 | 53.4 |
| N | 904 | 1,080 | 1,452 | 1,379 |

SOURCE: Japan, 1995 SSM, part A; Taiwan, 1996 TSC, part II.

All numbers are in percentages, except for the numbers of cases (N).

*Also includes respondents who were single and lived with their parents and extended relatives (e.g., grandparents).

TABLE B.2
Ordinary least squares regression analysis of log annual earnings.

| | JAPAN | | TAIWAN | |
|---|---|---|---|---|
| | Men | Women | Men | Women |
| Educational level | | | | |
| University and above | 0.156 (0.047)** | 0.326 (0.119)** | 0.236 (0.073)** | 0.365 (0.088)** |
| Junior college | 0.033 (0.126) | 0.228 (0.095)* | 0.048 (0.062) | 0.088 (0.074) |
| High school | — | — | — | — |
| Middle school‡ | -0.058 (0.046) | -0.230 (0.079)** | -0.121 (0.059)* | -0.065 (0.079) |
| Primary and less | NA | NA | -0.297 (0.062)** | -0.300 (0.077)** |
| Work experience, log y | 0.246 (0.036)** | 0.345 (0.054)** | 0.068 (0.035)* | 0.109 (0.035)** |
| Employer changes, n | | | | |
| None | — | — | — | — |
| One | 0.021 (0.042) | -0.298 (0.086)** | 0.042 (0.060) | -0.068 (0.066) |
| Two | -0.069 (0.054) | -0.249 (0.093)** | 0.022 (0.062) | -0.128 (0.067)† |
| Three and more | -0.184 (0.056)** | -0.288 (0.101)** | 0.069 (0.061) | -0.030 (0.067) |
| Within-organization job-shifting experience | 0.081 (0.038)* | 0.296 (0.101)** | 0.064 (0.044) | 0.169 (0.054)** |
| Marital status | | | | |
| Never married | — | — | — | — |
| Married | 0.228 (0.054)** | -0.290 (0.097)** | 0.165 (0.060)** | 0.072 (0.068) |
| Divorced/widowed | 0.145 (0.110) | 0.233 (0.142) | -0.065 (0.118) | 0.042 (0.096) |
| Occupation | | | | |
| Managerial/professional | 0.317 (0.052)** | 0.586 (0.118)** | 0.216 (0.076)** | 0.422 (0.112)** |
| Semiprofessional | 0.138 (0.059)* | 0.309 (0.134)* | 0.160 (0.062)** | 0.388 (0.092)** |
| Clerical | 0.095 (0.060) | 0.307 (0.090)** | 0.044 (0.093) | 0.208 (0.080)** |
| Service/sales | -0.096 (0.058)† | 0.118 (0.085) | 0.022 (0.067) | 0.147 (0.078)† |
| Farm worker | -0.281 (0.097)** | -0.180 (0.208) | -0.863 (0.099)** | -0.789 (0.134)** |
| Manual labor | — | — | — | — |

|  | (1) | (2) | (3) | (4) |
|---|---|---|---|---|
| **Employment status** | | | | |
| Regular paid employee | — | — | — | — |
| Part-time/temporary employee | −0.535 (0.142)** | −0.701 (0.075)** | −0.122 (0.094) | −0.246 (0.104)* |
| Family employment | −0.235 (0.133)† | −0.236 (0.110)* | −0.168 (0.149) | 0.048 (0.114) |
| Self-employment with hiring | 0.003 (0.069) | 0.159 (0.181) | 0.372 (0.066)** | 0.436 (0.109)** |
| Self-employment without hiring | −0.075 (0.101) | −0.306 (0.140)* | 0.032 (0.066) | 0.058 (0.089) |
| **Firm size, no. of employees** | | | | |
| 1–9 | — | — | — | — |
| 10–29 | −0.016 (0.070) | 0.208 (0.100)* | 0.006 (0.064) | 0.001 (0.073) |
| 30–99 | −0.088 (0.070) | 0.252 (0.107)* | 0.204 (0.073)** | 0.129 (0.080) |
| 100–499 | −0.008 (0.071) | 0.380 (0.112)** | 0.137 (0.074)† | 0.079 (0.081) |
| ≥500 | 0.062 (0.064) | 0.391 (0.093)** | 0.278 (0.066)** | 0.165 (0.073)* |
| Constant | 14.359 (0.135)** | 13.254 (0.223)** | 12.552 (0.098)** | 12.109 (0.125)** |
| N | 741 | 536 | 1,090 | 701 |
| Adjusted $R^2$ | 0.321 | 0.500 | 0.304 | 0.362 |

SOURCE: Japan, 1995 SSM, part A; Taiwan, 1996 TSC, part II.

Numbers in parentheses are standard errors. NA, category is not available for the analysis because of small cell size.

†Includes four cases whose highest educational level was below middle school for Japan.

†$p < .10$, *$p < .05$, **$p < .01$.

TABLE B.3

*Discrete-time event history models predicting labor force exits at any point of time.*

|  | Japan | Taiwan |
|---|---|---|
| Work experience before current employment spell, y | −0.139 (0.022)** | −0.078 (0.015)** |
| Schooling, y | 0.080 (0.031)* | 0.049 (0.015)** |
| Birth cohorts, y |  |  |
| 25–34 | 0.181 (0.148) | 0.092 (0.104) |
| 35–44 | — | — |
| 45–54 | −0.640 (0.123)** | −0.103 (0.103) |
| 55–60 | −0.433 (0.157)** | 0.169 (0.149) |
| Urban residence | 0.341 (0.112)** | 0.083 (0.079) |
| Marital status |  |  |
| Never married | −0.842 (0.325)** | −1.825 (0.200)** |
| Married | — | — |
| Separated/divorced | 0.678 (0.577) | −0.438 (0.312) |
| Widowed | 0.691 (0.376) | −0.876 (0.377)* |
| Extended family support‡ | −0.605 (0.128)** | −0.072 (0.099) |
| Presence of preschool children | −1.528 (0.164)** | −0.939 (0.114)** |
| Year of first childbirth | 1.707 (0.213)** | 1.770 (0.138)** |
| Spouse's years of schooling§ | 0.099 (0.024)** | −0.030 (0.016) |
| Don't know spouse's education§ | 0.516 (0.498) | −0.235 (0.212) |
| Occupation¶ |  |  |
| Managerial/professional | −0.068 (0.205) | −1.330 (0.282)** |
| Semiprofessional | −0.101 (0.216) | −0.771 (0.182)** |
| Clerical | 0.465 (0.131)** | −0.271 (0.123)* |
| Service and sales | 0.163 (0.143) | −0.011 (0.118) |
| Agricultural | −1.488 (0.525)** | −0.911 (0.195)** |
| Manual labor | — | — |

TABLE B.3
(*continued*)

| | Japan | Taiwan |
|---|---|---|
| Firm size | | |
| 1–9 | — | — |
| 10–99 | 0.640 (0.136)** | 0.376 (0.111)** |
| 100–499 | 0.804 (0.160)** | 0.430 (0.126)** |
| ≥500 | 0.895 (0.143)** | 0.179 (0.143) |
| Don't know | 1.151 (0.185)** | 0.376 (0.151)* |
| Public-sector employment | −1.239 (0.253)** | −0.815 (0.178)** |
| Unemployment rate$^\perp$ | −0.720 (0.112)** | 0.089 (0.062) |
| Constant | −3.235 (0.588)** | −2.964 (0.293)** |
| Log likelihood | −2053.266 | −2843.652 |
| Person-year spells, n | 14,037 | 17,467 |
| Events, n | 615 | 782 |

SOURCE: Japan, 1995 SSM, part A; Taiwan, 1996 TSC, part II.

Numbers in parentheses are standard errors. All the models presented include a set of dummy variables for the duration of the given employment spell, but the coefficients are skipped to simplify the presentation.

‡If ever-married.

§If currently married.

¶Based on the 1988 International Standard Classification of Occupations (see Ganzeboom and Treiman [1996] for details). Made comparable by recoding three-digit occupational codes provided in the original surveys.

$^\perp$National unemployment rate reported in the given calendar year.

†$p < .10$, *$p < .05$, **$p < .01$.

## TABLE B.4
### Discrete-time event history models predicting labor force exit upon marriage.

| | JAPAN | | TAIWAN | |
|---|---|---|---|---|
| | Any break | Long break | Any break | Long break |
| Duration of marriage | | | | |
| Marriage year | — | — | — | — |
| First postmarital year | -1.187 (0.171)** | -0.985 (0.184)** | -1.688 (0.168)**‡ | -1.841 (0.198)**‡ |
| Second postmarital year | -1.484 (0.199)** | -1.682 (0.243)** | -1.650 (0.179)** | -1.780 (0.214)** |
| Third postmarital year | -2.157 (0.267)** | -2.499 (0.355)** | -2.086 (0.221)** | -2.526 (0.307)** |
| Years of schooling | -0.137 (0.046)** | -0.154 (0.052)** | 0.004 (0.025)‡ | -0.016 (0.028)‡ |
| Cohort (age in survey year) | | | | |
| 25–34 | 0.174 (0.246) | -0.261 (0.291) | -0.283 (0.277) | -0.105 (0.311) |
| 35–44 | 0.188 (0.228) | 0.036 (0.240) | -0.145 (0.254) | -0.036 (0.276) |
| 45–54 | -0.169 (0.221) | -0.133 (0.230) | 0.130 (0.257) | 0.281 (0.276) |
| 55–60 | — | — | — | — |
| Urban residence | 0.159 (0.155) | 0.258 (0.173) | 0.271 (0.123)* | 0.343 (0.141)* |
| Extended family support | -0.625 (0.154)** | -0.681 (0.173)** | -0.051 (0.128)‡ | -0.114 (0.149)‡ |
| Year of first childbirth | 0.373 (0.183)* | -0.023 (0.218) | 0.695 (0.139)** | 0.669 (0.156)**‡ |
| Spouse's years of schooling | 0.112 (0.034)** | 0.134 (0.037)** | -0.016 (0.024)‡ | -0.013 (0.027)‡ |
| Don't know spouse's education | 1.739 (0.511)** | 1.934 (0.557)** | -0.109 (0.305)‡ | 0.001 (0.333)‡ |
| Occupation | | | | |
| Managerial/professional | -0.042 (0.291) | 0.021 (0.331) | -1.618 (0.481)**‡ | -1.648 (0.583)**‡ |
| Semiprofessional | 0.023 (0.303) | 0.276 (0.338) | -0.881 (0.268)**‡ | -0.829 (0.320)**‡ |
| Clerical | 0.621 (0.201)** | 0.796 (0.227)** | -0.315 (0.188)†‡ | -0.479 (0.223)*‡ |
| Service and sales | 0.451 (0.224)* | 0.626 (0.250)* | -0.152 (0.187)§ | -0.155 (0.210)‡ |
| Agricultural | -1.595 (0.753)* | -1.224 (0.762) | -0.980 (0.276)** | -0.907 (0.295)** |
| Manual labor | — | — | — | — |

| | | | | |
|---|---|---|---|---|
| Firm size | | | | |
| 1–9 | — | — | — | — |
| 10–99 | 0.985 (0.197)** | 1.056 (0.220)** | 0.549 (0.172)** | 0.619 (0.196)** |
| 100–499 | 1.335 (0.227)** | 1.492 (0.255)** | 0.504 (0.195)**‡ | 0.405 (0.224)†‡ |
| ≥500 | 1.242 (0.207)** | 1.240 (0.232)** | 0.349 (0.216)‡ | 0.269 (0.251)‡ |
| Don't know | 1.163 (0.293)** | 1.363 (0.325)** | 0.094 (0.250)‡ | −0.075 (0.287)‡ |
| Public-sector employment | −1.494 (0.338)** | −1.622 (0.395)** | −1.031 (0.264)** | −0.688 (0.291)*§ |
| Constant | −1.613 (0.513)** | −1.963 (0.572)** | −0.716 (0.312)* | −0.868 (0.344) |
| Log likelihood | −775.156 | −629.436 | −943.354 | −735.272 |
| Person-year spells, n | 2,017 | 1,828 | 2,672 | 2,301 |
| Events, n | 396 | 310 | 405 | 307 |

SOURCE: Japan, 1995 SSM; Taiwan, 1996 TSC, part II.

Numbers in parentheses are standard errors. "Any break" indicates the experience of leaving the labor force for at least one full year, whereas a "long break" is defined as a job exit followed by five or more years away from the labor force. Also see Yu (2005) for details on data, variables, and measurement.

‡Statistically different from the corresponding coefficient for Japan at $p < .05$.

§Statistically different from the corresponding coefficient for Japan at $p < .10$.

†$p < .10$, *$p < .05$, **$p < .01$.

## TABLE B.5

### Discrete-time event history models predicting labor force exit around first childbirth.

| | JAPAN | | TAIWAN | |
|---|---|---|---|---|
| | Any break | Long break | Any break | Long break |
| Time | | | | |
| Pregnant with first child | — | — | — | — |
| Year of first birth | −0.563 (0.181)** | −0.817 (0.211)** | −0.353 (0.133)** | −0.439 (0.147)** |
| 1 year since birth | −1.528 (0.256)** | −1.569 (0.288)** | −1.881 (0.213)** | −2.275 (0.275)**§ |
| 2 years since birth | −2.746 (0.430)** | −4.343 (1.011)** | −1.920 (0.219)** | −2.343 (0.291)**§ |
| 3 years since birth | −2.918 (0.467)** | −3.598 (0.724)** | −2.418 (0.271)** | −2.471 (0.311)** |
| Years of schooling | −0.082 (0.056) | −0.136 (0.065)* | 0.013 (0.025) | −0.003 (0.028)§ |
| Cohort (age in survey year), y | | | | |
| 25–34 | 0.753 (0.306)* | 0.347 (0.363) | −0.125 (0.266)‡ | 0.050 (0.296) |
| 35–44 | 0.377 (0.292) | 0.248 (0.313) | −0.147 (0.246) | −0.084 (0.264) |
| 45–54 | −0.033 (0.284) | −0.022 (0.301) | 0.214 (0.247) | 0.285 (0.263) |
| 55–60 | — | — | — | — |
| Urban residence | 0.244 (0.190) | 0.262 (0.217) | 0.229 (0.118)† | 0.291 (0.135)* |
| Married | 0.009 (0.556) | −0.458 (0.639) | 1.639 (0.327)**‡ | 1.813 (0.372)**‡ |
| Extended family support | −0.674 (0.185)** | −0.675 (0.216)** | −0.006 (0.124)§ | −0.063 (0.143)‡ |
| Spouse's years of schooling | 0.077 (0.038)* | 0.120 (0.045)** | −0.035 (0.024)‡ | −0.025 (0.027)‡ |
| Don't know spouse's education | 1.392 (0.575)* | 1.651 (0.669)* | −0.202 (0.298)‡ | −0.046 (0.325)‡ |
| Occupation | | | | |
| Managerial/professional | 0.318 (0.337) | 0.390 (0.395) | −1.272 (0.428)**§ | −1.433 (0.529)**‡ |
| Semiprofessional | 0.440 (0.355) | 0.875 (0.402)* | −0.978 (0.267)**§ | −0.915 (0.312)**‡ |
| Clerical | 0.686 (0.251)** | 0.920 (0.294)** | −0.260 (0.178)§ | −0.427 (0.210)**‡ |
| Service and sales | 0.245 (0.279) | 0.407 (0.324) | −0.053 (0.178) | −0.062 (0.201) |
| Agricultural | −1.766 (1.044)† | −1.316 (1.059) | −0.913 (0.269)** | −0.859 (0.287)** |
| Manual labor | — | — | — | — |

| | | | | |
|---|---|---|---|---|
| Firm size | | | | |
| 1–9 | — | — | — | — |
| 10–99 | 0.643 (0.232)** | 0.811 (0.268)** | 0.718 (0.164)** | 0.761 (0.187)** |
| 100–499 | 0.901 (0.265)** | 1.112 (0.309)** | 0.703 (0.185)** | 0.557 (0.212)** |
| ≥500 | 1.038 (0.243)** | 1.019 (0.289)** | 0.303 (0.213)‡ | 0.163 (0.250)‡ |
| Don't know | 1.059 (0.355)** | 1.465 (0.388)** | 0.304 (0.233) | 0.116 (0.270)‡ |
| Public-sector employment | −1.404 (0.392)** | −1.195 (0.441)** | −1.106 (0.262)** | −0.809 (0.288)** |
| Constant | −2.241 (0.728)** | −1.955 (0.823)* | −2.415 (0.348)** | −2.689 (0.391)** |
| Log likelihood | −551.020 | −422.171 | −1040.445 | −679.668 |
| Person-year spells, n | 2,000 | 1,830 | 3,201 | 2,758 |
| Events, n | 252 | 183 | 416 | 315 |

SOURCE: Japan, 1995 SSM, part A; Taiwan, 1996 TSC, part II.

Numbers in parentheses are standard errors. "Any break" indicates the experience of leaving the labor force for at least one full year, whereas a "long break" is defined as a job exit followed by five or more years away from the labor force. Also see Yu (2005) for details on data, variables, and measurement.

‡Statistically different from the corresponding coefficient for Japan at $p < .05$.

§Statistically different from the corresponding coefficient for Japan at $p < .10$.

**$p < .01$, *$p < .05$, †$p < .10$.

*Discrete-time event history models predicting labor force reentry.*

| | Japan | Taiwan |
|---|---|---|
| Duration of homemaking, year | | |
| 1–2 | — | — |
| 3–6 | −0.252 (0.238) | −0.550 (0.182)** |
| 7–10 | 0.024 (0.263) | −0.682 (0.220)** |
| 11–15 | 0.152 (0.291) | −0.411 (0.239)† |
| ≥16 | 0.057 (0.335) | −0.799 (0.293)** |
| Years out of labor force before marriage | −0.056 (0.053) | 0.009 (0.041) |
| Income potential | | |
| Years of education | 0.013 (0.056) | 0.057 (0.027)* |
| Years of husband's education | −0.094 (0.036)** | 0.004 (0.025) |
| Don't know husband's education | −1.216 (0.572)* | 0.350 (0.319) |
| Spouse present | −0.748 (0.296)* | −0.678 (0.298)* |
| Family cycle and child rearing | | |
| No child | −0.316 (0.302) | 0.659 (0.298)* |
| Youngest child < 3 y | −1.343 (0.255)** | −0.681 (0.176)** |
| Youngest child age 3–6 y | −0.426 (0.196)* | −0.023 (0.182) |
| Youngest child > 6 y | — | — |
| Work commitment | | |
| Work experience, y | 0.062 (0.054) | −0.011 (0.047) |
| Work experience squared | −0.001 (0.002) | 0.124 (0.138) |
| Exiting labor force upon childbirth | 0.538 (0.199)** | −0.001 (0.002) |
| Previous job experiences | | |
| Previous occupations | | |
| Managerial/professional | 0.746 (0.310)* | 0.114 (0.415) |
| Semiprofessional | −0.744 (1.044) | −0.158 (0.292) |
| Clerical | 0.378 (0.220) | −0.044 (0.194) |
| Service and sales | 0.681 (0.222)** | −0.125 (0.176) |
| Manual labor | — | — |
| Agricultural | −0.518 (1.130) | 0.214 (0.338) |
| Previous employment status | | |
| Full-time employee | — | — |
| Part-time/temporary employee | 0.105 (0.212) | −0.640 (0.731) |
| Self-employed, hiring others | −0.260 (0.636) | −0.777 (0.762) |
| Self-employed, no hiring | 1.137 (0.416)** | 0.370 (0.261) |
| Family enterprise employee | −0.356 (0.438) | −0.296 (0.286) |
| No. of previous jobs | −0.003 (0.104) | 0.177 (0.060)** |
| Other control variables | | |
| Birth cohorts (age in survey year), y | | |
| 25–34 | 0.404 (0.284) | 0.219 (0.184) |
| 35–44 | −0.570 (0.173)** | −0.332 (0.165)* |
| 45–54 | −1.092 (0.254)** | −0.358 (0.248) |
| 55–60 | — | — |
| Nonfarm labor force growth rate | 0.171 (0.097) | 0.025 (0.032) |
| Unemployment rate | 0.072 (0.215) | −0.072 (0.124) |
| Constant | −1.620 (0.853) | −2.226 (0.578)** |
| Log likelihood | −1030.455 | −1157.321 |
| Person-year spells, n | 6,036 | 6,108 |
| Events, n | 271 | 310 |

SOURCE: Japan, 1995 SSM, part A; Taiwan, 1996 TSC, part II.

Numbers in parentheses are standard errors. See Yu (2006) for details on samples, models, and measurement.

†$p < .10$, *$p < .05$, **$p < .01$.

Multinomial logit models predicting married women's current work status in Japan.

| | No job | Part-time/ temporary workers | Nonemployee workers |
|---|---|---|---|
| Educational level | | | |
| University or more | −2.176 (0.485)** | −2.421 (0.585)** | 0.122 (0.520) |
| Junior college | −1.238 (0.423)** | −1.181 (0.447)** | 0.299 (0.455) |
| High school | −1.143 (0.317)** | −0.627 (0.298)* | −0.298 (0.324) |
| Middle school or less | — | — | — |
| Years of work experience | −0.110 (0.013)** | −0.037 (0.012)** | 0.071 (0.016)** |
| Preschool children present | 1.342 (0.333)** | −0.613 (0.414) | 1.019 (0.406)* |
| Family type | | | |
| Nuclear family | 1.002 (0.229)** | 0.970 (0.239)** | 0.170 (0.244) |
| Extended family | — | — | — |
| Husband self-employed | 0.016 (0.380) | −0.370 (0.388) | 1.729 (0.303)** |
| Log husband's income | 0.106 (0.068) | 0.156 (0.059)** | 0.040 (0.063) |
| Husband's income unknown‡ | 1.089 (0.514)* | 1.695 (0.463)** | 0.410 (0.494) |
| Urban residence | 0.818 (0.247)** | 0.812 (0.255)** | 0.604 (0.267)* |
| Gender attitude§ | −0.672 (0.157)** | −.392 (0.160)* | −0.869 (0.176)** |
| Gender attitude unknown | −0.226 (0.319) | 0.101 (0.314) | −0.120 (0.348) |
| Age group, y | | | |
| 25–34 | — | — | — |
| 35–44 | 0.519 (0.339) | −0.030 (0.401) | 0.222 (0.446) |
| 45–54 | 1.233 (0.420)** | −0.624 (0.458) | 0.146 (0.541) |
| 55–60 | 2.235 (0.531)** | −0.957 (0.570)† | −0.271 (0.667) |
| Entering current status after marriage | −1.444 (0.236)** | 1.423 (0.298)** | 0.617 (0.274)* |
| Age entering current status ≥ 45 y | −0.960 (0.493) | 1.179 (0.351)** | −0.627 (0.450) |
| Constant | 0.507 (0.640) | −1.805 (0.676)** | −3.446 (0.754)** |
| Log likelihood | | −859.015 | |
| N | | 941 | |

SOURCE: Japan, 1995 SSM, part A; Taiwan, 1996 TSC, part II.

Full-time paid employment is the baseline category for the model. Numbers in parentheses are standard errors.

‡Indicates that respondents had no husband at the survey time or failed to report their husbands' income.

§Estimated by a factor analysis based on respondents' reports on how much they agreed with the following statements: (1) Men should work outside the home and women should be responsible for the family, (2) male and female children must be raised differently, (3) women are better at household work and child rearing than men, (4) the work of full-time housewives means much to society, (5) women should value their own work lives and careers highly, and (6) full-time housewives enjoy their lives more and are happier than women working outside the home. Larger values represent stronger support for traditional gender roles.

†p < .10, *p < .05, **p < .01.

Multinomial logit models predicting women's current occupational status.

| | JAPAN | | | TAIWAN | | |
| | No job | Office job | Service job | No job | Office job | Service job |
|---|---|---|---|---|---|---|
| | | vs. factory job | | | vs. factory job | |
| Years of schooling | 0.155 (0.037)** | 0.323 (0.047)** | 0.200 (0.045)** | 0.156 (0.032)** | 0.609 (0.048)** | 0.154 (0.044)** |
| Marital status | | | | | | |
| Never married | — | — | — | — | — | — |
| Married | -0.164 (0.335) | -0.736 (0.338)* | -0.437 (0.358) | -0.809 (0.413)* | -0.167 (0.452) | -0.397 (0.509) |
| Divorced/widowed | 0.344 (0.389) | -0.066 (0.424) | 0.261 (0.428) | -0.403 (0.490) | 0.747 (0.624) | -0.207 (0.652) |
| Age group, y | | | | | | |
| 20–29 | — | — | — | — | — | — |
| 30–39 | -0.330 (0.367) | 0.323 (0.379) | -0.272 (0.397) | -0.337 (0.392) | 0.758 (0.419)† | -0.394 (0.473) |
| 40–49 | -0.216 (0.392) | 0.348 (0.403) | -0.127 (0.419) | 0.438 (0.415) | 0.904 (0.468)† | 0.137 (0.509) |
| 50–59 | -0.344 (0.388) | -0.341 (0.407) | -0.151 (0.414) | 0.874 (0.437)† | 1.467 (0.533)** | -0.268 (0.579) |
| ≥60 | 1.689 (0.398)** | -0.784 (0.451)† | -0.406 (0.445) | 1.640 (0.492)** | 1.162 (0.730) | 0.316 (0.643) |
| Preschool child present | 1.537 (0.333)** | 0.022 (0.354) | 0.170 (0.376) | 0.618 (0.232)** | -0.177 (0.317) | 0.216 (0.329) |
| Urban residence | 0.329 (0.164)* | 0.444 (0.202)* | 0.147 (0.192) | 0.370 (0.189)* | 0.121 (0.248) | 0.257 (0.260) |
| Constant | -1.344 (0.591)* | -3.341 (0.713)** | -1.770 (0.688)** | -0.617 (0.522) | -7.017 (0.744)** | -1.596 (0.685)* |
| Log likelihood | | -2124.022 | | | -1045.891 | |
| N | | 2,027 | | | 1,020 | |

SOURCE: Japan, 2003 JGSS; Taiwan, 2002 TSC, part I.

Numbers in parentheses are standard errors. An "office job" is defined as a job in a managerial, professional, semiprofessional, or clerical occupation; a "service job" is one in a sales and service occupation, and a "factory job" is one in a manufacturing occupation. Because their numbers are very small, I included those with agricultural jobs in the group of women with factory jobs.

†$p < .10$, *$p < .05$, **$p < .01$.

TABLE B.9

Multinomial logit models predicting women's current organizational locations.

| | JAPAN | | | TAIWAN | | |
|---|---|---|---|---|---|---|
| | Nonemployment | Small firm | Medium firm | Nonemployment | Small firm | Medium firm |
| | vs. large-firm employment | | | vs. large-firm employment | | |
| Years of schooling | -0.163 (0.047)** | -0.163 (0.048)** | -0.233 (0.056)** | -0.297 (.039)** | -0.278 (.041)** | -0.087 (0.057) |
| Marital status | | | | | | |
| Never married | — | — | — | — | — | — |
| Married | 0.822 (0.295)** | 0.824 (0.300)** | 0.615 (0.326)† | -0.406 (.373) | 0.011 (.376) | 0.588 (0.519) |
| Divorced/widowed | 0.500 (0.392) | 0.251 (0.403) | 0.415 (0.451) | -0.157 (.599) | -0.035 (.618) | -0.677 (1.212) |
| Age group, y | | | | | | |
| 20–29 | — | — | — | — | — | — |
| 30–39 | -0.416 (0.317) | 0.317 (0.345) | -0.512 (0.345) | -1.380 (.352)** | -0.992 (.354)** | -1.227 (0.466)** |
| 40–49 | -0.531 (0.345) | 0.066 (0.371) | -0.773 (0.377)* | -0.405 (.414) | -0.481 (.423) | -0.620 (0.548) |
| 50–59‡ | -0.314 (0.355) | 0.355 (0.378) | -0.968 (0.394)* | 0.182 (.464) | -1.045 (.491)* | -1.583 (0.714)* |
| ≥60 | 3.330 (0.492)** | 2.240 (0.520)** | -0.332 (0.577) | NA | NA | NA |
| Preschool child present | 1.750 (0.336)** | 0.446 (0.357) | 0.216 (0.391) | 0.446 (.302) | -0.184 (.311) | 0.053 (0.423) |
| Urban residence | 0.271 (0.203) | -0.038 (0.203) | 0.456 (0.247)† | -0.129 (.261) | -0.516 (.263)* | -0.505 (0.349) |
| Constant | 1.932 (0.715)** | 1.705 (0.737)* | 2.762 (0.832)** | 5.394 (.625)** | 5.168 (.645)** | 1.219 (0.892) |
| Log likelihood | -1950.996 | | | -998.789 | | |
| N | 1,952 | | | 1,006 | | |

SOURCE: Japan, 2003 JGSS; Taiwan, 2002 TSC, part I.

Numbers in parentheses are standard errors. "Large firm" refers to one with more than 500 employees; "medium firm," 30–499 employees and "small firm," 1–29 employees.

NA, category is not available for the analysis.

‡This category is for age 50 and older for Taiwan. Because of small cell size, dividing this category further into two age groups leads to unstable results.

†p < .10, *p < .05, **p < .01.

# TABLE B.IO
## Multinomial logit models predicting women's current employment status.

| | JAPAN | | | TAIWAN | | |
|---|---|---|---|---|---|---|
| | Nonemployment | Part-time/ temporary employment | Nonemployee status | Nonemployment | Part-time/ temporary employment | Nonemployee status |
| | vs. full-time regular employment | | | vs. full-time regular employment | | |
| Years of schooling | −0.031 (0.041) | −0.058 (0.044) | 0.019 (0.049) | −0.136 (0.028)** | 0.070 (0.050) | −0.116 (0.033)** |
| Marital status | | | | | | |
| Never married | — | — | — | — | — | — |
| Married | 0.845 (0.267)** | 1.093 (0.274)** | 0.752 (0.364)* | −0.226 (0.294) | −0.660 (0.492) | 1.335 (0.443)** |
| Divorced/widowed | 0.327 (0.347) | 0.771 (0.356)* | −0.280 (0.452) | −0.542 (0.429) | −1.332 (0.827) | 0.120 (0.604) |
| Age group, y | | | | | | |
| 20–29 | — | — | — | — | — | — |
| 30–39 | −0.519 (0.274)† | −0.416 (0.285) | 0.556 (0.534) | −0.802 (0.268)** | −0.393 (0.497) | −0.489 (0.389) |
| 40–49 | 0.015 (0.311) | 0.295 (0.312) | 1.081 (0.548)* | 0.114 (0.309) | 1.277 (0.516)* | 0.171 (0.418) |
| 50–59‡ | 0.085 (0.316) | −0.205 (0.323) | 1.837 (0.536)** | 1.793 (0.373)** | 1.981 (0.637)** | 1.178 (0.478)* |
| ≥60 | 4.189 (0.460)** | 1.293 (0.487)** | 4.698 (0.639)** | NA | NA | NA |
| Preschool child present | 1.736 (0.278)** | 0.534 (0.288)† | 0.013 (0.475) | 0.499 (0.237)* | 0.421 (0.434) | −0.237 (0.286) |
| Urban residence | 0.292 (0.181) | 0.264 (0.188) | 0.003 (0.215) | 0.070 (0.186) | −0.427 (0.322) | −0.296 (0.226) |
| Constant | −0.423 (0.623) | −0.099 (0.652) | −2.814 (0.822)** | 1.766 (0.427)** | −2.385 (0.769)** | −0.197 (0.558) |
| Log likelihood | −2039.768 | | | −1006.891 | | |
| N | 2,023 | | | 1,021 | | |

SOURCE: Japan, 2003 JGSS; Taiwan, 2002 TSC, part I.
Numbers in parentheses are standard errors. "Nonemployee status" refers to self-employment and family enterprise employment. NA, category is not available for the analysis as a result of small cell size. Although women with higher additional income may choose to work part-time, adding the husband's income to the models does not affect the results presented here (and it may cause potential problems of multicollinearity).

†This category is for age 50 and older for Taiwan, since dividing them into two age groups leads to unstable results.

†p < .10, *p < .05, **p < .01.

*Chapter One*

1. The upper secondary educational level refers to high school and the equivalent, or about twelve years of formal schooling. Tertiary education refers to any formal schooling beyond the high school level, including junior college, technical college, and university.

2. Here, the Tokyo metropolitan area is defined broadly, consisting of not only Tokyo city, but Saitama, Chiba, and Kanagawa prefectures as well.

3. Both Japan and Taiwan, however, have begun to recruit more women from lower income countries in Southeast Asia as care workers in recent years. Despite this change, Japan and Taiwan maintain relatively restrictive quotas for immigrant workers. Such restrictions have made the use of foreign maids far less common than in other industrialized economies in Asia, such as Singapore and Hong Kong.

4. In general, female respondents were less likely to agree with statements supporting traditional gender roles than male respondents in both Japan and Taiwan, but the gender differences in the responses were small. When men's and women's responses are examined separately, the gaps between the two countries regarding attitudes toward the statements described are essentially the same as those demonstrated in Figure 1.4.

5. As discussed in Chapter 6, the Japanese tax system does encourage women's marginal employment by providing an extra tax incentive for households with part-time employed wives. To be specific, Japan's tax system allows the husband to receive dependent spousal and supplementary allowances that offset his tax liability when his wife earns less than a certain threshold. Calculated from the average hourly pay for women reported by Japan's Ministry of Labour (1997), the tax threshold allowed a wife to work 22 to 30 hours a week in 1995 (without her husband losing dependent spousal and supplementary allowances), depending on the geographical area, industry, and enterprise scale. The supplementary allowance remains available if the wife's earnings fall between the threshold and the next level (i.e., between ¥1,030,000 and ¥1,410,000). This regulation thus reduces the incentive for women with part-time jobs to work long hours, because their husbands may in turn lose the tax allowances and both will pay a greater income tax. It is noteworthy that this regulation is only relevant to wives with part-time employment status. Moreover, providing an incentive for part-time working wives to work fewer hours is not equal to discouraging women from taking full-time jobs

in Japan, because part-time employment refers to status rather than hours of work in that country. Part-time employees cannot be considered and treated as full-time ones regardless of how many hours they spend at work.

6. The changes in tax regulations and maternity leave for employed married women both occurred so late in Taiwan that they could not be the cause of married women's increasing labor force participation. Rather, it is likely that they result from the increasing number of married women in the workplace, which might have pressured the government to lift some barriers to female employment.

7. The numbers of women involved in home-based piecework are quite small in the surveys used for most of my analyses. For this reason, I did not create a separate category for this group of workers. Instead, in analyses when employment status is concerned, I combine this group with those who reported to be self-employed without hiring others.

8. Both Lu's (2001) research and my own interview notes indicate that women working at family enterprises often act as co-owners of the businesses, while reporting their husbands as the owners and themselves as employees nominally. In this sense, family enterprise work may still empower women even when it does not pay them regularly.

9. Specifically, I spent a year and a half, from 1995 to 1997, in the Tokyo metropolitan area, and an additional three months in 2002 in the Kansai area to conduct fieldwork for Japan. The interviews for Taiwan were conducted solely in the Taipei metropolitan area in 1994 and 1998. Some of my ethnographic observations also came from the various time periods since 1996 when I resided in Taipei. Although selecting large urban centers as fieldwork sites may cause an urban bias in my qualitative data, the comparison of urban women's work and life experiences in the two countries is particularly meaningful because the Japan–Taiwan differences in gender inequality manifest in urban areas (see Figure 1.2). Besides, I use the interview data only to supplement the statistical analysis of survey data; thus, it is less problematic that my interview samples are not representative of the entire population.

## Chapter Two

1. The SSM sample contains individuals age 20 to 69 years, whereas the TSC sample includes those age 25 to 60 years. For this study I therefore selected respondents age 25 to 60 years in the survey years: 1995 for Japan and 1996 for Taiwan. Consequently, the analytical samples consist of men and women born from 1935 to 1970 for Japan and from 1936 to 1971 for Taiwan. For the Japanese sample, the four cohorts are composed of respondents born 1935 to 1940, 1941 to 1950, 1951 to 1960, and 1961 to 1970. Because the Taiwanese data were collected one year later, the cohort definitions are also shifted to one year later. The so-called 1930s cohort in the Taiwanese sample was born 1936 to 1941, and the 1940s cohort was born 1942 to 1951. Likewise, the 1950s cohort was born 1952 to 1961, and the 1960s cohort was born 1962 to 1971 for Taiwan.

2. The definition of labor force participation is based on survey respondents' self-reports of involvement in market work, regardless of whether they are regularly paid. In addition, participation in the labor force may include performing either agricultural or industrial work.

3. I calculated the average proportions of time men and women spent in market work since their first job entry with respondents who have ever been married.

I excluded those who have never been married because the difference in the length of work experience between single men and women is minimal in both countries. I also excluded those who had never participated in the labor market until after marriage because such cases were rather unusual. By comparing only respondents who began their employment careers before marriage, we can better assess the extent to which men and women with similar starts of their working lives eventually differed in their total experiences of labor force participation.

4. Taiwanese men are required to serve in the military for about two years on average during the postwar period. A sizable proportion of men in the sample started their first job before the military service and had to interrupt their work trajectories around age 20 to serve in the military.

5. I calculated the labor force participation rate during the first stage, before marriage, as the percentage of respondents who ever had participated in market work at any time before marriage. For the other stages, the labor force participation rate was calculated as the percentage of respondents who reported to have ever held a job for any amount of time during the year when the given life course event occurred, if they had ever experienced it. The SSM did not distinguish first from current marriage, so I have to assume that the two were the same marriage for all married respondents throughout this study. I expect this assumption to cause only a small bias, because the divorce rate is low for the generations included in the sample.

6. An exit from the labor force is defined as a job exit followed by a year of absence from the labor market. A job exit leading to only a few months of non-employment is not considered a labor force exit because the individual may never intend to (and may never actually) leave the labor force in such a scenario.

7. This trend is supported by two other surveys of individuals' work histories: the Survey of Occupational Mobility and Processes conducted in 1983 and the National Survey of Occupation and Family Life in 1991. Both surveys were conducted by the Japan Institute of Labour (currently the Japan Institute for Labour Policy and Training).

8. That the late 1970s was the turning point in terms of Taiwanese postmarital women's employment can also be observed in Chapter 6 (see Figure 6.1).

9. The only exception was that managers and professional workers in these countries tended to be those who had changed employers particularly infrequently.

10. In most cases, Japanese women moved to the nonstandard employment sector after employment interruption, when reentering the labor force. See Chapter 6 for more details on women's job options upon labor force reentry.

11. Specifically, I estimate the earnings for the following five groups of workers: (1) regular full-time employees, (2) part-time and temporary employees, (3) family enterprise workers, (4) self-employed workers who hire others to work at the same establishment, and (5) self-employed workers who do not hire others. I divide the self-employed into two groups because solo self-employed workers tend to have different profiles and earnings from entrepreneurs who employ others (Yu and Su 2004).

12. In Figure 2.6, the hypothetical worker appears to have similar or higher earnings than a standard employee with the same characteristics if he or she is self-employed and hires others. However, this comparison does not take into account the fact that self-employed workers who hire others often have to invest substantial capital in their businesses. After the returns to such capital investment

are excluded, the returns to self-employment are likely to be smaller than those to standard employment.

13. Because the 1995 SSM did not ask respondents' hours of work, I could not control for working hours in the regression analysis of annual earnings. Nevertheless, it is noteworthy that, in Japan, part-time or temporary employment generally indicates the status of work more than the hours spent at work. Part-time employees can work as many hours as full-time employees but maintain part-time status (Houseman and Osawa 1995). I address Japan's design of part-time and temporary employment status and its implications for women in Chapter 6.

14. The gender differences in earnings would be smaller for Japan in Figure 2.6 if the hypothetical person is single. However, given that men and women are likely to move to nonstandard jobs after marriage, the assumption that the hypothetical person is married is more appropriate for comparing gender differences in earnings across various types of employment.

## Chapter Three

1. Although a woman who leaves a job that strongly conflicts with her family obligations may move to a less difficult job, she is more likely to head for full-time wifehood or motherhood, because finding a new job when experiencing heavy family burdens is rather stressful.

2. Labor demand in the 1960s, the peak of Japan's economic growth, was nevertheless higher than that in other postwar years in Japan. Prior research reports greater bargaining power for workers against management during this period (Cole 1971; Evans 1984). According to my own interviews, Japanese women who entered the labor market in the 1960s also reported encountering more flexible recruitment policies at the time of their labor force entry. Such a difference suggests that overall labor demand plays a crucial role in workplace policies. The figures shown in Chapter 2 also corroborate that the Japanese cohort entering the labor market in the 1960s had a stronger tendency to remain in their jobs after marriage. However, the increase in labor demand in the 1960s was not large and did not last long enough to cause a more permanent change in Japanese workplaces.

3. As indicated by official statistics for 1955, 10 percent of Japanese who completed compulsory education were able to attend universities or junior colleges (Yanotsuneta Kinenkai 2000).

4. Although these calculations of higher education opportunities in Taiwan exclude those who attained higher education after age 21, I noted earlier that educational systems in Taiwan generally had age barriers to each level and few people could return to school after having passed the normative school age. Hence, the proportions of the population age 18 to 21 in higher education serve as fairly accurate estimates for the advancement rates in this society. Besides, even if the actual advancement rates were slightly higher, the rates for Taiwan in the 1990s would still be lower than the rates for Japan in the 1970s, given that the differences were not trivial.

5. The expansion of higher education in Taiwan in the 1990s in part resulted from the democratization of the regime, which forced the government to respond actively to popular demands.

6. Specifically, job scarcity in the 1950s made the system more appealing to workers, whereas rapid economic growth in the 1960s and early 1970s allowed employers, even those of small firms, to afford the practices of long-term employ-

ment and seniority-based wage increases. Moreover, the relatively youthful labor force made the system seem beneficial to employers during the early postwar years, since the practices allowed them to deprive young workers of proper compensation until later in their firm careers.

7. Not only had labor shortages not been a concern since the 1950s, but the permanent employment system also became less affordable after the mid 1970s, when the economy slowed down. Moreover, the aging population also increased labor costs under the system, which tends to overpay senior employees. In the absence of an economic rationale, the reason to maintain the permanent employment system became a moral one for management. To give an example, in 1997, the president of a major Japanese enterprise spoke in public about the company's recent expansion to new industries as means to create new jobs for existing employees; the ultimate goal was to keep the promise of permanent employment during severe economic recession.

8. The Japanese labor market does not define regular full-time employees based simply on work hours. Full-time employment indicates that the job is not for a limited term or temporary, whereas part-time employment indicates an irregular short-term status regardless of the hours worked. More details on these definitions are provided in Chapter 6.

9. Nevertheless, the marriage bar existed in some firms during the early postwar period. Under the marriage bar policy, an employer would force female full-time workers to resign upon marriage. However, the introduction of a marriage retirement system was determined to be illegal after the ruling of *Suzuki v. Sumitomo Cement* in 1966 (Upham 1987). From then on, Japanese companies, by law, had to abandon the marriage bar and apply the long-term employment practice to every full-time standard employee.

10. To give an example of the dichotomous employment contracts, the popular discourse in the 1990s debating the replacement of the permanent employment system often mentioned the situation for professional sports, in which everyone was under term contracts as an alternative. Options in between the extremes were rarely mentioned.

11. The statistics discussed here are drawn from the same sources as those for Figure 3.4. The percentages for Taiwan include paid employees in the agricultural sector; those for Japan do not. Nevertheless, both countries had few agricultural employees. The percentage of paid employees in the agricultural sector in Japan has been less than 1 percent.

12. As shown in Appendix B, Table B.2, each successive year of work experience led to much greater earnings in Japan than in Taiwan for both men and women. The effect of one year of work experience on log earnings in Japan is three to four times as large as that in Taiwan.

13. When a female worker did stay in the firm after childbearing, her employer needed to pay for the additional labor cost incurred as a result of her maternity leave. In most cases, as I was told during my in-depth interviews in Taiwan, employers were reluctant to provide maternity leave. The additional cost may certainly have discouraged employers from retaining female workers after marriage. However, because there was no law mandating small- to medium-size firms to offer maternity leave before the late 1980s, most employers were able to offer only a minimal period of leave, depending on how busy the business was. This condition made the cost of maternity leave somewhat more acceptable by employers.

*Chapter Four*

Part of this chapter is based on my earlier article (Yu 2005).

1. The examples provided by no means suggest that all Taiwanese workplaces were highly family responsive. Rather, both labor shortages and a relatively informal workplace atmosphere, as discussed in the previous chapter, have compelled Taiwanese employers to be somewhat tolerant toward female employees with heavy family burdens.

2. The regression models used event history techniques (Yamaguchi 1991), with both the predictors and outcomes varying with women's duration of exposure to the possibility of leaving the labor force. Precisely, the models estimated the log odds of a specified event occurring at time $t$, given that the event has not occurred through $t - 1$.

3. The odds of the occurrence of a given event are defined as the probability of the event occurring divided by the probability of the event not occurring (i.e., $p/[1 - p]$). An odds ratio is a ratio of the odds of a certain outcome for one group to the odds of the same outcome for another group (usually the reference group). Hence, an odds ratio larger than one indicates that the estimated event is more likely to occur among the group under examination than the reference group, whereas an odds ratio less than one indicates the event is less likely to occur among the first group than the second group.

4. Although the coefficients corresponding to service and sales occupations are somewhat consistent with the labor market conditions discussed in Japan and Taiwan, I do not consider them as part of the supporting evidence because the job contexts for this occupational category were particularly heterogeneous. A large proportion of service and sales jobs for women was associated with contingent work arrangements or family-owned retail stores in both Japan and Taiwan.

5. Before the implementation of the EEOA in 1986, most large Japanese firms automatically excluded women from jobs in the career track that required job rotation.

6. As indicated in Figure 4.3, Japanese women in larger firms were significantly more likely to leave their jobs than those employed in smaller firms. For the regression model on employment exits upon marriage, the coefficients corresponding to firms with 100 to 499 employees and those with 500 and more employees are not significantly different, but firms with 100 and more employees had significantly larger exit rates than smaller firms (those with 10–99 employees).

7. In recent years, there has been an increase in married Japanese women who remain in their jobs until their first pregnancy. Nevertheless, a survey conducted during 2002 by the National Institute of Population and Social Security Research (2004) in Japan found that it is still common for women to leave their jobs around the time of marriage, if not staying in the labor force throughout their early child-rearing years.

8. During the period of economic growth in postwar era Japan and Taiwan, layoffs were highly uncommon. However, in the case of Taiwan, many small-scale firms have shorter lives than one's working life. When a firm terminates, its workers have to end their employment.

9. To elaborate, we need to know the husband's exact earnings at each time point when the wife is in the labor force to analyze the effect of the husband's income on the wife's decision to leave the labor market at a particular time.

10. Although I have no information regarding whether those who lived with an extended family member at the survey time had lived with the same person throughout the years under examination, I argue that current coresidence suggests a relatively close relationship between respondents and their extended kin even in previous years. Such respondents are therefore more likely to receive their relatives' help throughout their child-rearing years.

11. It is noteworthy that a husband's education may also decrease his support for traditional gender roles, thus reducing the wife's difficulty with combining work and family demands. I cannot examine this possibility without retrospective data regarding the husband's income or attitudes. However, in the case of Japan, the positive effect of husbands' education on women's likelihood of leaving the labor force suggests that the greater income resulting from husbands' higher education overshadowed the effect of gender attitudes. By contrast, the two opposite effects of a husband's education led to the weak overall impact of this factor on his wife's employment exit in Taiwan. This cross-national difference is consistent with the argument that work environments imposed greater barriers to women's continuous employment after marriage in Japan.

12. The reason for choosing these two groups for a comparison is that most of them had experienced marriage and participated in the nonagricultural sector. Comparing them allows us to assess the impact of the redistribution of single women's jobs in the nonagricultural sector on their postmarital job continuity. Nevertheless, grouping women with different birth years did not change the trends in the two countries.

## Chapter Five

1. I do not intend to suggest that Japanese men would devote much more time to domestic work if they were to work fewer hours. As noted in Chapter 1, the household division of labor is highly gendered in both countries. Women are responsible for the majority of domestic chores and childcare, and their husbands share only a small proportion of the household work (Lee et al. 2000; Tsuya and Bumpass 1998). My argument is simply that a husband working fewer hours will arrive at home earlier at night. When there is a young child in the family, a husband's presence alone will increase the wife's time flexibility and hence alleviate her burden.

2. One exception for working relatively regular hours applies to the self-employed in Taiwan. Self-employed workers tend to work long hours, often at night (Yu and Su 2004). However, a sizable proportion of the self-employed in Taiwan are able to combine the home and the workplace (Yu 2001b). This arrangement alleviates some conflict between their working hours and family responsibilities. It is also noteworthy that overtime work has increased among Taiwanese in upper white-collar occupations in recent years, because the transformation of the economy has brought in a greater number of "promising" jobs in capital-intensive industries. I discuss this change and its impact in Chapter 8.

3. The fee charged by public childcare centers, however, is not low by an absolute measure. A few Japanese women with whom I spoke said that they considered the cost of the public daycare centers a burden. Roughly speaking, having two children enrolled in public daycare centers would cost most of the wage of a full-time working mother. Private daycare centers tend to be much more expensive.

4. In a few conversations I observed in Taiwan, grandmothers who decided not to take care of their young grandchildren even became the targets of criticism by others. It appears that the grandmothers' help is taken for granted among many Taiwanese families.

5. The percentages among respondents from northern European countries, which provide better social welfare for parents, were even lower. For example, only 30 percent of Swedish respondents felt that mothers with preschool children should stay at home rather than taking a job. Unfortunately, the ISSP conducted in 1994 did not include Taiwan.

6. The percentage calculated for Taiwan includes respondents who felt that mothers of young children should decide about their employment whichever way they prefer. This option was available only in Taiwan. Interestingly, according to the 2002 ISSP, Taiwanese respondents were more likely to agree that "a preschool child is likely to suffer if his or her mother works" than their Japanese counterparts (Figure 1.4), although they also reported a higher level of support for the employment of mothers with preschool children. Somewhat consistent with these tendencies, among those believing that a preschool child may suffer from his or her mother's employment, a larger proportion of respondents in Japan (rather than Taiwan) reported that mothers with preschool children should not work. Thus, for Taiwanese people, whether mothers should work appears not to depend heavily on whether their preschool children may suffer. As discussed later, the family's need for the wife's income may also affect Taiwanese adults' views regarding mothers' employment.

7. From the 1970s to the 1980s, the amount of time a Japanese mother spent on each child must have increased slightly, because marital fertility declined gradually during this period (Ogawa and Retherford 1993; Retherford et al. 1996).

8. Most Japanese women who have interrupted their employment careers face a substantial income reduction or a considerable decrease in occupational status upon their labor force return (see Chapter 6 for a thorough examination). As my interviews suggest, many Japanese women are aware of this possibility. In this sense, most homemaking women in Japan recognize that they have given up their opportunities to develop a career for their family.

9. This type of household division of labor does not necessarily require the three generations to live under one roof. The oldest generation may live alone, but remains close to the nuclear family composed of the succeeding two generations.

## Chapter Six

A portion of this chapter was drawn from my earlier article (Yu 2006).

1. An average Japanese woman born in 1936 to 1940 would marry around age 24 and have her first child by age 26. In contrast, an average Taiwanese woman in this birth cohort married around 22 years old and experienced her first childbirth around 23 years old. These differences in the ages of first marriage and childbirth reflect the large gap in women's education during the early postwar period between the two countries. Japanese women of this cohort typically have at least nine years of education, the mandatory educational level. Most of their Taiwanese counterparts, by contrast, had finished schooling by age 12 and started to work even before they turned 15 years old. As women's educational levels increased, the average ages of first marriage and childbirth among Taiwanese women became more similar to those in Japan.

2. There is no significant difference in the mean education, age of marriage, length of premarital work experience, or number of children between Japanese women with and without homemaking experience. However, Japanese women with continuous work trajectories are more likely to live with extended kin. In contrast, Taiwanese women with continuous work patterns have higher education, marry later, have more highly educated husbands, and have fewer births compared with those with full-time homemaking experience (see Table 1 in Yu [2006] for details).

3. I measured a woman's homemaking duration as the number of years that have passed since both of the following two requirements were met: (1) she entered her most recent marriage and (2) she was out of the labor force. I only considered those who had been jobless for a full year as being out of the labor force. Because the statistical analysis presented in this section is concerned with labor force reentry, only women with premarital work experience were used in the analytical samples.

4. The estimations are based on the coefficients from the full models in Appendix B, Table B.6, and use the combined means from both samples for all independent variables, except for duration and family cycles.

5. Other than this replacement, the models are identical to the full models shown in Appendix B, Table B.6. A complete description of these additional models and results is included in my earlier work (Yu 2006).

6. It is theoretically possible that the occupational opportunities for Taiwanese reentrants are better because only those who are able to find good enough jobs return to work in that country, whereas the selection mechanism is different in Japan. However, based on Appendix B, Table B.6, there is no evidence that Taiwanese women with better occupational experience previously were more likely to resume employment. On the contrary, among Japanese women, those who had held professional or managerial occupations were more likely to reenter the labor force. Hence, if anything, the selection mechanisms should ensure that Japanese reentrants experience less downward occupational mobility than their Taiwanese counterparts.

7. In many ways, the practices of the Taiwanese government and its affiliated enterprises are highly similar to those of the Japanese permanent employment system.

8. A separate analysis further indicates that married women's timing of their return to the labor force was independent of the type of employment they reentered in both Japan and Taiwan. That is to say, those taking part-time jobs upon reentry do not necessarily resume their employment in a more timely fashion than those obtaining full-time jobs.

9. Ironically, despite the nature of their employment contracts, Japanese part-timers do not necessarily have less job attachment or more frequent turnovers. During my fieldwork in Japan, I encountered a few part-timers who had held the same job continuously for more than a decade. Thus, a part-timer can sometimes be entitled to work like a full-time employee, only without the same benefits and long-term opportunities.

10. A survey (*Gyōkyō to Koyō ni Kansuru Anketo Chōsa* [Business Situation and Employment Survey]) conducted in 1996 by a job advertisement company in Tokyo, AIDEM, reported that even among small- to medium-size firms, more than half specified upper age limits when recruiting regular full-time employees.

I obtained the survey report directly from AIDEM during my field research in To-kyo in 1997.

11. State policies have also made nonstandard employment more appealing in Japan (Gottfried and Hayashi-Kato 1998; Gottfried and O'Reilly 2002). The income tax system provides a good example. The tax system provides a relatively high tax threshold, which makes part-time jobs seem tax free and hence attractive (Ishii 1993; Shoven 1989; Wakisaka and Bae 1998). To be specific, based on the regulations in 1995, one individual would be free from income tax if he or she earned ¥1,030,000 (about US$10,300) or less. This amount would be equal to the annual earnings of a woman with a part-time job and working 22 to 30 hours per week (depending on her geographical location, industry, and enterprise scale). Moreover, because of the addition of "special allowances for spouses" in 1987, husbands with wives who earned less than ¥700,000 a year could receive twice the spousal deduction, and husbands of wives who earn up to ¥1,410,000 annually could still receive tax deductions of various amounts. Thus, a married woman who reenters the labor force into a part-time job can virtually expect no increase or only a small increase in her family's income tax as a result of her employment.

12. In a separate analysis, not shown here, I found that the age of entering the current status had no significant effect on married women's likelihood of being in part-time employment rather than full-time employment, as long as their entry occurred before age 45. Thus, although returning to the labor force at a relatively old age (>45 years) decreases a woman's chance of having a full-time job, returning much earlier than age 45 does not improve this chance any further.

## Chapter Seven

1. For example, Japanese government statistics on educational advancement rates among high school graduates include only those who attend universities and junior colleges. Entering a special training school after high school graduation is not considered educational advancement. Therefore, in this chapter I pay little attention to special training schools in Japan.

2. Graduates from three-year junior colleges may take examinations to "transfer" into four-year universities. Although those who take such examinations have usually completed their junior college education, it is considered transferring because they start with the second or third year of their university education if they pass the examinations. Such transfers, however, are uncommon because Taiwanese universities generally allow a very small number of transfers from all types of schools.

3. Taiwan's educational reforms since the late 1990s have led to the increases in general high school and university enrollment (Wang 2003). With these increases, the demand for five-year junior colleges has declined. Hence, most of the more prestigious five-year junior colleges transformed into four-year colleges or universities and began to admit only high school graduates.

4. In this sense, vocational high schools hold less promise for tertiary education than general high schools and five-year junior colleges, which makes them the worst option for educational advancement.

5. In 2002, the number of students enrolled in general high schools surpassed that in vocational high schools for the first time since 1970 (Ministry of Education, Republic of China various years). This change had to do with the rapid increase in academic high schools since the late 1990s, which is part of the government's plan to expand university education.

6. Recent educational reforms have made it possible for students to obtain university admission without taking the entrance exams in both countries. Nevertheless, most students in higher education were still admitted through the traditional channel: university entrance exams. Therefore, my discussion of the road to university education in a later section focuses on this channel of obtaining university admission.

7. Japan traditionally distinguishes national (*kokuritsu*) from public (*kōritsu*) universities, with the former sponsored by the central government and the latter by local governments. However, for convenience, I refer to both types as public universities.

8. As Luoh (2002) shows, a considerable proportion of the students admitted to National Taiwan University are recent high school graduates. I elaborate on the difference in the reasons for undertaking *rōnin* study between Japan and Taiwan in a later section.

9. Here, *high school* refers to both general and vocational high schools because the Japanese government generally reports the high school advancement rate using the combined category. Japan's proportion of vocational high schools is relatively small, and the ratio of boys to girls among vocational high school students is relatively even (Fujimura-Fanselow and Imanura 1991). Therefore, using the combined advancement rate does not affect the overall picture regarding gender inequality in the opportunities for receiving a high school education.

10. Because the exact numbers of male and female students who advanced to different types of schools after middle school completion are only available from 1987 onward, I used the number of students enrolled in middle and equivalent schools compared with the numbers of students enrolled in general high schools, vocational high schools, and the first three years of five-year junior colleges three years later to estimate the advancement rates to each of these upper secondary educational institutions. The estimated results are highly similar to the detailed upper secondary educational advancement rates reported by the Ministry of Education since 1987. My estimated rates are slightly higher (<5%), especially for the vocational and junior college advancement rates, because they include those who attend high school or junior college after *rōnin* study.

11. Before 1987, the Taiwanese government did not even report the educational advancement rate for vocational high school students because it was negligible. Moreover, when vocational high school students do study further, they are unlikely to go to universities. According to official statistics, between 1987 and 1997 less than 3 percent of vocational high school graduates advanced to universities (Ministry of Education, Republic of China various years). Most vocational high school students who advanced to the next level went to two- or three-year junior colleges.

12. The ratios of the seats at three-year junior colleges to those at four-year universities were 28:72 in 1975 and 22:78 in 1985, according to educational statistics reported by the Ministry of Education in Taiwan. The enrollment of three-year junior colleges, however, declined rapidly in the 1990s (Ministry of Education, Republic of China various years). This level of school no longer existed by the late 1990s.

13. Specifically, the advancement rate of Japanese male high school students has been fluctuating within the range of 35 to 45 percent since 1975 (Brinton and Lee 2001).

14. Yu and Chu (1998) also argue that the higher ability of students in prestigious universities, rather than the better quality of elite universities, accounts for the positive relation between university prestige and labor market outcomes. This argument is plausible in both Japan and Taiwan, given that university admission is solely determined by exam performance. Regardless of why elite university graduates have better job prospects, this association nevertheless indicates the importance for women to have equal access to elite higher education in these countries.

15. Generally speaking, those who major in nature sciences and engineering take different entrance exams from those who intend to major in social sciences, business, arts, and humanities.

16. One such example is National Tsing Hua University in Taiwan, also known as the Massachusetts Institute of Technology of Taiwan, which traditionally has had few nonscience departments.

17. All information regarding National Taiwan University's student compositions in this chapter is provided by Ming-Ching Luoh, based on his study (Luoh 2002) of the enrollment in that university.

18. In both Japan and Taiwan, there are several public high schools in each school district, and these schools are not equally desirable. Therefore, students must compete intensely to enter the best high school in the district. The admission to Taiwan's high schools is based solely on entrance exam scores. Some school districts in Japan, however, also take into account applicants' middle school grades and their teachers' recommendations, but these other criteria count much less than examination scores in determining school admission (Rohlen 1983).

19. The top ten high schools are all gender segregated except for the Affiliated Senior High School of National Taiwan Normal University, which has a student body that is, nevertheless, predominantely male. For convenience, I refer to this school as a boys' high school.

20. The discussion here about Taiwan's public high schools and their admission policies concerns only general, academic high schools, because vocational high schools hold entrance exams separately. Besides, Taiwan's vocational high schools are mostly private owned (Woo 1991).

21. As part of the government's effort to eliminate the public consensus on the ranking of high schools, there is no public record of the minimum entrance scores to high schools each year. Nonetheless, I was able to collect this information from newspaper coverage from 1980 to 1997.

22. The lack of a gender-specific admission quota for universities suggests that the gendered admission system for public high schools originated from the single-sex policy of a few elite high schools, rather than the government's attempt to ensure female access to education.

23. Because of Taiwan's rapid expansion of higher education since the late 1990s, university admission is no longer the privilege of students from top-ranked high schools. Nevertheless, being admitted to an elite university remains difficult. For simplicity the discussion in this chapter focuses on the conditions before recent educational expansion and reforms. I address the effects of Taiwan's educational reforms in the next chapter.

24. National universities offer two university-specific, second-stage entrance exams annually within the entrance exam season, whereas universities affiliated with local governments, which are usually less prestigious, offer three opportunities for the second-stage exam every year.

25. According to the School Basic Survey conducted in 1978, the number of female applicants for national universities decreased by nearly four thousand from the previous year, whereas male applicants increased by about two thousand. The same source also indicates that from 1955 to 2005, the numbers of male and female applicants for national universities almost always changed in the same direction from one year to the next (MEXT, Japan various years). Therefore, the change in 1978 indicates an unusual decline in women's willingness to try taking entrance exams for national universities that year.

26. My own experience during the late 1980s also suggests that the percentage of National Taiwan University entrants with *rōnin* experience was relatively small, perhaps between 10 and 15 percent.

## Chapter Eight

1. Interestingly, Hiroshi Ishida (1993) shows that attending higher prestige universities actually enhances men's occupational attainment and income much more in the United States than in Japan. In this sense, Japanese men's endeavor to attend elite universities perhaps reflects more of how important university prestige is believed to be, rather than how important it actually is.

2. As of 2007, the 2003 wave of the JGSS is the most recent one accessible by the public at the Inter-University Consortium for Political and Social Research. Also see Appendix A for details about the JGSS.

3. The detailed results from these models are shown in Appendix B, Tables B.8 through B.10.

4. When I fit the same models to the male sample in the 2003 JGSS, marital status has no significant effects on their current occupations or firm size. Japanese men's likelihood to be in part-time or temporary jobs rather than full-time standard jobs, however, is significantly less if they are married. Thus, the results for men are completely different from those for women. In this sense, marriage is still the key factor shaping gender differences in employment trajectories in Japan.

5. However, it is noteworthy that age groups have hardly any significant effects on Japanese women's job locations in the regression results presented in Appendix B, Tables 8 through 10, suggesting that there is little alteration in women's employment opportunities and behaviors over time. I also found virtually no interaction effect between marriage and age groups. This finding corroborates that women's postmarital employment patterns have not changed much in recent years.

6. To increase the sample size, the data used here are drawn from both questionnaires A and B of the 1995 SSM, whereas in previous chapters only part A of the SSM sample was used for analyses. As explained in Appendix A, the reason to use only part A has to do with the requirement of work and life history data in event history analyses. I utilize both parts of the SSM here because only cross-sectional information is necessary.

7. I combine manufacturing and agricultural occupations into the same group because there was only one respondent in these samples who reported having an agricultural job. I therefore refer to this group as "women in manufacturing occupations," despite the inclusion of farm workers.

8. Like the 2003 wave of the JGSS, the 2002 TSC did not collect information on respondents' full work and life histories (see Appendix A for details regarding this data set). I therefore must rely on cross-sectional analyses for estimating women's job exit patterns.

9. Here, *working age* refers to between 20 and 55 years old.

10. In a separate analysis, I calculated the percentage in the labor force among women age 20 to 45, as well as among those with preschool children, by their first occupation. The results are generally similar to those shown in Figure 8.3. Nevertheless, limiting the sample by women's or their children's age leads to relatively few cases for each occupational category. The percentages estimated from such samples are therefore less stable and meaningful than those shown in Figure 8.3.

11. The fact that Japanese men's working hours have only increased since the mid 1990s, as shown in Chapter 5, corroborates this argument.

12. For example, based on the experiences of a few professional women, a *Wall Street Journal* report on July 23, 2007, suggests that as a result of the changing demographic structure, a shift in Japanese companies' attitudes toward women workers is under way.

# REFERENCES

Ahmadjian, Christina L., and Gregory E. Robbins. 2005. A clash of capitalisms: Foreign shareholders and corporate restructuring in Japan. *American Sociological Review* 70:451–471.

Allmendinger, Jutta. 1989. *Career mobility dynamics: A comparative analysis of the United States, Norway, and West Germany*. Berlin: Max-Planck-Institut für Bildungsforschung.

Becker, Gary S. 1964. *Human capital*. New York: National Bureau of Economic Research, Columbia University Press.

Becker, Gary S. 1981. *A treatise on the family*. Cambridge: Harvard University Press.

Berger, Peter L., and Hsin-Huang Michael Hsiao, ed. 1988. *In search of an East Asian development model*. New Brunswick, NJ: Transaction Publishers.

Biddlecom, Ann, Napaporn Chayovan, and Mary Beth Ofstedal. 2002. Intergenerational support and transfers. In *The well-being of the elderly in Asia: A four-country comparative study*, ed. Albert I. Hermalin, 185–230. Ann Arbor: The University of Michigan Press.

Blossfeld, Hans-Peter, Alfred Hamerle, and Karl Ulrich Mayer. 1989. *Event history analysis: Statistical theory and application in the social sciences*. Hillsdale, NJ: Lawrence Erlbaum Associates.

Boling, Patricia. 2007. Policies to support working mothers and children in Japan. In *The political economy of Japan's low fertility*, ed. Frances McCall Rosenbluth, 131–154. Stanford: Stanford University Press.

Bongaarts, John. 2001. Fertility and reproductive preferences in post-transitional societies. *Population and Development Review* 27:260–281.

Bourguignon, François, Martin Fournier, and Marc Gurgand. 2004. Distribution, development, and education in Taiwan, China, 1979–94. In *The microeconomics of income distribution dynamics: In East Asia and Latin America*, eds. François Bourguignon, Francisco H. G. Ferreira, and Nora Lustig, 313–356. Washington, DC: World Bank.

Brinton, Mary C. 1988. The social–institutional bases of gender stratification: Japan as an illustrative case. *American Journal of Sociology* 94:300–334.

Brinton, Mary C. 1989. Gender stratification in contemporary urban Japan. *American Sociological Review* 54:549–564.

Brinton, Mary C. 1993. *Women and the economic miracle: Gender and work in postwar Japan*. Berkeley: University of California Press.

Brinton, Mary C. 2001. Married women's labor in East Asian economies. In *Women's working lives in East Asia*, ed. Mary C. Brinton, 1–37. Stanford: Stanford University Press.

Brinton, Mary C., and Sunhwa Lee. 2001. Women's education and the labor market in Japan and South Korea. In *Women's working lives in East Asia*, ed. Mary C. Brinton, 125–150. Stanford: Stanford University Press.

Brinton, Mary C., Yean-Ju Lee, and William L. Parish. 1995. Married women's employment in rapidly industrializing societies: Examples from East Asia. *American Journal of Sociology* 100:1099–1130.

Broaded, C. Montgomery. 1997. The limits and possibilities of tracking: Some evidence from Taiwan. *Sociology of Education* 70:36–53.

Bureau of Statistics, Office of the Prime Minister, Japan. 1971. *1970 population census of Japan*. Tokyo: Author.

Cabinet Office, Government of Japan. Various years. *Annual reports on national accounts*. Tokyo: Author.

Chang, Mariko Lin. 2000. The evolution of sex segregation regimes. *American Journal of Sociology* 105:1658–1701.

Chang, Mariko Lin. 2004. Cross-national variation in sex segregation in sixteen developing countries. *American Sociological Review* 69:114–137.

Chang, Ming-Cheng, Ronald Freedman, and Te-Hsiung Sun. 1987. Trends in fertility, family size preferences, and family planning practices in Taiwan, 1961–85. *Studies in Family Planning* 18:320–337.

Charles, Maria, and Karen Bradley. 2002. Equal but separate? A cross-national study of sex segregation in higher education. *American Sociological Review* 67:573–599.

Charles, Maria, and David B. Grusky. 2004. *Occupational ghettos: The worldwide segregation of women and men*. Stanford: Stanford University Press.

Chen, Fen-ling. 2000. *Working women and state policies in Taiwan: A study in political economy*. Houndmills, NY: Palgrave.

Cheng, Lucie, and Ping-Chun Hsiung. 1994. Women, export-oriented growth, and the state: The case of Taiwan. In *The role of the state in Taiwan's development*, ed. Joel D. Aberbach, David Dollar, and Kenneth L. Sokoloff, 321–353. Armonk and London: M.E. Sharpe.

Cheng, Mariah Mantsun, and Arne L. Kalleberg. 1996. Labor market structures in Japan: An analysis of organizational and occupational mobility patterns. *Social Forces* 4:1235–1260.

Cheng, Mariah Mantsun, and Arne L. Kalleberg. 1997. How permanent was permanent employment? Patterns of organizational mobility in Japan, 1916–1975. *Work and Occupations* 24:12–32.

Chu, C. Y. Cyrus, Yu Xie, and Ruoh-Rong Yu. 2007. Effects of sibship structure revisited: Evidence from intrafamily resource transfer in Taiwan. *Sociology of Education* 80:91–113.

Clark, Rodney. 1979. *The Japanese company*. New Haven: Yale University Press.

Cole, Robert E. 1971. The theory of institutionalization: Permanent employment and tradition in Japan. *Economic Development and Cultural Change* 20:47–70.

The College Entrance Examination Center (Taiwan). 2001. Statistics of individuals admitted to a university, 2001. www.ceec.edu.tw/UnionEntrance/90uni_report/t7.htm (accessed September 16, 2008).

The College Entrance Examination Center (Taiwan). 2003. Statistics of university applicants, 2003. www.ceec.edu.tw/AppointExam/AppointExamStat/91ApExamStat/1.htm (accessed September 18, 2008).

The College Entrance Examination Center (Taiwan). 2008. Statistics of university applicants over time. www.ceec.edu.tw/AppointExam/AppointExamStat.htm (accessed September 18, 2008).

Cotter, David A., JoAnn Defiore, Joan M. Hermsen, Brenda Marsteller Kowalewski, and Reeve Vanneman. 1998. The demand for female labor. *American Journal of Sociology* 103:1673–1712.

Crawcour, Sydney. 1978. The Japanese employment system. *Journal of Japanese Studies* 4:225–245.

Cumings, Bruce. 1987. The origins and development of the northeast Asian political economy: Industrial sectors, product cycles, and political consequences. In *The political economy of the new Asian industrialism*, ed. Frederic C. Deyo, 44–83. Ithaca: Cornell University Press.

Department of Household Registration Affairs, Ministry of Interior, Republic of China. Household registration statistics. The specific data used in the book are from http://sowf.moi.gov.tw/stat/year/y02-02.xls, www.ris.gov.tw/ch4/static/st10-10.xls, and www.ris.gov.tw/ch4/static/st10-17.xls (accessed September 1, 2008).

Department of Statistics, Ministry of Interior, Republic of China. 2007. Monthly bulletin of interior statistics. http://sowf.moi.gov.tw/stat/month/m1-01.xls (accessed September 10, 2008).

Desai, Sonalde, and Linda J. Waite. 1991. Women's employment during pregnancy and after the first birth: Occupational characteristics and work commitment. *American Sociological Review* 56:551–566.

DeSoto, Hernando. 1989. *The other path: The invisible revolution in the third world.* New York: Harper and Row.

Directorate-General of Budget, Accounting and Statistics (DGBAS), Executive Yuan, Republic of China (Taiwan). 1979. *Report on fertility and employment of married women, Taiwan area, Republic of China.* Taipei: Author.

DGBAS. 1988. *The report on the time utilization survey.* Taipei: Author.

DGBAS. 1995. *The report on the time utilization survey.* Taipei: Author

DGBAS. 1996. *Social indicators, Taiwan area, Republic of China.* Taipei: Author.

DGBAS. 2000. *Yearbook of manpower survey statistics: Taiwan area, Republic of China.* Taipei: Author.

DGBAS. 2001a. *The report on 2001 industrial and commercial census in Taiwan-Fukien area, the Republic of China.* Taipei: Author.

DGBAS. 2001b. *Survey of social development trends (time use), Taiwan area, Republic of China.* Taipei: Author.

DGBAS. 2003. Women's Marriage, Fertility, and Employment Survey. www.dgbas.gov.tw/ct.asp?xItem=11661&CtNode=3304 (accessed September 1, 2008).

DGBAS. 2005a. Manpower Survey. www.dgbas.gov.tw/ct.asp?xItem=17286&ctNode=3246 (accessed September 1, 2008).

DGBAS. 2005b. Social indicators. www.dgbas.gov.tw/public/Data/411711484071.xls (accessed September 1, 2008).

DGBAS. 2006. *Yearbook of manpower survey statistics: Taiwan area, Republic of China.* Taipei: Author.

DGBAS. 2007. *Statistics yearbook of the Republic of China, 2006.* Taipei: Author.

http://eng.dgbas.gov.tw/public/Data/710417195871.pdf (accessed September 18, 2008).

DGBAS. Various years. *National income in the Taiwan area of the Republic of China*. Taipei: Author.

DGBAS. Various years. *Social indicators, Taiwan area, Republic of China*. Taipei: Author.

DGBAS. Various years. *Yearbook of manpower survey statistics, Taiwan area, Republic of China*. Taipei: Author.

Diamond, Norma. 1973. The middle class family model in Taiwan: Woman's place is in the home. *Asian Survey*. 13:853–872.

Diamond, Norma. 1979. Women and industry in Taiwan. *Modern China* 5:317–340.

Doeringer, Peter B., and Michael J. Piore. 1971. *Internal labor markets and manpower analysis*. Lexington, MA: Health Lexington Books.

Drobiniö, Sonja, Hans-Peter Blossfeld, and Götz Rohwer. 1999. Dynamics of women's employment patterns over the family life course: A comparison of the United States and Germany. *Journal of Marriage and the Family* 61:133–146.

Edwards, Linda N. 1988. Equal employment opportunity in Japan: A view from the West. *Industrial and Labor Relations Review* 41:240–250.

Eissa, Nada. 1996. Labor Supply and Economic Recovery Tax Act of 1981. In *Empirical foundations of household taxation*, ed. Martin Feldstein and James M. Poterba, 5–38. Chicago: University of Chicago Press.

Esping-Anderson, Gøsta. 1990. *The three worlds of welfare capitalism*. Princeton, NJ: Princeton University Press.

Esping-Anderson, Gøsta. 1999. *Social foundations of postindustrial economies*. Oxford: Oxford University Press.

Estevéz-Abe, Margarita. 2007. Gendering the varieties of capitalism: Gender bias in skills and social policies. In *The political economy of Japan's low fertility*, ed. Frances McCall Rosenbluth, 63–86. Stanford: Stanford University Press.

Evans, Robert, Jr. 1984. Pay differentials: the case of Japan. *Monthly Labor Review* 107:32–36.

Even, William E. 1987. Career interruptions following childbirth. *Journal of Labor Economics* 5:255–277.

Feeney, Griffith, and Andrew Mason. 2001. Population in East Asia. In *Population change and economic development in East Asia: Challenges met, opportunities seized*, ed. Andrew Mason, 61–95. Stanford: Stanford University Press.

Feldstein, Martin, and Daniel R. Feenberg. 1996. The taxation of two-earner families. In *Empirical foundations of household taxation*, ed. Martin Feldstein and James M. Poterba, 39–76. Chicago: University of Chicago Press.

Fujimura-Fanselow, Kumiko, and Anne E. Imamura. 1991. The education of women in Japan. In *Windows on Japanese education*, ed. Edward R. Beauchamp, 227–258. Westport, CT: Greenwood.

Fujita, Mariko. 1989. "It's all Mother's fault": Childcare and the socialization of working mothers in Japan. *Journal of Japanese Studies* 15:67–91.

Fuwa, Makiko. 2004. Macro-level gender inequality and the division of household in 22 countries. *American Sociological Review* 69:751–767.

Ganzeboom, Harry B. G., and Donald J. Treiman. 1996. Internationally comparable measures of occupational status for the 1988 International Standard Classification of Occupations. *Social Science Research* 25:201–239.

Gao, Bai. 2001. *Japan's economic dilemma: The institutional origins of prosperity and stagnation*. Cambridge: Cambridge University Press.

Gelb, Joyce. 2000. The equal employment opportunity law: A decade of change for Japanese women? *Law & Policy* 22:385–407.

Genda, Yuji, and Masako Kurosawa. 2001. Transition from school to work in Japan. *Journal of the Japanese and International Economies* 15:465–488.

Gender Equality Bureau, Cabinet Office, Japan. 2003. *Report on cross-national comparative surveys on gender equality*. Tokyo: Author.

Gender Equality Bureau, Cabinet Office, Japan. 2007. *Josei no raifupuranningu shien ni kansuru chōsa hōkokusho* [*Survey report on the support for women's life planning*]. Tokyo: Author. www.gender.go.jp/danjo-kaigi/kansieikyo/raifupuran1903.pdf (accessed September 18, 2008).

Gerson, Kathleen. 1985. *Hard choices: How women decide about work, career, and motherhood*. Berkeley: University of California Press.

Gindling, T. H., and Way Sun. 2002. Higher education planning and the wages of workers with higher education in Taiwan. *Economics of Education Review* 21:153–169.

Glass, Jennifer. 1992. Housewives and employed wives: Demographic and attitudinal change, 1972–1986. *Journal of Marriage and the Family* 54:559–569.

Glass, Jennifer, and Valarie Camarigg. 1992. Gender, parenthood, and job–family compatibility. *American Journal of Sociology* 98:131–151.

Glass, Jennifer L., and Sarah Beth Estes. 1997. The family responsive workplace. *Annual Review of Sociology* 23:289–313.

Glass, Jennifer, and Lisa Riley. 1998. Family responsive policies and employee retention following childbirth. *Social Forces* 76:1401–1435.

Gold, Thomas B. 1988. Colonial origins of Taiwanese capitalism. In *Contending approaches to the political economy of Taiwan*, ed. Edwin A. Winckler and Susan Greenhalgh, p. 101–120. Armonk, NY: M.E. Sharpe.

Goldin, Claudia. 1990. *Understanding the gender gap: An economic history of American women*. New York: Oxford University Press.

Goldin, Claudia. 1995. The U-shaped female labor force function in economic development and economic history. In *Investment in women's human capital*, ed. T. Paul Schultz, 61–90. Chicago: University of Chicago Press.

Goldin, Claudia. 1997. Career and family: College women look to the past. In *Gender and family issues in the workplace*, ed. Francine. D. Blau and Ronald G. Ehrenberg, 20–58. New York: Russell Sage Foundation.

Gornick, Janet C., and Marcia K. Meyers. 2003. *Families that work: Policies for reconciling parenthood and employment*. New York: Russell Sage Foundation.

Gottfried, Heidi, and Nagisa Hayashi-Kato. 1998. Gendering work: Deconstructing the narrative of the Japanese economic miracle. *Work, Employment and Society* 12:25–46.

Gottfried, Heidi, and Jacqueline O'Reilly. 2002. Reregulating breadwinner models in socially conservative welfare systems: Comparing Germany and Japan. *Social Politics* 9:29–59.

Greenhalgh, Susan. 1985. Sexual stratification: The other side of "growth with equity" in East Asia. *Population and Development Review* 11:265–314.

Gustafsson, Siv. 1992. Separate taxation and married women's labor supply: A comparison of West Germany and Sweden. *Journal of Population Economics* 5:61–85.

Gustafsson, Siv. 1995. Public policies and women's labor force participation: A comparison of Sweden, Germany, and the Netherlands. In *Investment in women's human capital*, ed. T. Paul Schultz, 91–112. Chicago: University of Chicago Press.

Hakim, Catherine. 1995. Five feminist myths about women's employment. *The British Journal of Sociology* 46:429–455.

Hamilton, Gary G., and Nicole Woolsey Biggart. 1988. Market, culture, and authority: A comparative analysis of management and organization in the Far East. *American Journal of Sociology* 94:s52–s89.

Hermalin, Albert I., and Li-Shou Yang. 2004. Levels of support from children in Taiwan: Expectations versus reality, 1965–99. *Population and Development Review* 30:417–448.

Hirao, Keiko. 2001. Mothers as the best teachers: Japanese motherhood and early childhood education. In *Women's working lives in East Asia*, ed. Mary C. Brinton, 180–203. Stanford: Stanford University Press.

Hirao, Keiko. 2007. The privatized education market and maternal employment. In *The political economy of Japan's low fertility*, ed. Frances McCall Rosenbluth, 170–197. Stanford: Stanford University Press.

Hochschild, Arlie. 1989. *The second shift*. New York: Avon Books.

Hodson, Randy, and Robert L. Kaufman. 1982. Economic dualism: A critical review. *American Sociological Review* 47:727–739.

Houseman, Susan N. 1998. Labor standards in alternative work arrangements. *Labor Law Journal* September: 1135–1141.

Houseman, Susan N., and Katharine G. Abraham. 1993. Female workers as a buffer in the Japanese economy. *The American Economic Review* 83:45–51.

Houseman, Susan N., and Machiko Osawa. 1995. Part-time and temporary employment in Japan. *Monthly Labor Review* 118:10–18.

Houseman, Susan N., and Machiko Osawa. 2003. The growth of nonstandard employment in Japan and the United States. In *Nonstandard work in developed economies: Causes and consequences*, ed. Susan N. Houseman and Machiko Osawa, 175–214. Kalamazoo, MI: W.E. Upjohn Institute.

Hsiung, Ping-Chun. 1996. *Living rooms as factories: Class, gender, and the satellite factory system in Taiwan*. Philadelphia: Temple University Press.

Hsu, Chiung-Wen, and Hsueh-Chiao Chiang. 2001. The government strategy for the upgrading of industrial technology in Taiwan. *Technovation* 21:123–132.

Huang, Fung-Mey. 2001. Education, earnings, and fertility in Taiwan. In *Population change and economic development in East Asia: Challenges met, opportunities seized*, ed. Andrew Mason, 279–299. Stanford: Stanford University Press.

Hunter, Janet. 2003. *Women and the labour market in Japan's industrialising economy: The textile industry before the Pacific War*. London, UK: Routledge Curzon.

International Labour Office (ILO). 1990. *Yearbook of labour statistics, 1945–89*. Geneva: ILO.

International Monetary Fund, World economic outlook database. www.imf.org/external/ns/cs.aspx?id=28 (accessed September 6, 2008).

Ishida, Hiroshi. 1993. *Social mobility in contemporary Japan: Educational credentials, class and the labor market in a cross-national perspective*. Stanford: Stanford University Press.

Ishida, Hiroshi. 2004. Entry into and exit from self-employment in Japan. In *The reemergence of self-employment: A comparative study of self-employment dynamics and social inequality*, ed. Richard Arum and Walter Müller, 348–387. Princeton: Princeton University Press.

Ishii, Hiromitsu. 1993. *The Japanese tax system, second edition.* Oxford: Clarendon Press.

The Japan Institute of Labour (JIL). 1991. *Paato Taimu Rōdō Jitai Chōsa Kenkyū Hōkokusho* [*Report for survey on part-time labor force participation*]. Tokyo: JIL.

The Japanese Public Opinion Database. www.ropercenter.uconn.edu/jpoll/JPOLL .html (accessed September 10, 2008).

Johnson, Chalmers. 1987. Political institutions and economic performance: The government–business relationship in Japan, South Korea, and Taiwan. In *The political economy of the New Asian industrialism*, ed. Frederic C. Deyo, 136–164. Ithaca: Cornell University Press.

Kalleberg, Arne L., and James R. Lincoln. 1988. The structure of earnings inequality in the United States and Japan. *American Journal of Sociology* 94 (Suppl.):s121–s153.

Kalleberg, Arne L., and Aage B. Sørensen. 1979. The sociology of labor markets. *Annual Review of Sociology* 5:351–379.

Kariya, Takehiko, and James E. Rosenbaum. 1999. Bright flight: Unintended consequences of detracking policy in Japan. *American Journal of Education* 107:210–230.

Kato, Takao. 2001. The end of lifetime employment in Japan? Evidence from national surveys and field research. *Journal of the Japanese and International Economies* 15:489–514.

Kelly, William W., and Merry I. White. 2006. Students, slackers, singles, seniors, and strangers: Transforming a family–nation. In *Beyond Japan: The dynamics of East Asian regionalism*, ed. Peter J. Katzenstein and Takashi Shiraishi, 63–84. Ithaca : Cornell University Press.

Koike, Kazuo. 1983. Internal labor markets: Workers in large firms. In *Contemporary industrial relations in Japan*, ed. Tashirō Shirai, 29–62. Madison: University of Wisconsin Press.

Koike, Kazuo. 1987. Human resource development and labor–management relations. In *The political economy of Japan*, vol. 1, ed. Kōzō Yamamura and Yasukichi Yasuba, 289–330. Stanford: Stanford University Press.

Komaba-50-Year-History Editorial Committee. 2001. *Komaba no gojōnen* [*The 50-year history of Komaba campus*]. Tokyo: The University of Tokyo.

Kung, Lydia. 1994. *Factory women in Taiwan.* New York: Columbia University Press.

Lam, Alice. 1993. Equal employment opportunities for Japanese women: Changing company practice. In *Japanese women working*, ed. Janet Hunter, 198–223. London: Routledge.

Lee, Yean-Ju, Willian L. Parish, and Robert J. Willis. 1994. Sons, daughters, and intergenerational support in Taiwan. *American Journal of Sociology* 99:1010–1041.

Lee, Mei-Lin, Ya-Chieh Yang, and Chin-Chun Yi. 2000. The division of household labor: Employment reality or egalitarian ideology. *Taiwanese Journal of Sociology.* 24:59–88.

Leibowitz, Arleen, and Jacob Alex Klerman. 1995. Explaining changes in married mothers' employment over time. *Demography* 32:365–378.

Lin, I-Fen, Noreen Goldman, Maxine Weinsten, Yu-Hsuan Lin, Tristan Gorrindo, and Teresa Seeman. 2003. Gender differences in adult children's support of their parents in Taiwan. *Journal of Marriage and Family* 65:184–200.

Lincoln, James R., and Kerry McBride. 1987. Japanese industrial organization in comparative perspective. *Annual Review of Sociology* 13:289–312.

Lincoln, James R., and Yoshifumi Nakata. 1997. The transformation of the Japanese employment system: Nature, depth, and origins. *Work and Occupations* 24:33–55.

Loveband, Anne. 2006. Positioning the products: Indonesia migrant women workers in Taiwan. In *Transnational migration and workers in Asia*, ed. Kevin J. Hewison and Ken Young, 75–89. Abingdon, Oxon: Routledge.

Lu, Yu-Hsia 2001. The "boss's wife" and Taiwanese small family business. In *Women's working lives in East Asia*, ed. Mary C. Brinton, 263–297. Stanford: Stanford University Press.

Luoh, Ming-Ching. 2002. Who are NTU students? Differences across gender and ethnic groups and urban/rural discrepancy. *Taiwan Economic Review* 30:113–147.

Mammen, Kristin, and Christina Paxson. 2000. Women's work and economic development. *The Journal of Economic Perspectives* 14:141–164.

Mason, Andrew. 2001a. Population and economic growth. In *Population change and economic development in East Asia*, ed. Andrew Mason, 1–30. Stanford: Stanford University Press.

Mason, Karen Oppenheim. 2001b. Gender and family systems in the fertility transition. *Population and Development Review* 27:160–176.

Melkas, Helinä, and Richard Anker. 2003. *Towards gender equality in Japanese and Nordic labour markets: A tale of two paths.* Geneva: ILO.

Miller, Alan S., and Satoshi Kanazawa. 2000. *Order by accident: The origins and consequences of conformity in contemporary Japan.* Boulder, CO: Westview Press.

Mincer, Jacob. 1985. Intercountry comparisons of labor force trends and of related developments: An overview. *Journal of Labor Economics* 3:1–32.

Mincer, Jacob, and Yoshio Higuchi. 1988. Wage structures and labor turnover in the United States and Japan. *Journal of the Japanese and International Economies* 2:97–133.

Ministry of Education, Republic of China. 1998. *Survey report on the life and study of students in middle school and below in Taiwan.* Taipei: Author.

Ministry of Education, Republic of China. 2001. *Survey report on the life and study of students in middle school and below in Taiwan.* Taipei: Author.

Ministry of Education, Republic of China. Various years. *Educational statistics of the Republic of China.* Taipei: Author.

Ministry of Education, Culture, Sports, Science, and Technology (MEXT), Japan. 2004. *Heisei 15 School Basic Survey.* www.mext.go.jp/b_menu/toukei/001/04011501/index.htm (accessed September 18, 2008).

MEXT, Japan. Various years. *School Basic Survey.* Tokyo: Author.

Ministry of Health, Labour, and Welfare, Japan. 2003. *Survey report regarding social policies for child-care support.* Tokyo: Author.

Ministry of Interior, Republic of China. 1970. *Household and residence census.* Taipei: Author.

Ministry of Labour, Japan. 1996. *Report of basic survey on wage structure*. Tokyo: Author.

Ministry of Labour, Japan. 1997. *Yearbook of labour statistics, vol. 48, 1995*. Tokyo: Institute of Labour Administration.

Mizoguchi, Toshiyuki, and Yuzo Yamamoto. 1984. Capital formation in Taiwan and Korea. In *The Japanese colonial empire, 1895–1945*, ed. Ramon H. Myers and Mark R. Peattie, 399–419. Princeton: Princeton University Press.

Moen, Phyllis. 1985. Continuities and discontinuities in women's labor force activity. In *Life course dynamics: Trajectories and transitions, 1968–1980*, ed. Glen H. Elder, Jr., 113–155. Ithaca: Cornell University Press.

Morgan, Philip S., and Kiyoshi Hirosima. 1983. The persistence of extended family residence in Japan: Anachronism or alternative strategy? *American Sociological Review* 48:269–281.

Mori, Hiromi. 1997. *Immigration policy and foreign workers in Japan*. New York: St. Martin's Press.

Nagase, Nobuko. 1997. Wage differentials and labour supply of married women in Japan: Part-time and informal sector work opportunities. *The Japanese Economic Review* 48:29–42.

Nippon Hōsō Kyōkai. 1996. *Detabukku: Kokumin seikatsu jikan 1995* [*Databook on national time utilization survey 1995*]. Tokyo: Nippon Hōsō Shuppan Kyōkai.

Nippon Hōsō Kyōkai. Various years. *Kokumin seikatsu jikan choōsa* [*National time utilization survey*]. Tokyo: Nippon Hōsō Shuppan Kyōkai.

National Institute of Population and Social Security Research, Japan. 2004. *The processes of marriage and fertility among married couples in our country, 2002: The 12th national fertility survey*. Tokyo: Health and Welfare Statistics Association.

Noble, Gregory W. 1998. *Collective action in East Asia: How ruling parties shape industrial policy*. Ithaca: Cornell University Press.

Ogasawara, Yuko. 1998. *Office ladies and salaried men: Power, gender, and work in Japanese companies*. Berkeley: University of California Press.

Ogawa, Naohiro, and Robert D. Retherford. 1993. The resumption of fertility decline in Japan: 1973–92. *Population and Development Review* 19:703–741.

Ojima, Fumiaki. 2001. Shinro sentaku ha donoyōni kawatta noka [How have high school students' advancement choices changed?]. In *Gendai kōkōsei no keiryō shakaigaku* [*Quantitative sociology of contemporary high school students*], ed. Fumiaki Ojima, 21–61. Kyoto: Mierva.

Okano, Kaori, and Motonori Tsuchiya. 1999. *Education in contemporary Japan: Inequality and diversity*. Cambridge: Cambridge University Press.

Okunishi, Yoshio. 2001. Changing labor forces and labor markets in Asia's miracle economies. In *Population change and economic development in East Asia: Challenges met, opportunities seized*, ed. Andrew Mason, 300–331. Stanford: Stanford University Press.

Ono, Hiroshi. 2004. Are sons and daughters substitutable? Allocation of family resources in contemporary Japan. *Journal of the Japanese and International Economies* 18:143–160.

Oppenheimer, Valarie K. 1970. *The female labor force in the United States: Demographic and economic factors governing its growth and changing composition*. Berkeley: University of California Press.

Organisation for Economic Co-operation and Development (OECD). 2006. *OECD factbook 2006: Economic, environmental and social statistics.* Paris: OECD publishing.

Osawa, Mari. 2005. Japanese government approaches to gender equality since the mid-1990s. *Asian Perspective* 29:157–173.

Padavic, Irene, and Barbara Reskin. 2003. *Women and men at work.* Thousand Oaks, CA: Pine Forge Press.

Pampel, Fred C., and Kazuko Tanaka. 1986. Economic development and female labor force participation: A reconsideration. *Social Forces* 64:599–619.

Parish, William L., and Robert J. Willis. 1993. Daughters, education, and family budgets: Taiwan experiences. *The Journal of Human Resources* 28:863–898.

Piore, Michael J., and Charles F. Sabel. 1984. *The second industrial divide: Possibilities for prosperity.* New York: Basic Books.

Polachek, Solomon W. 1979. Occupation segregation among women: Theory, evidence, and a prognosis. In *Women in the labor market,* ed. Cynthia B. Lloyd, 137–157. New York: Columbia University Press.

Portes, Alejandro. 1994. The informal economy and its paradoxes. In *The handbook of economic sociology,* ed. Neil J. Smelser and Richard Swedberg, 427–449. Princeton: Princeton University Press.

Portes, Alejandro, and Lauren Benton. 1984. Industrial development and labor absorption: A reinterpretation. *Population and Development Review* 10:589–611.

Pyle, Jean Larson. 1990. *The state and women in the economy: Lessons from sex discrimination in the Republic of Ireland.* Albany: State University of New York Press.

Pyle, Kenneth B. 1978. *The making of modern Japan.* Lexington, MA: D. C. Heath.

Raymo, James M., and Miho Iwasawa. 2005. Marriage market mismatches in Japan: An alternative view of the relationship between women's education and marriage. *American Sociological Review* 70:801–822.

Raymo, James M., Miho Iwasawa, and Larry L. Bumpass. 2004. Marital dissolution in Japan: Recent trends and patterns. *Demographic Research* 11:395–420.

Reskin, Barbara. 1993. Sex segregation in the workplace. *Annual Review of Sociology* 19:241–270.

Reskin, Barbara. 2001. Labor markets as queues: A structural approach to changing occupational sex composition. In *Social stratification in sociological perspective,* ed. David B. Grusky, 719–733. Boulder, CO: Westview Press.

Reskin, Barbara F., and Debra Branch McBrier. 2000. Why not ascription? Organizations' employment of male and female managers. *American Sociological Review* 65:210–233.

Retherford, Robert D., Naohiro Ogawa, and Satomi Sakamoto. 1996. Values and fertility change in Japan. *Population Studies* 50:5–25.

Rindfuss, Ronald R., and Karin L. Brewster. 1996. Childrearing and fertility. *Population and Development Review* 22:258–289.

Rindfuss, Ronald R., Minja Kim Choe, Larry L. Bumpass, and N. O. Tsuya. 2004. Social networks and family change in Japan. *American Sociological Review* 69:838–861.

Roberts, Glenda S. 1994. *Staying on the line: Blue-collar women in contemporary Japan.* Honolulu: University of Hawaii Press.

Rohlen, Thomas P. 1980. The Juku phenomenon: An exploratory essay. *Journal of Japanese Studies* 6:207–242.

Rohlen, Thomas P. 1983. *Japan's high schools*. Berkeley: University of California Press.

Rosenbaum, James E., and Takehiko Kariya. 1989. From high school to work: Market and institutional mechanisms in Japan. *American Journal of Sociology* 94:1334–1365.

Rosenfeld, Rachel A. 1992. Job mobility and career processes. *Annual Review of Sociology* 18:39–61.

Rosenfeld, Rachel A. 1996. Women's work histories. *Population and Development Review* 22:199–222.

Rosenfeld, Rachel A., and Gunn Elisabeth Birkelund. 1995. Women's part-time work: A cross-national comparison. *European Sociological Review* 11:111–134.

Russell, Nancy Ukai. 1997. Lessons from Japanese cram schools. In *The challenge of eastern Asian education: Implications for America*, ed. William K. Cummings and Philip G. Altbach, 153–170. Albany: State University of New York Press.

Sakamoto, Arthur, and Daniel A. Powers. 1995. Education and the dual labor market for Japanese men. *American Sociological Review* 60:222–246.

Salaff, Janet W. 1994. Foreword to the Morningside Edition. In *Factory women in Taiwan*, L. Kung, xi–xx. New York: Columbia University Press.

Schoppa, Leonard J. 2006. *Race for the exits: The unraveling of Japan's system of social protection*. Ithaca: Cornell University Press.

Shieh, Gwo-shyong. 1992. *"Boss" island: The subcontracting network and micro-entrepreneurship in Taiwan's development*. New York: Peter Lang.

Shirahase, Sawako. 2007. Women's economic status and fertility: Japan in cross-national perspective. In *The political economy of Japan's low fertility*, ed. Frances McCall Rosenbluth, 37–62. Stanford: Stanford University Press.

Shoven, John B. 1989. The Japanese tax reform and the effective rate of tax on Japanese corporate investments. *Tax Policy and the Economy* 3:97–115.

Shu, Xiaoling, and Yanjie Bian. 2003. Market transition and gender gap in earnings in urban China. *Social Forces* 81:1107–1145.

Statistics and Information Department, Minister's Secretariat, Ministry of Health, Labour and Welfare, Japan. Vital statistics database. www.mhlw.go.jp/english/database/db-hw/index.html (accessed September 6, 2008).

Statistics Bureau, Management and Coordination Agency, Japan. 1987. *Historical statistics of Japan*. Tokyo: Japan Statistical Association.

Statistics Bureau, Management and Coordination Agency, Japan. 1997. *Nihon no tokei* [*Statistics of Japan*]. Tokyo: Author.

Statistics Bureau, Management and Coordination Agency, Japan. Various years. *Annual report on the Labour Force Survey*, various years. Tokyo: Author.

Statistics Bureau, Ministry of Internal Affairs and Communications, Japan. 2001. The 2000 population census. www.e-stat.go.jp/SG1/estat/ListE.do?bid=000000030587&cycode=0 (accessed September 10, 2008).

Statistics Bureau, Ministry of Internal Affairs and Communications, Japan, 2005. The 2005 population census. www.e-stat.go.jp/SG1/estat/NewList.do?tid=000001007251 (accessed September 6, 2008).

Statistics Bureau, Ministry of Internal Affairs and Communications (Statistics Bureau of the Management and Coordination Agency prior to 2001), Japan. Various years. *Japan statistical yearbook*. Tokyo: Author.

Statistics Bureau, Ministry of Internal Affairs and Communications, Japan. Various years. Labour Force Survey. www.stat.go.jp/data/roudou/2.htm (accessed September 6, 2008).

Statistics Bureau, Ministry of Public Management, Home Affairs, and Posts and Communications, Japan, 2001. *2000 population census of Japan.* Tokyo: Author.

Stevenson, David Lee, and David P. Baker. 1992. Shadow education and allocation in formal schooling: Transition to university in Japan. *The American Journal of Sociology* 97:1639–1657.

Stier, Haya, Noah Lewin-Epstein, and Michael Braun. 2001. Welfare regimes, family-supportive policies, and women's employment along the life-course. *American Journal of Sociology* 106:1731–1760.

Taira, Koji. 1970. *Economic development & the labor market in Japan.* Cambridge: Cambridge University Press.

Tang, Wenfang, and William L. Parish. 2000. *Chinese urban life under reform: The changing social contract.* Cambridge: Cambridge University Press.

Thelen, Kathleen, and Ikuo Kume. 1999. The effects of globalization on labor revisited: Lessons from Germany and Japan. *Politics and Society* 27:477–505.

Thistle, Susan. 2006. *From marriage to the market: The transformation of women's lives and work.* Berkeley: University of California Press.

Tsurumi, Patricia. 1977. *Japanese colonial education in Taiwan, 1895–1945.* Cambridge: Harvard University Press.

Tsuya, Norika O., and Larry L. Bumpass. 1998. Time allocation between employment and housework in Japan, South Korea, and the United States. In *The changing family in comparative perspective: Asia and the United States,* ed. Karen Oppenheim Mason, Noriko O. Tsuya, and Minja Kim Choe, 83–104. Honolulu: East-West Center.

United Nations. 2007a. *Demographic yearbook 2004.* New York: Author.

United Nations. 2007b. *Demographic yearbook 2005.* New York: Author. http:// unstats.un.org/unsd/demographic/products/dyb/dyb2005.htm (accessed September 6, 2008).

Upham, Frank K. 1987. *Law and social change in postwar Japan.* Cambridge: Harvard University Press.

Van der Lippe, Tanja, and Liset Van Dijk. 2002. Comparative research on women's employment. *Annual Review of Sociology* 28:221–241.

Wakisaka, Akira. 2001. Daisotsu josei no genjō to koyōkanri no henka [Current conditions of female university graduates and changes in employment]. In *Daisotsu josei no hatarakikata [The work patterns of female university graduates],* ed. Akira Wakisaka and Yasunobu Tomida, 1–20. Tokyo: Nihon Rōdō Kenkyu Kiko (JIL).

Wakisaka, Akira, and Haesun Bae. 1998. Why is part-time rate higher in Japan than in South Korea? In *Part-time prospects: An international comparison of part-time work in Europe, North America, and the Pacific Rim,* ed. Jacqueline O'Reilly and Collette Fagan, 252–264. New York: Routledge.

Walsh, Janet. 1999. Myths and counter-myths: An analysis of part-time female employees and their orientations to work and working hours. *Work, Employment, & Society* 13:179–203.

Wang, Ru-Jer. 2003. From elitism to mass higher education in Taiwan: The problems faced. *Higher Education* 46:261–287.

Woo, Jennie Hay. 1991. Education and economic growth in Taiwan: A case of successful planning. *World Development* 19:1029–1044.

Wood, Adrian. 1994. *North–South trade, employment and inequality: Changing fortunes in a skill-driven world*. Oxford: Clarendon Press.

Wright, Eric Olin, Janeen Baxter, and Gunn Elisabeth Birkelund. 1995. The gender gap in workplace authority: A cross-national study. *American Sociological Review* 60:407–435.

Yamagata, Hisashi, Kuang S. Yeh, Shelby Stewman, and Hiroko Dodge. 1997. Sex segregation and glass ceilings: A comparative statics model of women's career opportunities in the federal government over a quarter century. *American Journal of Sociology* 103:566–632.

Yamaguchi, Kazuo. 1991. *Event history analysis*. Newbury Park: Sage Publications.

Yamakawa, Ryuichi. 2001. Labor law reform in Japan: A response to recent socio-economic changes. *The American Journal of Comparative Law* 49:627–651.

Yanotsuneta Kinenkai [Yanotsuneta Memorial Foundation]. 2000. *Japan's 100 years*. Tokyo: Yanotsuneta Kinenkai.

Yi, Chin-Chun. 1994. Childcare arrangements of employed mothers in Taiwan. In *Women, the family, and policy: A global perspective*, eds. Ester Ngan-Lin Chow and Catherine White Berheide, 235–256. Albany: State University of New York Press.

Yu, Ruoh-rong, and Cyrus C.Y. Chu. 1998. Does National Taiwan University add more value to her students than other colleges? Estimating the performance of college graduates in Taiwan. *Taiwan Economic Review* 26:65–89.

Yu, Wei-hsin. 1999. *Unequal employment, diverse career paths: Gender stratification in Japan and Taiwan*. PhD thesis. Chicago: Department of Sociology, The University of Chicago.

Yu, Wei-hsin. 2001a. Family demands, gender attitudes, and married women's labor force participation: Comparison between Japan and Taiwan. In *Women's working lives in East Asia*, ed. Mary C. Brinton, 70–95. Stanford: Stanford University Press.

Yu, Wei-hsin. 2001b. Taking informality into account: Women's work in the formal and informal sectors in Taiwan. In *Women's working lives in East Asia*, ed. Mary C. Brinton, 233–262. Stanford: Stanford University Press.

Yu, Wei-hsin. 2002. Jobs for mothers: Married women's labor force reentry and part-time, temporary employment in Japan. *Sociological Forum* 17:493–523.

Yu, Wei-hsin. 2004. Gender, family, and form of labor force participation: Woman and nonstandard employment in Japan and Taiwan. In *Old challenges, new strategies? Women, work, and family in contemporary Asia*, ed. by Leng Leng Thang and Wei-hsin Yu, 27–59. Leiden: Brill Academic Publishers.

Yu, Wei-hsin. 2005. Changes in women's postmarital employment in Japan and Taiwan. *Demography* 42:693–717.

Yu, Wei-hsin. 2006. National contexts and dynamics of married women's employment reentry: The cases of Japan and Taiwan. *The Sociological Quarterly* 47:215–243.

Yu, Wei-hsin, and Kuo-hsien Su. 2004. On one's own: Self-employment activity in Taiwan. In *The reemergence of self-employment: A comparative study of self-employment dynamics and social inequality*, ed. Richard Arum and Walter Müller, 388–425. Princeton: Princeton University Press.

Yu, Wei-hsin, and Kuo-hsien Su. 2006. Gender, sibship structure, and educational inequality in Taiwan: Son preference revisited. *Journal of Marriage and Family* 68:1057–1068.

Yu, Wei-hsin, and Kuo-hsien Su. 2008. Intergenerational mobility patterns in Taiwan: The case of a rapidly industrializing economy. In *Social stratification and social mobility in late-industrializing countries*, ed. Hiroshi Ishida, 49–78. Sendai: The 2005 Social Stratification and Social Mobility Survey Research Committee.

Zahidi, Saadia. 2007. *The global gender report 2006*. Geneva: World Economic Forum.

Numbers followed by *f* or *t* indicate material in figures and tables.

Lightning Source UK Ltd.
Milton Keynes UK
UKHW011338280422
402155UK00003B/42/J